Mother with Child

Transformations through Childbirth

KATHRYN ALLEN RABUZZI

INDIANA UNIVERSITY PRESS
Bloomington and Indianapolis

The paper used in this publication meets the minimum requirements of American National Standard for Information Sciences—Permanence of Paper for Printed Library Materials, ANSI Z39.48-1984.

♾

Manufactured in the United States of America

Library of Congress Cataloging-in-Publication Data

Rabuzzi, Kathryn Allen.
Mother with child : transformations through childbirth / Kathryn Allen Rabuzzi.
p.   cm.
Includes bibliographical references (p.   ) and index.
ISBN 0-253-34769-6 (cloth : alk. paper).—ISBN 0-253-20827-0 (pbk. : alk. paper)
1. Motherhood. 2. Self. 3. Pregnancy—Psychological aspects.
4. Childbirth—Psychological aspects. I. Title.
HQ759.R2   1993
306.874'3—dc20   92-45765

1 2 3 4 5 97 96 95 94

Contents

PREFACE

This book has alternately fascinated and frustrated me, its thirty-year gestation feeling inordinately long. "Conceived" at the birth of my first child in 1959, it owes its existence to faulty anaesthesia. In the late fifties, spinal injections, known as caudals, were favored for obstetrical anaesthesia because they permit continued consciousness while numbing a woman's lower body. Because my caudal failed, I had an unanticipated "natural" childbirth, which resembled nothing I had ever previously experienced. As my baby crowned, I felt myself expand infinitely outward. This did not exactly hurt; it was on "the other side" of pain, where *pain* is no longer an appropriate word. Possibly *ecstasy* will do.

By whatever name, my unusual feeling simultaneously contracted me inward with such intensity that I felt myself compacting into a very dense version of my habitual self. A few years later I recalled this strange phenomenon when I read a description of a dwarf star, a star so imploded that, assuming an original circumference of a square mile, it is now the size of an orange. Yet it retains its original million pounds of weight. I recognized in this odd condensation an image of my childbearing experience. How I could simultaneously feel *both* movements, I did not know. Accompanying them was a loud "pop," which seemed to both trigger and form a part of the two opposed movements. At the same time, I was also "dying," "being born," and giving birth. At age twenty, none of this made much sense to me. Certainly the only pregnancy and childbearing book I had read at the time, the then-popular *Expectant Motherhood* by Nicholson J. Eastman, M.D., revealed nothing of this sort. Nor did anyone I knew ever mention birth, death, and giving birth converging like this. By late-fifties standards, experiencing childbirth mystically—not that I then recognized it as such—was peculiar; nonetheless, I valued the experience. In the difficult period of adjusting to motherhood, though, I more or less forgot about it. Not until my final childbirth, when I experienced the same pattern of sensations, my middle delivery having been obliterated by total anaesthesia, did my original curiosity return.

This repeated experience of infinite outward and inward expansion accompanied by the "popping" sound and simultaneous sensations of dying, being born, and giving birth initiated a lifelong quest for answers: Why did this happen? What does it mean? Am I unique, or have others felt this way, too? This book is one attempt to provide some answers.

In the process of writing, I have received invaluable help from various colleagues: Thomas Moore, Paul Johnson, Ellen Umansky, and Diane Jonte-Pace.

As always, I could not have finished this work without the loving support of my family: Daniel, Deborah, Matthew, Yvonne, Douglas, Jennifer, and especially my husband, Dan.

INTRODUCTION

Becoming a mother necessarily alters a woman's pre-existing self-concept. This is so regardless of whether a woman "turns into a mother" by giving birth following an act of heterosexual intercourse, adopts a child, or becomes a mother through some sort of technological procedure such as in vitro fertilization, surrogate motherhood, self-administered insemination, or the like. Some women, whose sense of personal identity does not hinge on it, may find approaching motherhood disturbing, even damaging, to their selfhood. Others, anticipating it, may find that conception, pregnancy, labor, delivery, or awaiting the arrival of an adoptive child all heighten their selfhood. Either way, motherhood challenges a woman's accustomed sense of self, as these words from an anonymous woman well illustrate: "I was eighteen when Krissie was born, and there I was alone, and there's that fear, you know, the feeling of 'I might die.' And of being swept up in a force of nature so powerful *that your ordinary experience of yourself is gone*" [italics added].[1] This disappearance of the "ordinary experience of yourself" epitomizes self-transformation. Whether negative or positive or both, such transformation critically characterizes childbirth when it is understood as the deeply spiritual gynecocentric experience it potentially is.

Unfortunately, however, many women miss out on the positive ramifications of their own self-transformation because numerous patriarchal denials, distortions, and appropriations make it into quite a different experience. Unless women can variously reach beneath, set aside, or deconstruct these diverse patriarchal layers, we can neither retrieve nor (re)construct childbirth into the intensely meaningful experience it can readily become when patriarchal obstructions do not intrude. A major purpose of this book is to show how such retrieval and (re)construction are possible.

While *retrieval* may offend some feminists for its implicit essentialism, the term is historical as well as biological. Furthermore, the ability to bear children does constitute an unavoidable biological difference which, to date, still differentiates fertile women from all men. Thus, despite current deemphasis on biology in favor of social construction as a "cause" of presumed sexual differences, it is nonetheless wise to bear in mind that historically sexual difference construed biologically has mattered enormously. And to the extent that such thinking still permeates most people's awareness at some level, it makes sense to at least reformulate it: Rather than follow the accepted distinction that separates the sexes into woman and man, it seems more logical to separate mothers from nonmothers as a strategy useful for altering the more traditional polarization. No other difference, it seems to me, so dramatically separates the sexes, as they are usually defined. It is my thesis, therefore, that the transformation of woman into mother is far more disruptive of human sameness, hence of human cultures, than the more usual distinction based on possession or lack of a penis.

Childbirth as Instrument of Self-Transformation

Most traditional cultures understand the deeply important transformational power that childbearing exerts not just on women but on men as well. But modern individuals blithely assume we can make babies without pausing, going right on with our "real" work almost as if nothing had happened. By contrast, parents in some traditional cultures even change their names in recognition of the great inner change that childbirth effects. In the words of an informant from the Wagenia tribe of Kisangani, Zaire,

> after the birth of our eldest son I was often addressed as Isakalimasi, or "father of Kalimasi," the latter being the Wagenia name for him. My wife, who had until then been addressed as Mokalaandele, wife of Andre, henceforth bore the name M'makalimasi, "mother of Kalimasi."[2]

What is accepted in Wagenia culture as a positive symbol of self-transformation would surely be rejected as an ignominious reminder of self-loss by many people in our own culture. But what exactly is involved in such transformation? Although "transformation" commonly describes religious events, especially mystical experiences, its exact nature is rarely detailed. Consequently, the concept often remains abstract—something one talks about but cannot relate to experientially.

Fairy tales provide some useful images, for many portray exactly such deep alterations of self. Tales of swan maidens, mermaid wives, and bear-men, for example, variously dramatize alternative or temporary transformations of self. And stories of cinder children, of which Cinderella is the best-known variant, tell of the deep transformation of self most of us wish for at times. On one level such tales merely depict a superficial shift from rags to riches. On another, they show a dramatic life change, as when Cinderella abandons the selfhood imposed by her abusive family to openly assume her latent princess identity.

Such stories suggest how self-transformation touches the very deepest levels of a person's being; it is no superficial alteration of self but one which, as so many myths and rituals affirm, involves both death and rebirth. Most of us living in contemporary postindustrial cultures find such rituals notably missing from our lives. How, we may wonder, can a young boy living in a premodern context, when separated from his tribe for a three-month period of isolation followed by ritual "rebirth" from the tribal "Fathers," really forget his past life or see it as another existence entirely? Is that not just a metaphorical way of speaking, as we do when we return from an extended journey to a foreign culture feeling renewed and strongly altered? The answer, as this book seeks to show, is no.

Childbirth as Symbol and Ritual

In traditional world views untouched by modern questioning of symbols, during all stages of childbearing from conception through delivery, women function in a curiously twofold way. On the one hand, as embodiments of the abstraction "woman," we *symbolize* to others the creative process whereby human life is generated on earth. As such, we *re*-present an eternal religious (as well as biological) "truth." At the same time, however, we are experiencing firsthand, without recourse to any artificially constructed, human-made ritual, immediate contact with "the sacred" as creative life-force. Thus, our experience is representational and symbolic. It is "derived" from, and representative of, some earlier event. But it is also presentational—it is the event itself. Whatever childbirth is, it cannot be separated from the meaningful and felt experience that it symbolizes.

Like such well-known symbols as the Cross or the Flag, childbirth traditionally symbolizes an immensely complex phenomenon. Unlike them, in and of itself, childbirth is not a physical object but a process. Therefore, it implies time— the time required for the process to complete itself. Yet within childbirth a static, representational counterpart to the Cross or the Flag does exist: the image of a pregnant woman. Alternatively, though rarely in Western cultures, that woman is shown giving birth. Thus, some visual representations of pregnancy and birth giving do exist, functioning much the way both Cross and Flag do. There is a difference, however. Both Cross and Flag require a specific cultural context to be understandable. But a pregnant or laboring woman is not culture-specific. Unlike the particular context of the Cross or the Flag, that of childbirth is universal.

This universality is critical. It means that images depicting childbirth *as such* are not symbols in exactly the same sense as either the Cross or the Flag. Even if, as some philosophers contend, all representations are symbolic by definition, some more closely interconnect with their referents than others. Thus, the Cross with a capital *C* is meaningful because of its role in the larger story of Christianity; similarly, the Flag is meaningful relative to the values of the particular country for which it stands. By contrast, childbirth is readily understandable in a general sense, regardless of cultural particularity.

The symbolic meanings that have been attached to childbirth in diverse patriarchal cultures extend widely. The fact that childbirth holds so many meanings is a paradox: Why has childbirth, seemingly a "natural miracle" in and of itself, not functioned historically in world religions as a symbol equivalent to such celebrated visual images as the Cross or the Star of David?

One can, of course, deny the charge and say, "But there *is* a symbolic parallel to all those visual symbols—the Madonna and Child." And furthermore, unlike the other symbols, the Madonna and Child image occurs in many traditions from numerous Mystery religions of the classical world to contemporary Hinduism. But have you ever seen a nonprehistoric Western Madonna *giving birth?* Often she gives suck. But giving birth? Until the past decade, never! This is a crucial distinction, especially relative to the ritual aspects of childbirth.

Ritual characterizes all religious traditions, often as enactment of the sacred stories that give a particular tradition its reason for being. One thinks of Passover in Judaism, which celebrates the exodus of the Israelites from bondage in Egypt; or the Hadj in Islam, which repeats the journey of Mohammad to Mecca; or Holy Communion in Christianity, which reenacts the last supper of Jesus and his disciples before he was taken away and crucified.

Childbirth differs significantly, and this difference suggests an answer to the question of why childbirth as such has not functioned historically as an equivalent to such other world symbols as the Cross or Star of David: In childbirth, story and ritual are one and the same. When the mother gives birth, she repeats the age-old story of bringing new life into the world, while her act of giving birth is itself a symbolic ritual found in countless religions. Yet we have no "world religion" focused on giving birth. Moreover, in the combined process of this repeated story and ritualization of childbearing, something very strange happens. Instead of the story and the ritual remaining focused on or deepening women's experience of childbearing, both have been altered significantly throughout history. Rather than the story of giving birth, we hear two variants: of *being* born and, more commonly in religious contexts, of being *re*born.

If resurrection or rebirth is so central to most religious traditions, why is childbirth not equally celebrated? This omission strikes me as very peculiar. Part of the answer lies in the fact that meanings of symbols shift. Usually they do so slowly and accidentally, accreting new meanings that enlarge but do not negate the symbol's original significance. But occasionally, as with the swastika (originally an almost universal sun sign symbolizing life), a shift is deliberate, the result of one group's conscious appropriation of a symbol "belonging" to another.

This is what has happened, throughout patriarchal history, to images of childbirth. These have been snatched from women and attached to men. Thus, one of the most common of all religious images, that of *rebirth,* has been repeatedly used in such a way as to place males rather than females in the role of childbearers.

Denigration, Denial, and Devaluation

Originally revered by women and men alike, the act of giving birth once seemed "naturally" to symbolize the miracle of life. As patriarchies grew dominant, however, childbirth was not only reinterpreted as "rebirth" but it also ceased to symbolize women's powers of mystery, creativity, and eroticism. Over time, this positive, woman-centered symbol became deformed, first by patriarchal thought, then by modernist tendencies to desacralize all symbols, and more recently by some antiessentialist streams of feminist thought. Consequently, many women over the centuries have lost touch with our own power: Often we ourselves have participated in this process of "misconceiving" childbirth. A further purpose of this book, therefore, in addition to retrieving and (re)constructing the symbolic power of childbirth and demonstrating its spiritually transformative nature, is to trace some of the complex threads forming this fascinating, yet terrifying, pattern whereby patriarchal thought has "stolen" one of women's most fundamental symbols.

Patriarchy

How did images of childbirth, this potent transformative symbol of women's power, become so destructively altered under the onslaught of patriarchy? Answers to this question are not simple. They relate to the knotty issue of just what defines patriarchy. *Patriarchy* is a complex, troublesome term. Part of its complexity comes from its evolution over time. The traditional, fairly narrow definition is insufficient to cover what many contemporary feminists mean by it. As feminist historian Gerda Lerner points out, "In its narrow meaning, patriarchy refers to the system, historically derived from Greek and Roman law, in which the male head of the household had absolute legal and economic power over his dependent female and male family members." But, Lerner continues, patriarchal dominance does not emerge fullblown during the period of classical antiquity. Rather, "it begins in the 3rd millennium B.C., and is well established at the time of the writing of the Hebrew Bible." In the wider sense commonly used today, *patriarchy* refers to institutional, familial, and social dominance whereby women are systematically denied access to the power of social institutions. "It does *not* imply that women are either totally powerless or totally deprived of rights, influence, or resources," Lerner concludes.[3]

In contemporary poststructuralist thought influenced by such French thinkers as Lacan, Irigaray, and Cixous, *patriarchy* is now often replaced by *phallocracy* or *phallogocentrism*. Both terms focus on the power of the phallus, a symbolic abstraction of the penis understood not as a body part but as the primary power image and conveyor of meaning in culture. As such, the phallus is understood to be the central image through which all existing cultures are constructed. The term *phallogocentrism*, combines the Greek *logos,* meaning "word," and the phallus. Both are thought to coexist in the sense that all our speaking takes place in terms of male-centered modes of growing, thinking, learning, perceiving, and understanding. These male-centered modes are based on common patterns of socialization into families wherein women "mother" and men "father." That means that little boys must struggle to differentiate themselves from their mothers, who represent all women, with the result that our shared cultural constructs reflect their Oedipal struggle, not ours.[4]

Sacrality

Central to patriarchy's role in determining interpretations of childbirth is the concept of sacrality. Although sacrality does not necessarily leap to mind to characterize experience in a postindustrial context, in traditional societies it is taken for granted that a reality larger than that controlled by humans exists. The usual adjective for this reality is *transcendent*—from *trans* and *scandere,* to climb. The word *transcendent* immediately becomes suspect, however, once we ask a key question: What mode of sacrality—feminine or masculine?

Until the seventies, this question did not often arise. Sacrality was considered a neutral, nonsexualized category. But, as many feminist thinkers have pointed out, it was defined in inherently patriarchal terms which, like *transcendence,* are attached to gods but rarely to goddesses. Closely associated attributes reflect height—sky, mountains, peaks—and high places—thunder, lightning, rain, and so forth. These are qualities exemplified by weather gods such as the Hindu Indra or the Greek Zeus, whose dwelling places are always "up there." Equally important to patriarchally defined sacrality is *primordiality,* a word referring to the basic stuff of creation. This "stuff" may variously be nothingness, darkness, water, earth, a world-egg, and so on. In patriarchal religions such as Judaism, Islam, and Christianity, it is a male god who creates this stuff. Another major aspect of masculine sacrality is its permanence, a sharp contrast to the fluidity of actual life, which historically connotes women and feminine sacrality. Thus, in Judaism, Christianity, and Islam, for example, God is eternal and unchanging, whereas this world in which we live is forever changing. Implicitly, if not necessarily explicitly, these terms denigrate "this world," which is often represented by woman, as in Christianity, which sees Mother Nature as fallen. By contrast, patriarchal religions typically venerate an ideal, revised version implicitly equated with man.

In contrast to masculine qualities of sacrality are those which mirror women's bodies and our traditional activities. These constitute what some think of as sacrality in a feminine mode. Thus, whereas height and sky are typically considered masculine, depth, interiority, and earth are correspondingly feminine. Both the surface of the earth and its interior—caves, fissures, the imagined under-earth realm of Hell—also exemplify feminine sacrality. The interior nature of our bodies with their capacity to gestate and bear children makes vessels important symbols of feminine sacrality as well. Our natural ability to contain and gestate similarly connects seeds and the whole fertility cycle of nature to feminine sacrality. Also closely related is transformation, reflected by the changes mothers help facilitate in our growing children. Such transformational, "this-worldly" capabilities contrast strongly with the permanence characteristic of sacrality construed in a masculine mode.

Birth-Death

For any event to be fully transformative, it must involve the shedding of old images to the extent that these images actually die. Otherwise, nothing new—that is, no transformation—can take place. At the very deepest level, then, the transformation occasioned in a woman by childbirth is death. These words, spoken by an Italian peasant woman, are illustrative: "Every time one of my babies was about to be born I'd think to myself, You're going to die! This time you're going to die! Then it'd come out. Somehow—I don't know how to explain it—but somehow it was like I had been born again."[5] The close approximation of birth to death described in this account is also reversible according to numerous accounts of near-death experiences. Scientist Carl Sagan, for instance, in his essay "The Amniotic Universe," argues that the remarkable similarity across cultures of so-called near-death experiences can be explained with reference to birth experiences. To make his case, he draws on the work of physician Stanislav Grof.[6] Using LSD to regress his patients back to their births, Grof divides the process into four perinatal stages, variously representing the preborn's experience in the womb, onset of labor, birth, and the baby's first experience of the world outside the mother's body. It is in the third stage, when the infant is actually coming through the birth canal, that the closest similarities to near-death experiences occur. Consider, for example, a birth memory of a subject hypnotically regressed by psychologist David Chamberlain:

> I hear noises like sounds your stomach makes. And there's a long tunnel in front of me. I can't even see myself. I see in shadows, not pitch-dark, just a small amount of light. I found myself moving, and then there was a flash of light, but I was still back in the tunnel. There are sounds of different people talking. Muffled noises. I don't think I'm all crunched up now. . . . I don't know if I am moving down the tunnel or if the tunnel is coming to me. It seems to be getting lighter.[7]

Such tunneling toward light, often enclosing a transcendent figure, typifies near-death reports. Psychiatrist Raymond Moody, author of the popular *Life after Life,* says that the person near death finds him or herself disembodied, "floating or being propelled through a darkness sometimes described as a tunnel, becoming aware of a golden light, encountering and having a dialogue with . . . 'a being of light.' "[8]

If dying does recapitulate being born, then it stands to reason that any woman who feels herself simultaneously dying and being born as she labors to give birth must experience some of what is described above. The interconnectedness of childbearing, birth, and death highlights a central theme of this book: Childbirth, rescued from the contaminating influences of patriarchal thought, can spiritually transform women.

Of course, not all women who experience childbearing spiritually will describe their experiences the same way. Some liken childbearing to an archetypal descent instead of death per se:

> The friendly faces around Raven and the ferns and rough-hewn redwood walls receded from her consciousness. She felt she had descended beneath the world into interior chambers where she and Ken [her mate] existed in perfect and protected solitude. After very little effort and too soon for Raven, the baby was born. She reached down to feel between its legs to see if it was the girl she had wanted. Assured that it was, she fell into a state of bliss so intense that when Kitti [the attending midwife] told her she was "bleeding like a river," she didn't answer, but put the baby to breast in the time-honored manner and rapidly recovered as her uterus hardened.[9]

Whatever the exact words used to describe the important transformations that occur for women at various stages of pregnancy, labor, and delivery, childbearing is potentially a sacred experience.

Counteractives

To help counter the negativity that often causes victims of patriarchal thinking to misunderstand and misappropriate this fundamental women's symbol—childbirth—we must engage ourselves variously in retrieving and reframing it. To that end, I have assembled in what follows a representative, but not exhaustive, series of images of childbirth—some gynecocentric, most androcentrically distorted—to illustrate some of the connections between women's cultural contexts and our resultant experiences of childbirth. Their arrangement, beginning with "preconception" and progressing through the various phases of pregnancy, labor, and delivery, reflects the physiological pattern of women's "great secret." Each section typically begins with images strongly contaminated by patriarchal "misconceptions" and moves in so far as possible to positive reframings. In a few instances, sections focusing entirely on androcentric appropriations of a specific image are followed by positive reconstructions.

But presenting, retrieving, and reframing images does not take place in a vacuum. Since the second wave of feminism started in the late sixties, various books, feminist or otherwise, have begun to examine childbirth as a basis for philosophical and religious meanings. Representative of the earliest second-wave feminist books to seriously study motherhood is Dorothy Dinnerstein's influential *The Mermaid and the Minotaur,* which argues that overwhelmingly female-dominated childcare is responsible for "human malaise." [10] Since it emerged in the mid seventies, however, *Mermaid* has become dated. More couples do now share childcare more equally, making Dinnerstein's thesis slightly less generally applicable. Furthermore, much of what Dinnerstein asserts about childbirth has either changed or else reflects an unempirically grounded "inherited wisdom" characteristic of many theorists, which is troubling to many contemporary midwives and home-birthing parents. For example, Dinnerstein asserts that "it is in a woman's arms and bosom that the delicate-skinned infant—shocked at birth by sudden light, dry air, noises, drafts, separateness, jostling—originally nestles. In contact with her flesh it first feels the ecstasy of suckling, of release from the anguish of hunger and the terror of isolation. [11] Nowadays many birthing practices favor low lighting, muted sounds, and gentleness. As for the newborn's "anguish of hunger," Dinnerstein appears unaware that mother's milk does not come in until at least twenty-four hours postpartum. More disturbing, however, is Dinnerstein's grudging attitude toward maternity. She treats it as if it were merely to be "gotten through" as quickly as possible. This attitude is particularly conspicuous when she calculates the amount of time motherhood should take: "A generous estimate of the average number of children a maternally inclined woman would produce, if maternity were genuinely optional, is perhaps three. . . . Another generous estimate is that each birth might remove a woman from her sphere of activity for at most six months." [12] Continuing in this vein of measuring out minimal allotments of maternal "duty," Dinnerstein thus diminishes motherhood fully as much as some patriarchal thinkers have done. Implicitly, she presents "full human being" as something other than, or in addition to, "being a mother." Thus, despite the enormous influence of her book, Dinnerstein's attitude toward her subject matter is far removed from the sacred potential of childbearing. For that very reason, however, *Mermaid* presents a useful example of one strand of feminist thought against which to play off my own very different ideas.

Feminist Mary O'Brien has also provided some relevant childbearing theory in *The Politics of Reproduction*. As she makes clear, the idea that childbearing is a biological trap for women is an illegitimate distortion, for it ignores such equivalent "traps"—applicable to all humans, not just to women—as eating, sexuality, and dying. Each informs a major philosophy, as O'Brien points out. The need to eat, which requires work, informs Marxism; sexuality informs Freudianism; and death, always a topic of philosophers, specifically informs existentialism in the twentieth century. Yet, she argues, no comparable philosophy has emerged from the necessity of impregnated females to give birth. O'Brien also rightly points out that "we cannot analyse reproduction from the standpoint of any existing theory. The theories themselves are products of male-stream thought, and are among the objects to be explained."[13] To create such a necessary theory, O'Brien speaks of "reproductive consciousness," a condition experienced by both sexes, but in different ways. Using Hegel's well-known concept of dialectic, she reminds the reader that Hegel, though a misogynist, examines the dialectics of reproduction, seeing it as "unity, separated opposites, reunion." Then, taking issue with Hegel's assertion that the original seed "breaks free," in the form of the infant, from its matrix composed of the two parents into "a higher form of the embodied unity . . . of the parents," she stresses instead the act of labor by which a woman brings forth this new being.[14] This shift of emphasis is critical for maintaining a truly inclusive understanding of childbirth. Patriarchal thought, of which Hegel is but one representative, repeatedly focuses on the child, ignoring both the mother and the birthing process. Truly human-centered thinking must look inclusively at childbirth, seeing it as an event of great significance in and of itself and for laboring women, their mates, and their resultant children.

Another book significant for retrieving and reinterpreting childbirth is Emily Martin's *The Woman in the Body*.[15] Martin also uses Marxist metaphors to describe the alienation of women from our own reproductive labor, but from an anthropological, not a political, perspective. Based on interviews with 165 women of diverse backgrounds and ages, her study relates most directly to childbirth in its discussion of medical metaphors. Particularly chilling is the uterus, imaged as a machine to be tended by mechanical forceps. The result for contemporary medicine and technology, Martin argues, is general acceptance of an interventionist approach to childbirth: If the uterus is a machine, it must be regulated and fixed, not allowed to "run" on its own. Cesarean sections, she claims, are increasingly seen as "providing the best products"! Especially disturbing is the virtual disappearance of any woman, as the womb essentially displaces her. It follows that women's own experiences of giving birth are rendered insignificant and that mother and child, rather than being two players in a kind of dance, become separated out as antagonists locked in conflict.

Equally essential to serious consideration of women's reproductive experience is Sara Ruddick's *Maternal Thinking*, which engages the question, If "all thinking

. . . arises from and is shaped by the practices in which people engage, what then . . . is a woman's practice?''[16] Ruddick's answer is mothering because of its centrality in many women's lives and its effects on many others who identify with mothers. Basically a philosophy, the book moves from the general and abstract to the particular and concrete by focusing on certain "maternal" ways of thinking about the world reflective of cross-culturally common demands on mothers to protect, nurture, and train their children. Particularly noteworthy are Ruddick's frequently ambivalent observations on childbearing, as opposed to childrearing:

> Although birthing labor is an undeniably female activity, it is possible to minimize its importance to mothering as a whole. Adoptive or stepmothers are no less qualified maternal workers because they have not given birth. Nor is giving birth sufficient grounds for undertaking maternal work or doing it effectively. Pregnancy, birth, and lactation are different in kind from other maternal work and, measured by the life of one child, are brief episodes in years of mothering. A scrambling, temperamental toddler . . . a school child . . . a college student . . . are more emblematic of the demands on a mother than is a feeding infant, let alone a silent fetus.[17]

What is disturbing here is the disjunction Ruddick makes between gestation and childbirth on the one hand, and childrearing, on the other. Reassuring though her words may be for adoptive and stepmothers, Ruddick nonetheless minimizes the uterine stage of life, which is increasingly important in light of current findings in pre- and perinatal research.[18] What happens in utero, from the moment of conception, is now thought vital to the future well-being of a child. In contrast to Ruddick's assertion, mothering does start in pregnancy and good mothering should start there, even if, or perhaps especially if, the birth mother subsequently gives up her child for adoption. The separation of birthing from mothering needs to be examined carefully, for it is yet another version of the separations of mother from uterus, of women from our own experiences, that so negatively fragment our lives. As opposed to separating the two, and working from the abstract and general to the particular and concrete as Ruddick explicitly does, I have chosen to do the reverse: to stress the continuum of maternal experience reflected in coitus, conception, pregnancy, labor, childbirth, the postpartum period, and on into full-blown motherhood. I do so by working with and from the particularities of women's own experiences. In so doing, I have discovered that the interrelationship of mother-to-be, father-to-be, and preborn is such that it requires total reframing of childbirth.

A Feminist Archetypal Theology

This book is intended to provide such a reframing by developing a feminist archetypal theology of childbearing. One promising book for this enterprise is Penelope Washbourne's *Becoming Woman,* which examines various stages in women's lives for their role in creating ultimate meaning. In speaking of the spiritual and psychological changes brought about by pregnancy and birth, Washbourne emphasizes that pregnancy and birth "happen *through* a woman. "She does not appear in control of her body although she experiences the events."[19] This significant insight illustrates how greatly woman-centered spiritual experience differs from the patriarchal biblical imperative to have dominion over Nature.

Yet another text that helps begin the task of opening up the interconnected imagery of motherhood, pregnancy, childbirth, and sacrality is French feminist Julia Kristeva's essay "Stabat Mater." Kristeva makes the necessary, but not always acknowledged, distinction between woman and mother, emphasizing the psychological tendencies of Western cultures to conflate the two. After summarizing the development of the Cult of the Virgin, Kristeva establishes her main point: In today's "postvirginal" world, nothing replaces the Marian cult as a discourse of motherhood (a problematic assertion given such contemporary Marian devotions as pilgrimages to places like Zeitoun, Egypt, and Medjugorje in what used to be Yugoslavia). To help compensate for this loss, Kristeva calls for a "herethics" centered on "the dark area that motherhood constitutes for a woman," based on listening to mothers' own experiences of their bodies, language, and pleasure.[20] While Kristeva herself has not developed the theory or "herethics" she calls for, her focus on the psychological satisfaction the Virgin Mother once afforded women supplies a helpful point of departure.

More specifically archetypal is Sylvia Brinton Perera's essay "The Descent of Inanna: Myth and Therapy."[21] Perera views Inanna's archetypal feminine pattern of repeated descent from life into death and back into life from four different perspectives: as part of the rhythmic order of nature with its diurnal, seasonal, and vegetal transformations; as an initiation into the sacred realm of nature and the unconscious; as a pattern of feminine psychological wholeness for both women and men; and as a way of viewing what many now speak of as "a return of the goddess." All four perspectives, particularly the second and third, bear heavily on meanings of childbirth as many women experience it. The knowledge represented by Ereshkigal's terrifying realm, to which Inanna repeatedly descends, strongly opposes the kind of knowledge our technological world so values.

Like Perera's essay, portions of Patricia Reis's *Through the Goddess: A Woman's Way of Healing* also apply to the mysteries of childbirth, although in neither source is childbirth per se the focus. It is particularly in her chapter "The Mystery Is Always of the Body: A Mid-Life Meditation on the Villa of Mysteries at Pompeii" that Reis provides relevant insights. In the villa is a fresco of Ariadne, Mistress of the Labyrinth, holding the god Dionysus on her lap. As Reis says, "The journey to the center of the labyrinth has been imagined for millennia as the journey to the center of the soul, a symbol of 'the way.' "[22] But the labyrinth, as I point out in my book *Motherself,* is also the lived experience of childbearing.[23]

Perhaps the most comprehensive work that explicitly addresses the sacred aspects of childbearing is anthropologist Marta Weigle's *Creation and Procreation.* This collection of feminist reflections creates a "dialogue between myth as generally defined and women's mythology . . . as a more feminist complement and counterpart to the usual, largely sexist definitions of *mythos* as numinous, *ganz andere,* other and other worldly.''[24]

Childbearing as Religious Practice

Ultimately, these theoretical works, whether predominantly philosophical, sociological, or archetypal, useful as they are in pointing the way, are insufficiently anchored in the concrete process of childbearing to truly mirror women's lived experiences. Consequently, the sources I have found most useful are those which present childbearing variously in the words of childbirth educators, midwives, and, above all, women actually experiencing pregnancy and childbirth. Collectively, these words make it clear that, like birth and death, childbearing provides women with an important natural means of self-transformative power. Furthermore, unlike birth, which comparatively few people recollect, childbearing (unanaesthetized) can be remembered, and unlike death, it is a condition from which we normally "return." This means that women have been granted by nature "the secret of life" in two important ways: through our ability to conceive, gestate, and bear children and through our ability during labor and delivery to attain spiritual "knowledge" beyond that of everyday consensual reality. But historically this essentially empowering and transformative experience of women has been "stolen" from us. As women's experience, childbearing has been variously denigrated, denied, and devalued. Yet it has also been appropriated by being made the paradigm for religious rituals and initiations into male-dominated social realms. Thus, paradoxically, patriarchal thought frequently makes childbearing metaphoric of "higher" ritualized rebirth from which women have traditionally been excluded, while simultaneously distancing itself from actual childbirth. To counter these disturbing "thefts" of women's childbearing capabilities, women need to rename, reritualize, reinterpret, and reframe childbearing for ourselves and for our partners. This book is intended to help women do that.

Mother
with
Child

1 Preconception(s)

A definition of childbirth depends heavily on a mixture of the experience, imaginative power, and world view of the definer and his or her culture. Whether childbirth also depends on something "out there" believed independent of definer or participant is an unresolvable philosophical conundrum that current poststructuralist theories disallow. But to a great extent, childbirth depends on the preconceptions that any particular individual brings to bear on it.

Although not automatically construed as part of childbearing, preconceptions are just as important as the actual biological stages. So strongly do our preconceptions—the particular images of childbirth to which members of both sexes have been acculturated—influence us that they often determine a woman's experience of childbirth, including its physical manifestations, just as they do a man's expectations of what it is or should be. If a woman (or man) preconceives childbirth as so awe inspiring that "it is difficult to describe without becoming intensely poetic or religious,"[1] how different her experience will be from that of a woman who preconceives it, as does noted contemporary obstetrician Frederick Leboyer, as "the torture of an innocent."[2] And equally at odds with both is the common contemporary preconception that birth is merely a mechanical process.[3]

Preconceived notions necessarily cover an enormous range including beliefs that pregnancy and childbirth automatically fulfill a woman, labor is unbearably painful, or a baby will be deformed if its mother looks at any deformed creature in pregnancy. Some of these notions are clearly superstitious, some overtly religious, others ideological. To the extent that they inform the consciousness of a woman who plans to conceive and bear children, however, they all exert powerful influence.

"VALUE-FREE" CHILDBIRTH

In twentieth-century Western cultures, one of the most commonly held, pernicious preconceptions about childbirth considers it inherently "value-free." Value-free childbirth derives from a seemingly objective biological model, well described in that fount of "value-free" information, the *Encyclopaedia Britannica:*

> Childbirth, the act of bringing forth a child. Because this process requires considerable physical effort on the part of the mother it has been termed and is usually known as 'labour.' The term 'parturition' (a bringing forth) is also applied to the process of childbirth.
>
> About 280 days after the onset of the last menstruation in the human female, or 270 days after the fruitful coitus, the irregular intermittent contractions of the uterus (womb) that began in the early months of pregnancy become more regular and increase in frequency and intensity. This assumption of a rhythmic character by the uterine contractions marks the beginning of the process by which the maternal organism separates and expels the mature products of conception.[4]

This presumed value-free, seemingly natural biological model of childbirth exemplifies the interpretive problems at the heart of this book. Most people living in "advanced" technological cultures such as our own probably accept this model automatically; unquestionably, it is the one that most late-twentieth-century Westerners consider true to the facts of childbirth. Because pregnancy seems to result from successful male fertilization of an egg gestated inside a womb, the androcentric bias of the common biological model passes largely unnoticed. Yet when this process is viewed on film it is very much open to interpretation. What is typically seen in a value-free interpretation as a sperm penetrating the outer rim of an egg can just as well be seen as an egg choosing one sperm from the many and allowing it to enter. As anthropologist Robbie Davis-Floyd explained to me: "You can clearly see the egg reach out with a tentacle and draw the sperm into the inner area. Then the egg penetrates the top of the head of the sperm and blows it up. Then it explodes, and its genetic material is distributed throughout the egg. Thus, the two merge into one, but the egg's role is active, agentic." How greatly this view of the process departs from the supposedly value-free model that sees only the sperm as active!

Typically the value-free model is the only possibility, rather than merely one of many images of childbirth. By appearing to convey neutral information central to all humans, this implicitly androcentric, biological image has come to inform our foundational beliefs on the subject. In addition to its androcentric bias, there is another problem with this value-free model. From a modernist perspective it seems absolutely unassailable and totally lacking in mythic, religious, or ideological coloration. Yet this is not so.

Granting a value-free status to childbirth viewed through a biological lens is common to modern cultures. Premodern cultures, however, would abhor this view that most of us now automatically accept as natural. Various Australian aboriginal groups, for example, much like many contemporary New Agers, "know" that babies are "made" when an appropriate spirit child enters a woman.[5] To claim that men and women create babies on their own is absurd! Furthermore, it is sacriligious. How can mere mortals claim powers unique to deities? Even to think so risks grave offense.

At issue here is a serious, not specifically androcentric, problem of modernity—desacralization. Desacralization is the process by which accepted premodern connections linking this world to the divine world snap. What remains appears purely human. Thus, this world loses its special awe-inspiring capacity. In a poststructuralist view this is also the case because all meanings are believed to result solely from the language we use. To think that we can ever reach "beyond" language to the thing itself is absurdly delusive.

To a certain extent desacralization is implicit in the view that childbirth is a biotechnological process, that is, it occurs for totally explicable reasons. Premodern views—whether matrifocal emphases on parthenogenesis, or patrifocal revisions, alterations, or usurpations of childbirth—make childbirth sacred, albeit in different ways, although it may not be sacred as far as a particular laboring mother is concerned. Just as sacrality may be considered in terms of its feminine, depth and Earth-oriented qualities, or its masculine, height and Sky-oriented aspects, so with its opposite, desacralization. Given a supposedly value-free model of childbirth that desacralizes childbirth, the disturbed sacrality is not exclusively masculine.

One of the most archaic images of childbirth, which depicts women as sole possessors of the power of giving life, makes childbirth a great mystery. When we give birth, the powers of cosmic creation come into play. Yet biological descriptions reveal no trace of the awe traditionally associated with cosmic powers. As ordinarily worded, the language of a value-free model precludes the great mystery once believed unique to women. Thus, the desacralization reflected by a value-free biological model includes a gynecocentric as well as an androcentric perspective.

Given the sexually inclusive nature of desacralization, are women better off with a value-free biological model than with models that impose an inappropriate masculine sacrality on childbearing? This is the kind of question that divides some radical feminists from women with differing views. When childbirth is construed as sacred from a masculine perspective, the outcome of a woman's labor, her child, is sacred. Or, if not the child, the presumed central figure of the drama— its father. Or, if not the father, the deity responsible for the child's creation. Religious understandings of childbirth that focus on a Divine Child or a Divine Father unquestionably diminish its personal meaning for some women. Yet, even if religious meaning is variously bestowed on baby, father, or deity, a woman still knows herself to be instrumentally meaningful. Even if she personally does not play center stage, and even if she functions as a vessel, understood negatively (rather than positively as vessel imagery is when it reflects feminine sacrality), her part still matters. It contributes to the religious meaning that she, as a member of her culture, professes.

But meaning of this sort poses a serious problem. It is androcentrically biased toward the importance of child and/or father while simultaneously diminishing that of the mother. Such androcentric meaning has severely injured generations of women. Yet, despite this potential for harm, the question must be asked: Are women better off with androcentric sacrality than with no sacrality at all? Have all women who have seemingly enacted the role of passive birthgiver *vis-à-vis* their glorified spouses or offspring found their experiences negative? Events that many contemporary Western women consider degrading may not have seemed so to most premodern women. This point, of course, lies at the heart of consciousness raising. Before consciousness raising influenced hundreds of women's groups in Western cultures, few of us knew the extent of our own internalization of patriarchal preconceptions. In the past, cultural norms typically went unquestioned by all but the most feminist of women. At the same time, the assigned role of an individual of either sex mattered vitally for maintaining preindustrial cultures. While childbirth per se might not have ranked high in the past, it was clearly essential. Even if received wisdom overvalued men's roles at the expense of women's, women nonetheless played clearly defined, meaningful parts. Biblically speaking, a woman was destined to feel pain. This is certainly negative and undesirable from most contemporary feminist perspectives. But for women who believe the patriarchal Genesis story, this role confers spiritual meaning. The woman experiencing intensely painful labor at least knows why it hurts. If she is Jewish or Christian, she understands herself to be the most recent descendant of Eve.

By contrast, a seemingly value-free biological model of childbirth inhibits that kind of meaning. Unquestionably, many women find it a great relief to be freed from patriarchal meanings. Yet a biological model also "frees" women from the ancient, prepatriarchal meanings evident in woman-centered, parthenogenetic imagery of childbirth. With a biological model, women don't just lose the negative meanings conferred by patriarchy. We also lose the positive ones of feminine sacrality. This double loss raises an important question: Can we replace the spiritual meanings—whether androcentric or gynecocentric—erased by the value-free biological model with some other positive ones congruent with contemporary Westernized world views? Because the language surrounding the biological model makes the issue of *meaning* as such seem irrelevant, childbirth becomes an occurrence viewed primarily as necessary to ensure a product, the child. Consequently, a major interpretive issue is raised by a biological image of childbirth. Does a woman fare better when her world is informed by overtly mythic and religious meanings, even those precluding equality or excluding her from her culture's power structure? Or is she better off in a world devoid of such meanings, negative and positive alike? Does exchanging androcentric for mechanical meaning improve her lot?

Answering these questions requires distance from our own technological culture. Then what appears value-free becomes just another folk system of values and beliefs. But because our entire culture is so permeated by a scientific world view, it seems natural to most people who have grown up with that view. That makes it extremely difficult to see scientific models themselves as just some among many different models of "reality." The essay, "The Technocratic Body and the Organic Body: Cultural Models for Women's Birth Choices" by Robbie Davis-Floyd, helps clarify this issue. Based on interviews with forty middle-class women who have given birth, thirty-two in hospital, eight at home, the essay reveals markedly different belief systems in the two groups. Most striking are the differences in their attitudes toward mind/body and control. The women who chose hospital births did so because their world views so thoroughly reflect the Cartesian mind/body split that they feel their bodies are not identical with themselves. This statement of a woman named Georgia is representative: "You know, I think there is me and then there is what I'm like physically which can be changed or modified—clothes, makeup, exercise, hairstyles, food."[6] Most of the women who saw themselves as being separate from their bodies also viewed pregnancy negatively, as a time when they were out of control: "I didn't like it. It just overwhelmed me, the kinds and varieties of sensations and the things that happen to your body because of the pregnancy. I didn't like it at all. I felt totally alienated from my body." [7]

By contrast, the eight women who chose home birth were more in tune with their bodies. Not only did they not separate out body from self, they also experienced the growing fetus very differently, as what I call motherself, a binary-unity which is both two and one at the same time, its parts consisting of mother and child in varying degrees of relationship to each other.

Such close interrelationship of mother and child is not characteristic of the value-free model of childbirth. Although this model cannot legitimately be called either good or bad, what is potentially harmful is the way it so readily suggests that ultimately humans can control everything. "God" or "a cosmic force" or "nature" is replaced by the hubristic notion that nothing remains outside human control. A particular danger with this thinking for some childbearing women is that the associated technology they welcome to control a painful process may also serve to alienate them from their bodies, their womanhood—which already seems separate—and most disturbing, their own fetuses, which then become "products" emerging from their alienated bodies. The most serious question that this supposedly value-free model so painfully raises is whether what appears like progress is not at times a strong contributing factor in many of the diverse alienations so common to contemporary Westernized cultures. If so, the common preconception that childbearing is a neutral, value-free event deserves at the very least to be carefully reappraised as part of the process of reinterpreting childbirth.

DESTINY AND DUTY

A particularly prevalent patriarchal preconception holds childbearing to be woman's destiny. As feminist writer Gena Corea puts it in *The Mother Machine*, "The message comes down to women with the force of centuries-long repetition. The patriarchy gives us the message through games, stories, toys ('Sunny Suzy Suburban Doll House'). Our doctors give us treatments if our ovaries or wombs fail us. It is our cell-deep knowledge. We are here to bear the children of men. If we can not do it, we are not real women. There is no reason for us to exist." [8] Corea's words accentuate the line between destiny, ordinarily thought of as a predetermined course, and duty, usually considered what one is morally obligated to do. That line typically blurs in the case of childbearing.

It is primarily in the name of family that women's childbearing "destiny" turns into duty. But what exactly is family? Many Western individuals still imagine it as mother, father, several children, and a dog. But this Norman Rockwell image is only one—an increasingly problematic one, at that—of several possibilities. In most of the postindustrialized world the family has shrunk, just as conversely in the nonindustrialized world it still extends beyond a nuclear core to include mother, father, all unmarried children, eldest (sometimes youngest) son, his wife, and their children. Domestic groups that defy these nuclear or extended categories are variously stretched to fit, considered anomalous, or otherwise categorized as clans or tribes, thus skewing the experiences of many groups such as Amerindians, African Americans, and mothers and children living without an adult male. But however it is defined, "family" in a patriarchal context is the vehicle by which women's presumed destiny is turned into our "duty."

Women's duty to bear children for the sake of the family is difficult for women in patriarchies to avoid because patriarchies appropriate the family by defining it almost exclusively as the eldest male's, making every other family member subject to him. Each member contributes to the family as a whole, but only as a supporting player. As an individual, he or she does not matter. Only his or her role really counts. And who fills that role matters much less than the fact that it is filled.

Cultures that value the family over its individual members naturalize these family-ordained roles by acculturating members unquestioningly to play them. For a young woman, this means learning from birth that her primary function is to bear children, a duty typically not fulfilled unless she bears a healthy son. Moreover, in many traditional cultures, such as those dominated by Confucianism, Buddhism, and Hinduism, for example, this is not just a duty toward her husband or the oldest living male. It is ultimately an obligation to the revered ancestors. In many cultures this means that a woman's duty is to procreate primarily for the sake of past generations.

Such rigid past-orientation necessarily casts a childbearing woman into a rigid, preordained role: Only her labor prevents the family line from dying out. Seemingly this makes her indispensable. In fact, she is indispensable only in the sense that a productive cow is to its owner. If one fails, another can replace it, a situation exemplified in Genesis 16 when the Egyptian maid Hagar substitutes procreatively for the barren Sarai, albeit in this case at Sarai's urging. How strongly this ancient example foreshadows current surrogacy practices wherein any woman's womb will do for a fetal implant!

Viewing childbirth primarily as a duty to immortalize ancestors may initially startle contemporary Westerners. Yet this differs little from contemporary desires to immortalize ourselves, especially as presented through the eyes of sociobiologists. According to sociobiological theory, individual genes, much like children borne to ensure ancestral immortality, achieve immortality through reproduction.

Lest such concerns for attaining ancestral status—for either sex—seem far removed from contemporary Western life, consider that in the early days of its use AID (artificial insemination by donor sperm) was highly controversial precisely because it breaks a husband's link to his ancestors. Not only were AID children ruled illegitimate by Canadian, English, and U.S. courts, but AID was also considered adulterous behavior on the part of the woman! A 1921 Ontario Supreme Court case makes abundantly clear that the essential problem was "the possibility of introducing into the family of the husband a false strain of blood."[9] Similarly, a *Journal of the American Medical Association* editorial (May 6, 1939) comments that "the fact that conception is effected not by adultery or fornication but by a method not involving sexual intercourse does not in principle seem to alter the concept of legitimacy. This concept seems to demand that the child be the actual offspring of the husband of the mother of the child.'' The editorial goes on to suggest that because any child born of semen from a man other than the husband would apparently be illegitimate, a couple should actually safeguard their AID child's inheritance by adopting it![10] Such legalities about paternal genes ludicrously distort the already disturbing preconception that it is a woman's duty to bear her husband's children.

The harm done to women by this common patriarchal preconception is enormous. Not only does it reduce her to a single function, but it also makes her nothing but a means for perpetuating a man's family line. This restrictive preconception influences many women to reject motherhood and childbearing as possible venues for sacred, gynecocentric meaning. How is it possible then to reframe such a preconception?

Construed as ''duty,'' childbearing holds very little potential for retrieval. What has to be examined, however, is the subtext of ''women's childbearing duty.'' What are men really saying when they espouse the notion that women must conceive and bear children? What emerges from the subtext are fear, pain, and longing: fear that men may not produce children, and pain projected ahead as a sort of advance mourning for that terrifying possibility. This is not to exonerate the culturally embedded belief that women must have children, nor is it to deny that many women have suffered enormously from being forced into an unchosen role. But if one steps back a bit, it seems that many attitudes that have been interpreted as being *against* women may simply be *for* children. The two are not necessarily the same, even though they often appear suspiciously alike. Putting the emphasis on men's desires for children, as opposed to men's desires for keeping women ''barefoot and pregnant,'' may help in reinterpreting the idea of childbearing as women's duty. But an equally harmful notion must first be dealt with.

At the opposite extreme, some feminists, perhaps not wanting or having children themselves, have at times not only denied that childbearing is women's duty but also asserted that women should not have to bear children at all. Radical feminist Shulamith Firestone provides a good example when she calls for ''the freeing of women from the tyranny of their biology by any means available and the diffusion of the childbearing and childrearing role to the society as a whole.''[11] Seeing childbearing as so hateful that we must be ''freed'' from it scarcely improves on the notion it opposes, that childbearing is our duty.

I can't help but think of my own experience as an excellent answer to Firestone because as a child I, too, abhorred the idea that women were expected to become wives and mothers. I had other ambitions. I wanted to ''do something'' with my life. But after I had my first child I reevaluated my stance. So deeply meaningful to me were childbirth and the family it created that I find purely political feminist discussions of the topic as far removed from my personal experience as the patriarchal horrors those discussions are intended to address. Something is missing in both extremes: In neither do I hear that to be able to bear children is to be ''graced.'' Ultimately, the biological capacity that has been so variously twisted into an ugly condition is a great gift. Yet, as fairy tales often tell, when a great gift or secret is proffered in a form not immediately recognizable, sometimes it is mistakenly rejected.

Instead of either accepting or fighting the patriarchal "preconception" that childbearing is women's duty, it makes more sense to read the subtext of that imperative. When we do, we discover grace or privilege, a reinterpretation of duty touchingly apparent in these words of incest survivor Deborah Lipp, who has left her past to become a very concerned and aware mother: "In opening to the powerful forces of labor, we learn the difference between surrendering to nature and submitting to an abusive authority figure."[12] As Lipp so clearly states, reviling patriarchally imposed obligations is one thing; railing against a fact or gift of nature is quite another. Seeing the difference between them allows women to preconceive childbearing not as duty but as gift. That shift turns a negative preconception into a powerfully positive understanding of childbirth.

2 Conception

Throughout history and across cultures, various patriarchal preconceptions have strongly influenced beliefs about the childbearing cycle. Hence, many women experience tension between culturally accepted "knowledge" and our own bodily experiences. Some find that traditional "wisdom" overpowers body language, resulting in its silencing. Others, more independent perhaps, can listen to their own experiences. Thus, understandings of the various stages of childbearing typically run a gamut. Some reflect authentic gynecocentric experiences; others, patriarchally imposed interpretations. Conception, the first of the many stages of childbearing, is no exception.

Today we view conception primarily through a biological lens that teaches us that at birth a woman's ovaries contain their full quota of potential eggs, some half million or so. Fertilization requires an egg's male counterpart, a sperm, to swim up as the egg slides down during ovulation. Only if they meet and the sperm attaches to and is accepted by the wall of the egg does conception occur. From this pattern emerges a host of images: the persistent, active male principle opposes and supersedes its passive female counterpart; the chance meeting, out of millions of sperm, of this sperm with that egg becomes in countless love stories the chance meeting of this lover with that; the fusing of sperm and egg becomes the fusing of a kind of androgyne, and so on.

Conception signals the onset of, and thus often stands for, the entire process of giving life. Its signs include most notably eggs, sperm, and menstrual blood. These signs figure worldwide as symbols of creation, the egg frequently representing the source out of which all creation springs and blood representing the destruction believed prerequisite to anything new.

These images, derived from life-bestowing fluids, produce motifs that have been understood in vastly different ways. An archaic pattern of parthenogenesis ties these fluids almost exclusively to women's enormous power, and androgynous images make women's life-bestowing fluids seem to be the property of both sexes. A biologically more realistic view emerges in the ancient theme of the *hieros gamos,* the holy marriage, which strongly celebrates fertility as predominantly women's power. Then there are images that "reconceive" conception variously as world creation or the creation of artists. In the process of such reconception, women's life-bestowing fluids are transformed into male "property," although this negative reconception can sometimes by neutralized by the New Age practice known as "conscious conception." A sad commentary on the pervasiveness of male "theft" of women's power to conceive is found in assorted late twentieth-century technologies. Fortunately, gynecocentric counterclaims help to rescue childbirth from such patriarchal incursions.

THE POWER OF LIFE GIVING

"Earth first produced starry Sky equal in size with herself, to cover her on all sides." [1] Hesiod's parthenogenetic image of Earth, personified as a female conceiving and reproducing with no male participation, unequivocally demonstrates the great reproductive power of women. Today, we consider the image false because we know the "facts of life." These facts, however, like many we take for granted, are not immediately self-evident. Who, not knowing them, would automatically conclude that new life results from sexual intercourse? So much time separates the initial act from its outcome that prehistoric inability to recognize the male contribution is not surprising. A woman's belly does not swell revealingly for several months. And other signs—enlargement of breasts, darkening of nipples, morning sickness—mark pregnancy far less conspicuously and specifically. Consequently, although today we must actively imagine parthenogenesis as the principle of reproduction, its logic is undeniable. In fact, some plants—the dandelion, the cat's foot, and various algae and fungi—and some lower animals—the aphid, the parasitic wasp, and the thrip—do conceive parthenogenetically.

During human gestation, visible signs normally mark only the female. It is she whose belly enlarges, she whose breasts swell, she from whose body new life emerges. How natural then to see "woman," and by extension all women, as embodying some mysterious life-generating power. In any culture where women are believed sole possessors of procreative power, female images of divinity take precedence. Perhaps this is one key to the historical shift that reversed the ancient overemphasis on women's reproductive power in favor of men's biological capacities. Imagine the questions that must have vexed our remote ancestors: Why do women alone have this power? Why not men as well? What do women have that men do not? What can men do that will give them access to this secret?

Scientifically influenced cultures necessarily refer questions of this sort to the laboratory. But laboratory techniques provide a secularized approach to what others consider religious questions. Since Descartes, we in the West automatically split sacred from secular, religious from scientific. Many premodern cultures, however, assume the world is sacred. The concept of secularity simply does not exist. This does not mean that a sacred world is necessarily good, merely that it is infused with forces both divine and demonic.

When the world is understood in a religious sense, processes we now take for granted as natural inspire awe. Often they occasion ritual celebration. Thus, the replacement of cold hard winter by spring with its sunshine and sprouting greenery requires special thanks. Even the sun's daily return after darkness is a mystery to celebrate. How much more miraculous then is the periodic appearance of new human life from the bodies of women! It is scarcely surprising that prehistoric symbols of sacrality are overwhelmingly feminine—great goddess figures superseding gods.

Imaginatively entering such an archaic world view risks credibility, for evidence reconstructing prehistoric cultures is problematic. Even saying "an" archaic world view presumes an unverifiable unity of archaic cultures. It also coalesces periods that cannot be pinpointed precisely. Bearing these caveats in mind, some reasonably well informed speculation nonetheless seems feasible.

The earliest era to which the term *archaic* applies is the Ice Age, known variously as the Paleolithic or the Pleistocene.[2] At that time, before hominids had learned to polish stones, make pottery, or cultivate plants, they subsisted entirely by hunting, fishing, and gathering fruits and berries. This age is usually dated from the first appearance of humans—a date that shifts with each new archaeological find. We now place the Ice Age's inception about two and a half million years ago and its close at the beginning of the postglacial period, about 8000 B.C.E.

Material finds from the earliest time, the Lower Paleolithic, are extremely sparse and limited mainly to burials and a few traces of cave art. The lack of evidence makes speculation difficult. But the Middle Paleolithic, about 100,000 to 25,000 years ago, the time when Neanderthals dominated the human world, permits some comparatively authoritative statements, based on finds from the Shanidar Caves in Iraq. Neanderthals carefully buried their dead, typically in a crouching position along with food offerings and flint tools such as scrapers, awls, and hand axes; therefore, scholars generally assume these were ceremonial burials designed to send the dead adequately prepared to their afterlife..

By the Upper Paleolithic era (c. 25,000–8,000 B.C.E.), humans of our own species, Homo sapiens, had evolved. Evidence from their burials includes various round disks of ivory, bone, and stone, anthropomorphic figurines, and some rings. All suggest cultic significance. By now, cave art abounds. Mostly paintings of animals, this art appears to refer to the hunting then so central to existence. Some, however, depicts unmistakably feminine figures, called "Venuses" because they frequently overemphasize female body parts, showing gigantic breasts hanging over enormously pregnant bellies. Best known is the Venus of Willendorf from Lower Austria.

Besides such archaeological evidence, a second and far more speculative source for entering into possible prehistoric world views is provided by analogy with contemporary Stone Age tribes. The !Kung Bushmen of the Kalahari, for example, are still sufficiently isolated from other cultures that they give probable insight into life for Stone Age peoples generally.[3] In the absence of viable alternatives, this kind of piecing together by analogy is useful, provided that a warning is borne in mind: Despite apparent similarities with hunter-gatherers of the past, contemporary tribes have continued to develop and change over the centuries; therefore, comparisons will be far from exact.

For those who survive in contemporary Stone Age cultures, life typically lasts about thirty years. The total number of humans comprising a single band is so

small that reproduction is absolutely crucial to group survival. Without fairly regular births, extinction results. Because encounters with other bands are rare, enlargement by intermarriage or domination cannot substitute for careful reproduction. Our own highly urbanized, densely populated world makes this kind of species
survival hard to imagine (although potential nuclear holocaust or devastation by
AIDS may elicit comparable fears). Not directly competing for survival with deer,
elephants, and the like, we relate to the natural environment far differently. No
longer seeing ourselves as one of many competing animal species, we generally
believe ourselves masters of all.

But in a setting where individual, group, and even species survival is at stake,
bearers of human life are necessarily revered. The logic behind Paleolithic madon-
nas and Venus figures therefore seems clear. In a world unaware of the "facts of
life," women possess the secret power for recreating human life, a potent power
indeed.

As the secret of life, this power has often been conceptualized as a kind of
mystical substance, universally sought in myths and rituals. It is variously the
substance of immortality or the key to salvation—the holy grail, the waters of life,
the plant of immortality. Regardless of whether a particular religio-cultural matrix
calls it bodily immortality or salvation of the soul, its questers all seek the same
thing—a cosmic power, knowledge of which provides entry into, and intimacy
with, life itself. However, tales of this secret frequently degenerate into belief that
its possessors control all nature.

From a gynecocentric perspective, the nearly exclusive identification of this
power with women's sexuality appears perfectly logical. What, after all, but cosmic
force reproduces all life? Extend this line of thinking into a world view as yet
unaware of the connection between coitus and childbirth, and the reproductive
aspect of sexuality appears solely women's. Until sexual intercourse is specifically
connected with reproduction, what we call sexual attraction exists quite apart from
reproduction (much as it does now, for totally different reasons, in our own post-
pill culture).

In the minds of early humans, it is the power to conceive and bear that so
strongly separates women from men. No matter how much a prehistoric man might
blow into a lifeless object thinking that life resides in the breath, or how much he
might form pieces of mud and clay into human shapes, or how many body parts
he might lop off in hopes of generating new life from them, he still would not
possess the "secret" of women—the ability to conceive a child in the belly seemingly without recourse to any other human being. So miraculous must have seemed
the female power to conceive that it is not surprising that men have struggled for
so much of history to make it their own.

ANDROGYNOUS CREATION

Historically, one way men have sought to master women's "secret" powers
of conception is through obliterating sexual differentiation. The mythical andro-

gyne, from the Greek words *andros* (man) and *gune* (woman), does just that. Plato's well-known description of this phenomenon in *The Symposium* is apt:

> "The original human nature was not like the present. In the first place, the sexes were originally three in number, not two as they are now; there was man, woman, and the union of the two. . . ." Everything about these primaeval men was double: they had four hands and four feet, two faces, two privy parts, and so on. Eventually Zeus decided to cut these men in two, "like a sorb apple which is halved for pickling." After the division had been made, "the two parts of man, each desiring his other half, came together, and threw their arms about one another eager to grow into one."[4]

The relevance of this primal androgyne to conception is its harmonious combination of female and male as *one,* able to create in and of itself. The androgyne makes neither sex primary, better, stronger, nor more important, so neither can claim priority. Consequently, the androgyne appears promising for retrieving the sacrality originally attached to childbearing. This is not entirely the case, however, as myths of creation readily show.

Although initially world creation seems vastly unlike conception of babies, the two are analogous. So central is this parallel in most cultures that some consideration of mythic diversity is necessary to help untangle its interconnections. Religionist Charles Long suggests a typology whereby creation variously occurs from nothing, from chaos, from a cosmic egg, from world parents, through emergence (parthenogenesis), or by the help of an artisan.[5] Innocent as these categories may appear, most minimize women's powers to conceive and bear children. Consider creation from world parents, for instance—seemingly a straightforward, albeit divinized, image of copulation. Yet look at the following passage from Euripides:

> Heaven and Earth were once one form, but stirred
> and strove and dwelt asunder far away:
> And then, revelling, bore unto the day
> And light of life all things that are, the trees,
> Flowers, birds and beasts and them that breathe the seas,
> And mortal men, each in his kind and law.[6]

The significant words are *once one form.* One form differs greatly from a separate female (Earth) and male (Heaven). Such oneness inaccurately reflects the human situation we all experience from birth, certain physical anomalies such as hermaphroditism or transsexualism excepted. It shows primal oneness, making it an image of androgynous creation.

A similar image occurs in a description of the primal god Prajapati in a Vedic hymn of creation: "What time the mighty waters came, Containing the universal germ."[7] In this case, "conception" inheres from the start. The primal waters, a traditional mythic symbol of the original state of chaos, contain the germ of creation *(Hiranyagarbha).* When this germ hatches, it gives birth to Lord Prajapati, himself androgynous. But this androgyne is also presented as "he." Why is he not also Lady Prajapati, a "she"? The same problem occurs with the Hindu god Siva, another androgynous god—also a "he"—who generally dominates his female half, the goddess Parvati.

Even more overtly androgynous conception occurs in Winnebago Indian lore. Slightly different in kind, the androgynous figure in this myth is an extremely primitive trickster figure:

> Trickster now took an elk's liver and made a vulva from it. Then he took some elk's kidneys and made breasts from them. Finally he put on a woman's dress. . . . He now stood there transformed into a very pretty woman indeed. Then he let the fox have intercourse with him and make him pregnant.

The story proceeds to tell how Trickster attracts the attention of the chief's son, and then:

> Not long after Trickster became pregnant. The chief's son was very happy about the fact that he was to become a father. Not long after that Trickster gave birth to a boy.[8]

Trickster bears two more boys before his true identity becomes known to the village. He then runs away and resumes his interrupted life as a husband and father in a different village.

In this case, female and male do not fuse but chronologically alternate. Despite his frequent confusion about his sexual nature, Trickster is shown as experiencing "his" primary sexual identity as male. Not only is he spoken of as "he" except during his brief change but that change is a departure from "his" ordinary identity.

For those raised in a Western culture, the damage such conflation of androgyny with masculinity causes is readily apparent from the biblical account of creation in Genesis 1:27:

> So God created man in his own image, in the image of God he created him; male and female he created them.

As many feminist thinkers have pointed out, if God created man in his own image, and then created "them" male and female, then by implication God's image has to be androgynous. The problem is that in popular thought and in many theological discussions both Jewish and Christian, God is construed strictly as "He." Admittedly, some theologians acknowledge the androgyny of the biblical God both in his creative role and by virtue of his feminine Shekinah and Wisdom. But the popularly disseminated view nonetheless remains as overwhelmingly patriarchal as the version inherited from the ancient Hebrews, whose patriarchalism correlates with their pastoral way of life.[9] This kind of renaming of the unified "one," not as androgyne but as male, so common to myths of creation, therefore perpetuates an image of women's reproductive powers being men's.

The reverse situation does occasionally occur. A goddess, understood as "she," appears to create parthenogenetically, yet contains within herself a masculine element. This technically makes her an androgyne. This happens in myths of primal waters—usually deified as goddesses, as for example the Babylonian Tiamat—which split apart to create the cosmos. A primal seed (a masculine principle), inherent in these waters, makes the seemingly parthenogenetic "goddess" conceive. The Vedic lines quoted above, while not referring to a goddess as such, nonetheless illustrate this point: What the mighty waters conceal is the universal germ. Consequently, one myth seems to cancel out another. The problem is that in patriarchal cultures, goddess myths lack power; only the god myths, as in the Bible, are treated as "true"—whether literally as in fundamentalist belief or metaphorically as in more liberal thought.

What makes androgynous cosmogonies particularly influential to the ways women have been conceived, in ways that the many overtly male-dominated creation myths are not, is the misleading way they appear to give equal weight to both sexes. Myths of androgynous creation deceive by seeming to promise an exit from the endless war of the sexes. By presenting female and male equally, they counter the usual jealousy of one sex for the powers of the other. If the two are one, such jealousy lacks foundation. Not only does this idealistic image too smoothly gloss over the androcentrism often hidden beneath an androgynous facade but it also ignores an important biological fact: It *is* women, after all, not men, who conceive and give birth, despite the fact that both sexes combine to facilitate the process. Brushing over this circumstance, defenders of androgynous images inadvertently rob women of our actual biological powers. By thus altering the facticity of things-as-they-are into a patriarchally wished-for things-as-they-should-be, androgynous myths of creation may be seen as male cooptations that do nothing positive for images of women.

The covert androcentrism behind myths of androgynous creation misleadingly portrays reproduction and childbearing and deprives women of our natural role. These myths have also influenced the history of ideas in yet another more complex way. Most cosmogonies try to explain the creation of the world with the least possible number of elements—one. If the element is material, as in most myths, it might be variously earth, air, fire, water, or ether; if spiritual, a particular god, such as Zeus or Brahma; if abstract, as in many philosophies, chaos, time, or night. Some traditions make two elements primary. In that case, opposition almost invariably separates the two principles from the beginning. Typically this dualism values one element positively, the other negatively. The classic example is "good versus evil." Thus, for example, in the earliest Persian cosmogonies light and dark (good and evil) are opposed but equal from the start.

As long as no elements are sexualized, the number has no bearing on images of women or men. But most systems of thought connect primary principles to one sex or the other. With material elements, earth with its capacity to bear vegetation is almost always homologized to woman or, even more abstractly, to a "female principle," and sky, with its complementary capacity to fertilize through sun and rain, to man or a "male principle." If the primal element is spiritual, sexuality usually characterizes the particular deity. Earth, deified, signals a feminine first principle, assuming Earth is the primary element. Conversely, when a sky god is first—the Greek Zeus, the biblical Yahweh, the Indo-European Dyaus—the first principle is masculine. An androgynous deity theoretically equalizes the sexes. The problem, however, is exactly the same one that occurs with the now increasingly obsolete generic *he* and *mankind*. The supposedly inclusive term actually covers an androcentric bias that does not accord women equal status, nor does it even necessarily include us at all.

When the primal element has an opposing element, whether from the start, as in dualism, or subsequently, as in systems of modified dualism, the problem of valuation intensifies. Now one element represents absolute good, the other total evil, oppositions which extend, respectively, to commonly held ideas of men and women. In Western thought, the idea that female and male exemplify fundamental oppositions seems to appear first in the thought of Heraclitus (c. 540–480 B.C.E.).[10] Not until the time of the Pythagoreans (c. 530 B.C.E.), however, does any sort of classification of pairs of opposites occur. Aristotle gives a table, reputedly Pythagorean, in his *Metaphysics:*

> limit and absence of limit
> one and many
> male and female
> straight and curved
> good and bad
> odd and even
> right and left
> rest and motion
> light and dark
> square and oblong[11]

In each case, the first named member of the pair, the ''male,'' was valued positively by the Pythagoreans, the second, the ''female,'' negatively. In the sometimes esoteric, highly mathematical context of Pythagorean thinking, each secondary member was devalued because its opposite was so highly esteemed for its presumed perfection.

Unfortunately, for women, such classifications, with various alterations and reversals, continue to this day. By the time Aristotle was formulating his ideas, for example, the concepts of motion and rest had become reversed. He considered the male active, which he deemed good; the female, conversely, he considered passive or bad, a distinction he makes frighteningly clear when he says that ''the female is as it were a deformed male, the menstrual discharge is semen though in an impure condition: i.e., it lacks one constituent, and one only, the principle of soul. . . . This principle has to be supplied by the semen of the male.''[12] As anthropologist Robbie Davis-Floyd pointed out to me, this aspect of Aristotle's thought has strongly influenced Western medicine in this way: Eve's punishment is combined with Aristotle's passive female, and these two ideas together are added to the Cartesian mind/body separation and the industrial metaphor of body-as-machine. This complex of ideas then yields the following idea: The male body is the best machine, and the female body is a defective machine. It therefore follows that birth is a defective mechanical process.

This same sort of classificatory thinking, which automatically places woman on the negative side of every polarity, also appears insidiously nowadays in personality tests that make presumed male behaviors such as aggressiveness the norm and presumed female behaviors such as nurturance the deviation. Therefore, women who score high on female qualities are automatically "proved" less able than men. Seemingly, then, all a woman must do is check off stereotypical masculine traits to score well on such tests. But no. Then she deviates in a different way: She is not "feminine" enough. Thus, when it comes to classification of pairs of opposites, whether we look back to the Pythagoreans or remain in our own era, women typically lose out on all counts, especially with our childbearing function. If we are too "masculine," how can we possibly be good, nurturing mothers? If too "feminine," then how can we be assertive and strong enough to function effectively?

It is primarily in the history of ideas that androgyous images of conception and creation rob women of our experience. Women are shown, by androgynous creation, to be less important for physically reproducing humanity than biology indicates. Moreover, when the principle underlying reproductive capability is taken away and then elevated, as it is in many creation myths, to the level of primary cosmic significance, then women are deprived in ways that continue to have enormous consequences. As long as only the male principle is sufficiently important to account for all creation, then the male sex will be as elevated as the female is correspondingly denigrated.

If, instead of being unequal, however, two principles are considered equivalent, then invariably one is seen as good, the other as evil. In this case, too, in patriarchal cultures, it is invariably women, not men, who appear on the evil side. Androgynous images of conception, creation, and childbirth represent another example of men stealing women's ability to carry and bear children. What we need instead are images that are in fact what on one level androgynous images only pretend to be: images that truly value the generative capabilities of both sexes equally. Is it possible, then, to read androgynous images in some other way, thus reclaiming them as potentially positive images of childbirth? The answer is a qualified yes.

Read in another fashion, images of androgyny do not reflect things as they are but as the way things might be or even as they are when human imagination transfigures them. If, instead of starting from the image of polarity—that is, of totally separate women and men—we start with the image of a fused creature, then the actual biological separation appears to be a fall away from some original, "better" state of unity. And this, indeed, is how many readers, including the misogynist Freud, have read the Plato myth. What such a reading does, even if it is understandably galling to women who have endured hundreds of years of patriarchal thinking, is to right what must seem like a grievous biological wrong: If the capacity to bear children is as central to human meaning as logic and history indicate it is, then its lack in men's lives has to feel unjust to them.

On the one hand, it is natural for many women to want to gloat, to want to reclaim this process in its literal biological form, given our history of oppression. But such a response, despite its admitted appeal on one level, misses our real need at this stage. Thinkers of both sexes must heal the split between us rather than exacerbate it. To simply show the negative side, while helpful for understanding a patriarchal Western history of ideas, does not suggest a way out of this morass nor a way of positively reframing childbirth. Furthermore, it misses a major point of androgynous images of creation and childbearing—their encapsulation of male reproductive desire.

On the other hand, such images can just as easily be read as reflecting a deep human longing to *overcome* difference rather than, or as well as, to emphasize it. A central paradox inherent in reframing childbirth is that no matter how much women may want to retrieve it simply for ourselves, we cannot successfully do so, for such retrieval ultimately works against us. Rather than strengthening our position, it simply accentuates the issue of women's more prolonged and intimate role in reproduction, the very issue that so separates women from men in the first place. Unless we recognize the implicit message of images such as these of androgynes, which at one level seek to bridge the gap, we cannot reconstruct the symbol that also most separates us—that of childbirth. As the next section indicates, a more explicitly equalizing mythic concept is one known as the "holy marriage."

THE HOLY MARRIAGE

In contrast to parthenogenetic images that attribute reproductive powers solely to women or to androgynous figures of creation that obliterate sexual differentiation, the mythic "holy marriage" recognizes the role of both sexes. Often referred to by the Greek term *hieros gamos,* the holy marriage is enacted by two figures who, whether known by the Japanese names Izanagi and Izanami, the Greek Ouranos and Gaia, or any of the countless variations in other cultures, are the universal Father Sky and Mother Earth.

Of the two terms, Mother Earth is far more familiar nowadays; however, it remains relatively abstract to most of us. City dwellers scarcely see the Earth, let alone contact it directly, for concrete intervenes, separating them from Earth as living entity. Furthermore, although city dwellers know as well as their rural cousins that Earth nurtures the fruit and vegetables they eat, they rarely participate in the growing process themselves, so their knowledge of plant fertility remains largely theoretical. Without actually planting seeds and watching them come up, develop, and slowly ripen, an individual's appreciation for Earth as bountiful mother is slow to develop.

Similarly, sky becomes "Father" based on the way humans experience "Him" or "it." Whereas earth provides the base upon which we stand, sky affords an immeasurably distant cover for that base, a circumstance repeated in many myths through the image of "Father Sky" covering "Mother Earth" and enclosing and smothering everything in between. Whereas earth provides sustenance, sky less immediately connects to human needs, even though sky variously provides moisture and sunshine, darkness and light, wind and calm. Because it combines both infinite expanse and height, sky automatically evokes the feelings we intend by the word *transcendence:* It is infinitely beyond the scope and powers of humanity, dwarfing us by contrast.

Stories of the primal mating of earth and sky are nearly universal. A good example comes from Maori tradition, which tells of Rangi the Sky falling in love with Papa the Earth beneath him. To enact his love, Rangi approached Papa during the primeval darkness and, in so doing, squeezed everything between them into eternal darkness, including the children their lovemaking produced. The germ of this idea of the holy marriage of earth to sky goes back, archaeological evidence indicates, to the Paleolithic era. Andre Leroi-Gourhan, a specialist in prehistoric cave paintings, claims that some of the earliest traces of the male-female polarity that underlies the holy marriage come from such figures as the bison and the horse, which stand respectively, he argues, for the female and the male.[13] More open to dispute is the claim that other common cave figures of varied triangular shape are vulvas, for many scholars find them too ambiguous to identify. Far more suggestive evidence of the female-earth side of the polarity comes from the Venus figures mentioned earlier.

In contrast to these purely material objects, interpretation of which is always speculative, we have mythic evidence, which is more clearly defensible, from the Neolithic period. Dating from around 8000 to 3000 B.C.E, the Neolithic was a time of enormous climactic changes precipitated by the glaciers receding northward sometime around 10,000 to 9000 B.C.E.[14] As a result of these severe weather changes, the food supply basic to the earlier Paleolithic era altered. Once-flourishing herds of large herbivorous animals disappeared, to be replaced by far less abundant deer, boar, and numerous smaller animals. With this shift from big to small game, hunting lost its previous high status, and agriculture replaced it in many places.

Concomitantly, the nature of the *hieros gamos* and its primary players altered as well. What was once a marriage of Heaven and Earth now becomes much more explicitly a fertility drama with numerous variations in different parts of the world. The key players are no longer always the same. In the cults of Egypt, Syria, Mesopotamia, and Anatolia, three dominate: a rather shadowy male god whose cult is associated with a bull, a mother goddess, and her son. The male god, known variously as Baal and Hadad in Syria, is a horned weather god who controls the rain. But it is ultimately the goddess, known variously as Inana or Ishtar in Mesopotamia, Anat in Syria, Astarte in Phoenicia, and so on, who, along with her son-lover, matters most.

The story of the passionate attachment of the mother goddess and her son, with the son's inevitable death, is particularly significant for conception and childbearing. The son-consort is variously called Zababa of Kish, Ashur, An, and Dumuzi or Tammuz. As with most long-lived myths, many variants exist. The main features are the love affair and marriage of mother and son, followed by the mother goddess's descent to the underworld where, in some versions, she is humiliated by a loathesome Queen of the Dead who temporarily turns her into a corpse. Eventually she escapes, only to discover that her son-lover has not been mourning her. Enraged, she therefore has him dragged down to the underworld in her place. Despite variations in details, the essential story of the passionate love of these two, followed by the son-lover's death, remains constant, becoming the prototype for an annual ceremony to renew the vegetation. Eventually, in Sumer, it is the King who enacts this pattern, copulating ritually with a temple prostitute to induce fertility in the land, their intercourse symbolizing Dumuzi's resurrection, which brings joy to the people.

The countless variants of this myth found in diverse agricultural societies emphasize the enormous reproductive power of women. So strong is this power that it becomes the model for agricultural fertility. Following women's example, the land will likewise yield up its bounties. Yet this mythic celebration of women's reproductive powers common to ancient fertility and initiatory rites eventually mutated into an ugly tale. Such mutation typifies the reinterpretation repeatedly found as patriarchies diminish women's roles in various ways. A clue to this particular alteration appears in the odd, little-known character Baubo, of the Demeter story, celebrated in the ancient mysteries of Eleusis. According to Orphic tradition, while Demeter is wandering the earth, inconsolably lamenting the kidnapping of her daughter Persephone, her grief lessens when she laughs at the dirty jokes of Iambe and Baubo, the daughters of Celeus of Eleusis. While Iambe is said to cheer the grieving goddess with words, Baubo does so with a curious gesture. She lifts her skirts to reveal beneath them either the young Iacchos (Bacchus/Dionysus) or a surgical scar resembling a baby's face.

What Baubo represents is revealed by her name, which means vagina or mock vagina, a feature dramatized in terra cotta figurines showing her genitals so dominating her body that they appear directly beneath her mouth in place of her torso. What provokes laughter in the myth is the sight of a "baby" or "child" where genitals are logically expected. Either image—the one of the young Dionysus, the other of a baby replacing Baubo's genitalia—reinforces the close sexual bond of mother and child.

Considering that the Eleusinian mysteries celebrating the story of Demeter contained as part of their ritual a manipulation of sexual implements, Baubo's role in the myth strongly suggests what patriarchy considers the obscene, but not the erotic, side of the conception-childbearing process. According to anthropologist Bruce Lincoln, who interprets the myth of Demeter and Persephone as the story of women's initiation into the sexual mysteries of womanhood,

> what seems to be expressed in this fashion is the understanding that when a young woman comes of age, or when women come together in the absence of men, the force of their sexuality is so great that it can no longer be suppressed. Although social norms may severely inhibit the direct expression of female sexual energy under ordinary circumstances, at these special moments it bursts forth in "obscene" gestures, songs, and stories, whereby women collectively celebrate the appearance of reproductive power in a new woman. Thus, when Demeter mourns the loss of her daughter, she simultaneously celebrates her daughter's transformation.[15]

The significant fact here is the labeling of women's sexuality as "obscene." Such labeling, extended to fertility rites in general, characterizes the patriarchal attitude of Jewish and Christian tradition and raises the sticky issue of what exactly the word *obscene* means. Is it possible to speak of a generalized category, "the obscene," as we do of "the sacred," for instance? Although usually treated as a moral issue, the obscene is also an aesthetic category that raises issues almost identical to those posed by "found objects" elevated to the status of art. But obscenity, instead of being on the positive end of the aesthetic scale, rests on the negative; here, "ugliness," in all senses of the word—aesthetic, physical, and moral—enters in. Because obscenity brings together elements that not only repel us sensually, aesthetically, and morally but that also tend to incite lust, this is a particularly horrifying category to most people. Its threefold nature necessarily assaults sensibilities with triple the force of any one of these categories alone. Its repulsiveness, on the one hand, combined with incitement to lust, on the other, appeals to what is generally considered the basest aspect of human nature. Nonetheless, the obscene holds great fascination for many people.

This fascination is what sets the obscene apart as a category, making it closely akin to the sacred in its negative demonic manifestation. In fact, in some instances, the two categories overlap. It is the capacity to fascinate that gives both their power. To be fascinated, as opposed to merely interested, is to be held in thrall, as if by a force outside oneself. A category incapable of so holding an individual more or less regardless of will hardly has power. It may hold our interest at times, but it does not lock us in place, helpless to go about our business. In the case of the obscene, the fascination seems to arise out of an attraction to the forbidden, to whatever is culturally defined as existing beyond the bounds of acceptability. Thus, one is driven to exactly what the culture most fears and dreads. Although classifying women's reproductive power as obscene is not to be desired, such classification nonetheless signals a potent message. It attests to the great power and fascination of women's ability to create and bear children.

CONCEPTION "RECONCEIVED"

Women's great power to conceive, sometimes patriarchally masked as obscenity, is more openly acknowledged by myths, such as that of Zeus gestating Dionysus, of men bearing children, or in the ideas of young children. Both myth and psychology sometimes imagine males, not only as concealed behind the masks of androgynes but overtly as men in their own male bodies, conceiving and bearing life. Our early forebears imagined babies emerging from various body parts. Lacking "factual" evidence, what logic says only vaginas channel birth? Indeed, diverse body orifices readily become logical reproductive sites if we envision the body as a three-dimensional shape and not just as a person's visible aspect. Its solid mass is variously interrupted by openings of different shapes and sizes—little doorways into its otherwise solid structure. Eyes, ears, nostrils, mouth, anus, vagina, pores, penis, and even open wounds all become functionally equivalent. If new life can emerge from a woman's vagina, why not from any other body aperture? This view grants males equal childbearing powers and blurs accepted scientific distinctions between procreation and creation.

One of the oldest and most persistent images of male conception and child-bearing blurs the two by equating them with defecation. As Freud says, commenting on this association in children's thinking, "Their ignorance of the vagina also makes it possible for children to believe ⁚ . . . [that] if the baby grows in the mother's body and is then removed from it, this can only happen along the one possible pathway—the anal aperture. *The baby must be evacuated like a piece of excrement, like a stool.*[16]

But why stop with defecation? Indeed, mythic thinking does not. Any excretory function is just as likely: sweat, spit, tears, vomit, blood, and even regurgitation. For example, initiation rites from Oceania, West Africa, Lapland, and Finland dramatize birth/creation as swallowing and vomiting by a gigantic fish. Western cultures recognize this theme from the biblical story of Jonah and the Whale and numerous fairy-tale swallowings of heroes such as Tom Thumb.

Almost all body parts can serve mythically as sites of conception and childbirth. More anatomically equivalent to actual childbirth than eyes or armpits is the phallic birth found in many traditions, as when Zeus placed the infant Dionysus in his thigh, a euphemism for the penis, to keep him safe until birth. Stories of this sort suggest that cultures aware of the function of semen make the penis the logical counterpart of the womb.

Creation by masturbation, a prominent motif in the ancient Egyptian pyramid text, is more overtly phallic. Atum, the Creator god of Heliopolis, rather graphically describes his remarkable ability this way:

> yes I
> it was me
> grabbed my cock
> drained seedwater
> through my fist back into me
> I wrapped myself around cock
> joined in fucking my shadow
> fanning me under his cloud
> I rained seedwater
> Spewing it like barley from the earth
> into my mouth my own
> I sprouted windman Shu
> I dropped raingirl Shefnut.[17]

These material images are roughly equal in kind to the process of childbearing. Many others, more abstract, are not. Myths wherein breath is the sacred substance of life are simultaneously material and abstract, the now rather abstract concept of inspiration literally meaning "to blow" or "breathe upon." Thus, inspiration is clearly physical in its original meaning. Blowing is thought to bring the soul to life as, conversely, ceasing to breathe signals departure of the soul. This idea that breath or spirit creates life relates critically to ideas of childbirth. In the far more abstract sense that we now understand inspiration, it is still the "secret" of life that informs most religious traditions. As a kind of spontaneous eruption of spirituality, inspiration connects aspects of religion otherwise seemingly far removed from childbirth.

Even more abstract than breath as the secret life-creating force is "the word," an image found nearly everywhere, as in the Bible: "In the beginning was the Word" (John I), which gave rise to the Christian theology of the *Logos,* the Greek term for word. Particularly relevant is the Stoic version, *logos spermatikos,* the spermatic word. As in other traditions, this understanding of creation, or "birth," involves only a male god who holds within himself all the seminal *logoi* that govern each thing's production. Eventually, the Logos became identified with Jesus, aligning him with the Creator who "conceived" the world through speech.

Varying this idea that speech is the bodily substance of creation is the belief that males, with their hands instead of their mouths, can shape various substances into new life. Mud, dirt, earth, and clay typify the substances from which humans are thus born, as in man's creation from dust in Genesis 2:7 and from clay in African Yoruba and Blackfoot Indian myths.

Comparison of procreation and creation raises a special concern, especially for women. Creation by an artist supposedly involves external "making" as opposed to internal gestation. Patriarchal thought conceptualizes this external act of creation positively. For a man to fashion raw material in order to "birth" something new is "good." Not only does he affirm his worth by creating, he visibly establishes his superiority to his material—he controls it, shapes it, forms it, determines what it shall be. By contrast, gestation supposedly involves no willed action. It just happens. A woman cannot control the process once it starts, short of the drastic step of abortion. Whatever happens then is simply mediated through her without any active input on her part until after the baby is born. Unlike a creation, the baby emerges fully formed, rather than slowly, bit by bit. But does this contrast accurately reflect gestation?

If the contrast is accurate, and if dirt does function as a displacement of feces, the ability forcibly to shape it to its maker's will provides a disturbing image. Applied to childrearing, it suggests "shaping" a child to the parents' will. Furthermore, viewing woman as passive incubator suggests the equally pernicious idea that a woman contributes nothing but a warm, protective environment for gestating her children. Both images exaggerate their respective positions. A gynecocentric perspective, however, may reveal that a far greater creativity characterizes women's gestation than accepted wisdom admits. Presumed "helpless" passivity constitutes but a partial picture.

For an artist or artificer, the situation does not differ significantly, although superficially control seems more possible. But any practicing artist knows this is illusory: Depending on the degree of actual artistry involved, control may be nearly impossible. Following Coleridge's distinction, which makes imagination "the living power and prime agent of all human perception" and fancy "a mode of memory emancipated from the order of time and space," [18] an artist who uses fancy consciously knows what she is doing and can therefore control the outcome. By contrast, one who works from the imagination parallels gestation. The mental creation frequently assumes a life of its own beyond the artist's control. Novelists often speak of characters they have created dictating their own stories, sometimes to the authors' surprise. In much the same way as these characters grow and develop along their own lines, regardless of their authors' preconceived ideas, a fetus, too, except in extreme cases such as starvation or severe nutritional deficiency, grows despite its mother's personal eating habits. Yet the opposite position can be taken as well. No successful artist totally relinquishes control any more than a responsible mother totally ignores her behavior during pregnancy. Most caring mothers-to-be consciously try to "shape" their babies by controlling their own eating, drinking, and exercising patterns.

Thus, although patriarchal thought holds creation superior to gestation, the rationale for this argument is shaky. Both matter for any process that brings something new into being. To call one more important than the other is absurd. Without both, nothing new could ever emerge. This argument illustrates yet another instance of patriarchal thought seizing and attributing female powers of conception, gestation, and birth giving to males. Recognizing this pattern of appropriation makes clear just how central the stages of childbirth really are as symbols. Some women find reaching this awareness a major step in retrieving, hence eventually (re)constructing, images of childbirth. Others, however, are already moving beyond this point to engage in a very different kind of "reconception" of conception, the currently popular New Age process of "conscious conception."

Conscious conception, which deals with the physical rather than the artistic process, assumes that we all unconsciously recall the moment of our own conception. That means that parental thoughts, feelings, and attitudes at the time significantly affect the person-to-be and consequently must be consciously attended to. Typically, conscious conception involves rituals of greeting. As Dawson Church, author of *Communing with the Spirit of Your Unborn Child,* puts it, a major purpose of conscious conception is to "radiat[e] welcome . . . the first great blessing we can offer our baby. It is the first spiritual gift we can give. More will follow, but if the first gift is fully given, it establishes a pattern for the giving of everything else." [19] To consciously mark conception as soon as it is known is to incorporate this significant, but often overlooked, rite of passage into the parents' lives.

For some women, conscious conception is an extremely significant part of reconstructing childbirth. It can be the important first step in greeting the person-to-be whose eventual arrival makes such an enormous difference in the lives of its parents. Conscious conception can also connect the erotic, loving communion of this woman and that man with the often deeroticized, overly domesticated process of growing, birthing, and rearing a child. Such a connection to Eros not only provides a powerful counter to the mechanistic split of mind and body, technology and ritual endemic to Western cultures, but it also reminds both partners how special this particular moment is in their lives. As the following section indicates, counters to these splits are desperately needed if we are ever to reconstruct childbirth along more positive, life-affirming lines.

TECHNOLOGICAL CHILDBEARING

In many ways a great boon to women, technological childbearing is not without its problems. For one thing, it exacerbates Western tendencies to split ideas and experiences dualistically. For another, it may at times combine some of the worst excesses of mythic thinking with scientific prowess. For instance, onerous as are the themes and images connecting childbirth with obscenity that we examined at the close of the section on "holy marriage," they do not ordinarily, in and of themselves, physically harm women, although they may incite others to do so. Technological childbearing, however, is often quite a different matter. Cases that combine both obscenity and technology are fortunately still rare, but a major one so disturbing that it cannot be ignored concerns infertility doctor Cecil B. Jacobson, who was found guilty in May 1992 of inseminating his patients with his own sperm. Generally speaking, however, what technological childbearing does to women is devoid of Jacobsen's particular perversity, being far more apt to turn us into mechanical, rather than sex, objects.

Now that a fetus can be almost totally laboratory "conceived" and "carried," technological childbirth poses a real and immediate threat. As one experimenter puts it, "If I can carry a baby all the way through to birth in vitro, I certainly plan to do it, though obviously I am not going to succeed on the first attempt or even on the twentieth." [20] These words, so full of the hubris often associated with technology in a patriarchal context, reflect age-old male dreams of appropriating the "secret of life." Furthermore, they clearly show a desire to appropriate "woman's secret power" by controlling conception and childbirth.

Yet, despite the real danger that technology may thoroughly usurp and desacralize women's powers, this same technology can also help childbearing women and would-be fathers in countless ways. It can give women with fertility problems the chance to bear children successfully; it can help men with low sperm counts produce babies with their own genes; it can enable unmarried women to conceive children without sexual intercourse. These are just a few of the many "miracles" technology permits. Consequently, one cannot say that technology per se threatens women's powers; only technology (patriarchally) misapplied threatens to work against women's best interests and ultimately against those of all humans.

New as technological conception and childbearing appear to be, both have roots in medieval history. Their most direct practical antecedent is alchemy, the science devoted to turning base metals into gold and finding the elixir of immortality. Whereas myths merely tell of male appropriations of women's "secret powers," alchemy ritualized attempts to steal them. Developed in both the East and the West, the sexual form developed primarily in India from about the sixth century C.E. is particularly relevant to contemporary beliefs that human life can be reproduced in the laboratory. The goal of Indian alchemy, as of all alchemical practices, was immortality, believed attainable by properly mixing mercury and sulphur, understood respectively to be the seed of Siva in his male form and the blood of his female partner, Sakti. The sexual nature of the processes to which these two elements were subjected is readily apparent in the language used to describe them in the alchemical samskaras: "mercury pierces or penetrates *(vedhara)* sulphur in order that it may be killed *(mrta)* and be "reborn" into a purer, more stable state *(bandha)* where it has a greater capacity for transmuting other elements.[21]

As in the mystical "conception" of alchemy, twentieth-century laboratory reproductive techniques reveal motives for control, improvement, even perfection of life. The further alchemical motive of immortality, overtly stated by its language (the embryo), its implements (the cauldron), and its materials (the blood-colored mercury ore—blood being a prominent women's symbol because of menstruation and the blood accompanying childbirth), remains implicit in contemporary laboratory techniques.

Contemporary reproductive practices can similarly be interpreted as stealing the very essence of reproduction. Here again, language immediately reveals the nature of this theft: the products of technological reproduction have been called "test-tube babies." This image of a long sterile tube from which the fetus is "taken," not "born," makes the birth mother obsolete. One can argue that this is a false and therefore inappropriate image, but that makes little difference. The popular image exists and accurately reflects the Cartesian split that alienates body and self, mother and fetus in our culture.

Besides causing such linguistic shifts in the meaning of reproduction, the actual procedures of technology threaten to displace thousands of women from our biological ability to conceive and reproduce. Yet these are the very same techniques that can help infertile women fulfill their dreams of reproduction.

Oldest of the "new" laboratory techniques is artificial insemination—the method by which "Baby M" was created—which Arab sheiks are thought to have used for horse breeding as early as 1322 c.e.[22] In Europe, one of the earliest known attempts was made by Jan Swamerdam, a Dutch physician who tried unsuccessfully to fertilize fish eggs in 1780. Four years later, a professor of natural philosophy at Pavia, Abbe Lazzario Spallanzani, inseminated first an insect, then an amphibian, and finally a dog. In 1785, a London woman was inseminated by John Hunter. In the United States, Dr. J. Merion Sims, at the close of the Civil War, recorded fifty-five inseminations of six different women, which yielded one successful pregnancy. The next scientific account of the practice did not appear until 1907 in a publication by J. Ivanoff, a Russian physiologist discussing its use in animal breeding. By 1941, in the United States, close to ten thousand women had been artificially impregnated.

The process is relatively simple. The sperm donor masturbates to produce fresh sperm, which then must be inserted into the woman's vagina or, by laparoscopy, into her tubes within the next two hours. Otherwise, it must be frozen and stored in a sperm bank. A woman's detailed account of her husband's experience illustrates the desacralizing tendencies that opponents of technology believe characterize the whole process:

For the required sperm test he would have to masturbate into a cup. . . . He began to fret about his performance. With the mention of artificial insemination all sexual desire had gone. What if he was impotent? . . .

What if he failed? [His wife] suggested he stock up on "girlie" magazines and even proposed that they make the purchase a family outing. The night before the test the two of them ventured out to a newsstand that carried pornography. . . .

"I sweated bullets all weekend reading those dumb magazines. I read so many of them that by Sunday night when I was lying in bed all I could see were bodies in all sorts of positions. . . ." That night Glenn was so terrified of impotency that he couldn't sleep. When the alarm went off at 7:15 . . . he reached for the jar on his bedstand and wondered again whether he would be able to do it. The whole process took about thirty seconds.[23]

As this account suggests, although the technique for this procedure is simple, using it is not. Superficially, to "beget" a child like this in no way resembles procreation as an act of love fully shared by two potential parents. Instead, it becomes a humiliating, "dirty" procedure without a trace of sanctity—whether feminine or masculine. Yet what of the "natural" lovemaking that fertile couples, determined to conceive, may force upon themselves? For some people, preoccupation with calendars and thermometers may desacralize conception every bit as much as collecting sperm in a jar.

Various acronyms reflect the linguistically barren aspects of the new reproductive technologies. Some variants of artificial insemination too unsuccessful as yet to pose problems include POST (Peritoneal Oocyte-Sperm Transfer), CULAID (Cul-de-sac Artificial Insemination Detour), TITI (Transfimbrial Intratubal Insemination), and DIPI (Direct Intraperitoneal Insemination). Each requires sperm to be inserted in the location designated by the procedural name. Acronyms for the two most promising methods so far, AIH and AID, refer respectively to artificial insemination by husband and donor. AIH can circumvent male impotence or low sperm count and offset a fertile female's inability to conceive due to blocked tubes.

In the United States, AID usually takes place through registered sperm banks. Some physicians require marriage as a prerequisite. Others refuse if the woman is lesbian. Some feminist writers consider these physician responses automatically patriarchal and antilesbian. Often they may be, but the situation is too complex for automatic reduction to ideology. The clash of potentially conflicting rights—those of the not-yet-conceived child, those of the physician, and those of the would-be mother—illustrates the difficulty of evaluating any given image or interpretation of technological childbirth.

In this particular case the "rights" of the physician have typically prevailed because the single mother who is refused cannot force the sperm bank to alter the practitioner's decision. She may therefore resort to do-it-yourself insemination. All she needs is a willing donor. As stories of turkey basters suggest, implanting the sperm is simple. At this point, though, another major issue surfaces: What is the role of the father? In a cogent article by Ellen Lewin, "By Design: Reproductive Strategies and the Meaning of Motherhood," four lesbian women respond to this question. Each chose an anonymous donor primarily for fear of losing her child to its father if anonymity did not exist on both sides. While the specifics of each story vary, the situation of "Louise, a counterculture lesbian in her early twenties" is representative:

> She approached several gay men she knew and asked them if they would donate sperm; after several firm rejections, she found a man who was "thrilled" to be asked and obtained the necessary sample from him. She carried out the insemination alone in her room, with candle light and soft music, envisioning the insemination as "a perfect baby spirit entering her."[24]

It is easy to sympathize with Louise, a single woman who desperately wants to conceive children of her own. At the same time, from an opposing perspective, this artificial impregnation raises disturbing questions. Is this procedure, as described above, not precisely the nightmare that underlies much male hostility to women? This kind of separation of the sexes in reproduction surely turns the male donor into an object as much as prostitution does either women or men. For many men this alienation from any act of love, any contact with a future child, has to desacralize male sexual experience. Here, for all intents and purposes, is parthenogenesis at work in the twentieth century. Apart from his anonymously donated sperm, no man participates in this process. If women have been consistently deprived of our own starring role in the great drama of childbearing, AID almost completely reverses that deprivation. Does this kind of reversal ultimately help women? Or is this just another stage in the ongoing polarization of the sexes?

Other issues arise when artificial insemination is used to impregnate a surrogate mother. The now well publicized Baby M case illustrates one of the gravest problems—its effect on the surrogate. William and Elizabeth Stern, both professionals, hired as a surrogate the comparatively poor, relatively uneducated Mary Beth Whitehead, a then-married mother of two. She was impregnated with Stern's sperm and eventually gave birth to "Baby M." Instead of relinquishing her daughter to the Sterns and cashing their $10,000 check, Whitehead disappeared with the baby.

Quite apart from the issue of Whitehead's postdelivery refusal to relinquish the baby, whom she called "Sara" and the Sterns called "Melissa," there is the image of reproduction created by the initial agreement. Whatever else this arrangement may be, the contract drawn up between Whitehead and the Sterns makes absolutely clear that it is conception rendered commercial:

> Mary Beth Whitehead, Surrogate, agrees . . . that she will not abort the child once conceived except, if in the professional medical opinion of the inseminating physician, such action is necessary for the physical health of Mary Beth Whitehead or the child has been determined by said physician to be physiologically abnormal. Mary Beth Whitehead further agrees, upon the request of said physician, to undergo amniocentesis . . . or similar tests to detect genetic and congenital defects. In the event said test reveals that the fetus is genetically or congenitally abnormal, Mary Beth Whitehead, Surrogate, agrees to abort the fetus upon demand of William Stern, Natural Father, in which event, the fee

paid to the Surrogate will be in accordance with paragraph 10 [$1,000.00]. If Mary Beth Whitehead refuses to abort the fetus upon demand of William Stern, his obligations as stated in this agreement shall cease forthwith, except as to obligations of paternity as imposed by statute. . . .

. . . to adhere to all medical instructions given to her by the inseminating physician as well as her independent obstetrician. Mary Beth Whitehead also agrees not to smoke cigarettes, drink alcoholic beverages, use illegal drugs, or take nonprescription medication or prescribed medications without written consent from her physician. Mary Beth Whitehead agrees to follow a prenatal medical examination schedule.[25]

The commercialization of surrogate conception and childbearing is unmistakable. Much of the debate about the ethics of payment for surrogacy hinges on whether payment is for the service or for the baby. Either way, by the language of the contract, conception and giving birth have clearly lost any sense of being sacred. Instead, both have become business propositions, plain and simple. Childbearing "conceived" this way holds the same relation to childbearing resulting from love as an indulgence does to genuine repentance of sins. And as with the sale of indulgences, to hold either buyer or seller more "guilty" is absurd. The contract equally implicates both. The issue of Whitehead's "rights," or lack thereof, regarding the baby is separate. To enter into such a contract in the first place—whether as surrogate or adoptive mother (and actual father)—involves both parties equally. One can sympathize deeply with the anguish of an infertile couple (somewhat problematic in the case of the Sterns); one can also understand the urge to help another human procreate and to earn some money for it. But as far as the acts of conception and childbearing go, commercialization destroys their potential sacrality.

A variant process of technological conception uses a surrogate womb. This allows a woman wishing to avoid pregnancy or lacking a uterus but capable of producing eggs (as after a hysterectomy performed without an oophorectomy) to have her own biological child. She neither experiences conception nor bears the child herself. Her eggs are removed and fertilized with her husband's sperm and then placed in another woman's womb. The child thus biologically relates to both parents who raise it. The womb of the childbearing woman is "rented," as it were, for nine months. But again, if childbearing is a "cash and carry" procedure, what happens to its sacrality?

Somewhat different is the process of embryo transfer. Its purpose in humans is to ensure that an embryo, successfully conceived in a woman unable to carry to term, does not spontaneously abort. Thus, conception does take place within the biological mother's body. The idea of embryo transfer, which seems frighteningly modern, actually has mythical roots in Hindu and Jain legends of the extraordinary birth of the god Balarama, Krishna's elder brother. A demon's threat to kill all the male children of Balarama's mother caused Balarama to be saved by "embryo transplant."[26] Magically, he was transferred to the womb of another woman, making this perhaps the first recorded, albeit mythical, surrogate birth.

In the embryo transplant variant of surrogacy, whereby only the gestating womb is not that of the biological mother, the legal rights of the childbearer are not as strong as those of a woman who actually provides the eggs. What is very clear in the case of embryo transplant, however, is that unless the childbearing woman is providing her service out of humanitarian concern, she is selling her body. This variant makes a very clear case for the potential for exploitation inherent in all such procedures. As Andrea Dworkin puts it,

> Motherhood is becoming a new branch of female prostitution with the help of scientists who want access to the womb for experimentation and for power. A doctor can be the agent of fertilization; he can dominate and control conception and reproduction. Women can sell reproductive capacities the same way old-time prostitutes sold sexual ones but without the stigma of whoring because there is not penile intrusion.[27]

Another technological procedure with particularly ambiguous future implications for the way we experience and envision childbirth involves freezing and storing embryos. This process was originally used only to store experimentally or economically valuable strains of farm and laboratory animals so that they would not have to be continuously bred to maintain their particular desirable traits, but in 1984, the first human frozen embryo was born in Melbourne, Australia.[28] That same year, newspapers worldwide announced the world's first frozen-embryo "orphans," a situation that began in 1981, when eggs were taken from multimillionaire Elsa Rios at a Melbourne in vitro fertilization clinic, fertilized by an anonymous donor, and then frozen. Before a successful implant could take place, however, both Elsa Rios and her husband, Mario, died in a plane crash. Of various ethical issues to emerge from this circumstance, the one most frequently headlined concerned inheritance rights to the couple's $8 million estate. Close to one hundred women subsequently volunteered to carry and "adopt" the embryos, raising the issue of childbirth for monetary gain.

Another major issue—definition of human life—was raised by Australian right-to-life groups who brought sufficient pressure to bear that subsequent state legislation now mandates preserving abandoned embryos for use by some other infertile couple. To further complicate matters, physicians have been wary of implanting the Rios' embryos in any volunteer for fear of possible AIDS contamination because the sperm and eggs were not tested in 1981.

As a result of this case, the Australian state of Victoria, in 1987, passed the first legislation requiring IVF centers to maintain files on parents and donors so that information about possible genetic abnormalities and future incestuous relationships can be prevented. Law also requires a five-year limitation on storage of embryos to prevent implantation of a sibling embryo into a woman who was herself formed of the same frozen embryonic genetic material. Consent forms are now required so that potential parents must declare in advance what should be done with their frozen embryos in the event of untimely death.

An additional issue is dramatized by the well-publicized September 1989 judicial decision in the case of a U.S. couple, Mary Sue and Junior Davis. In this case, in the wake of a divorce, Junior Davis withdrew his consent for preserving and subsequently implanting seven frozen embryos. His ex-wife, Mary Sue, however, fought for their preservation and won custody on the ruling of a Tennessee judge. This decision raises the question of an ex-husband's legal and financial responsibilities. May one or all of the embryos he no longer wishes to preserve be subsequently implanted? If so, will he then be financially responsible for their upbringing?

Yet another unsettling technological manipulation of conception is cloning, which produces genetically identical individuals. Already, by the 1980s, cloning had produced a mouse and some frogs, but as yet it has not been actualized in humans despite a book by David M. Rorvik, in which he claims to have done so in 1978—*In His Image: The Cloning of a Man.* The oddity of this process is that what would result would not be precisely a child, nor would it be the original person nor even a sibling. According to Volpe, "It is its own parent reincarnated in new cytoplasm."[29] The experimenter begins the process of "conception" by stimulating an unfertilized egg in the intended recipient with a sharp needle. In response, the egg rotates, leaving its nucleus uppermost. This nucleus is then removed by a glass needle. Meanwhile, the donor material, consisting of some body cells, is prepared by first separating it into individual cells in a special solution and then isolating one cell from which a nucleus is carefully injected into the previously prepared recipient egg.

When it is successful, cloning results in a perfectly normal embryo. Furthermore, the process can be endlessly repeated to produce as many copies as the experimenter wants. This means no part of the ordinary sexual process occurs; no egg is fertilized by a sperm. Fortunately, only an embryo can provide this replacement nucleus because adult cells lose the ability of the embryonic cell to guide the development of an enucleated cell. Therefore, the kind of nightmare often envisioned when cloning is mentioned, in which adults endlessly "reproduce" themselves, is not actually possible. In principle, however, the cellular material of a single viable fetus could be endlessly reproduced. With this technique, not only are conception and childbearing desacralized but both are made totally obsolete.

Another disturbing phenomenon closely related, but in a sense opposite, to cloning results in a chimera. Originally the name of a mythical Greek monster with lion's head, goat's body, and serpent's tail, a chimera created in a laboratory combines two distinctly different genetic types in one body. Already, a combination sheep-goat exists![30] More commonly, however, the process remains confined to intraspecies manipulation. "Conception" occurs like this. A protein-splitting enzyme dissolves the *zona pellucida,* the protective membrane, of two different embryos. These two embryos are then put into a culture medium, touching each other. Their cells automatically connect, forming a composite blastocyst (an early stage of the embryo), at which point the combined (chimeric) embryo is implanted into the uterus of a foster mother. From 1965 to 1987, one thousand normal mouse chimeras in turn produced over twenty-five thousand progeny.

Such creation of life raises troubling issues for the way conception and childbearing are understood. Consider this case, for instance. A discovery that grew out of such experimental manipulation of cells is immunological tolerance, which refers to the way various organs can be transplanted from a donor to a host without rejection. But nonrejection only occurs with an embryonic donor, not an adult one. Aware of the potential application of this discovery, the wife of a twenty-eight-year-old engineer severely debilitated from kidney disease wished to help her husband. Knowing that his rare blood type made a transplant practically impossible, she volunteered to purposely create a matching donor. She would become pregnant, abort her fetus after six months, and then donate its kidneys![31] Had she been permitted to carry out her plan, she would have been altering the processes of conception and childbirth into horrifying procedures of sacrifice. Yet this child sacrifice is disturbingly familiar from years and years of patriarchal myths: It is the sacrifice of the son (or daughter) for the father. This particular image of technological reproduction therefore illuminates, more clearly than most, a split that can make desacralization of a gynocentric event sacred from a patriarchal perspective and vice versa.

Although all artificial techniques of conception can be ambivalent, frightening, or exciting, depending upon how they are interpreted, perhaps most difficult of all to construe, because on one level it so overtly threatens women's uniqueness as childbearers, is the creation of artificial placentae and wombs. These permit ectogenesis, external development, an image which Aldous Huxley's *Brave New World* has imprinted on the human imagination:

> One egg, one embryo, one adult—normality. But a bokanovskified egg will bud, will proliferate, will divide. From eight to ninety-six buds, and every bud will grow into a perfectly formed embryo, and every embryo into a full-sized adult, making ninety-six human beings where only one grew before. Progress.[32]

At present, only partial human ectogenesis has actually occurred.[33] In the typical in vitro procedure, it lasts only a few days at the very beginning of pregnancy. At the opposite end of pregnancy, although we do not usually envision it this way, ectogenesis also occurs when premature infants are maintained in the artificial "womb" of an intensive-care nursery. In mice, ectogenesis has lasted longer—for eight days of culture. By this time the mouse embryo has passed beyond the earliest stage of fetal development, when it is called a blastocyte, to the somite stage, in which its main body axis and major rudiments have developed. Scientists at Stanford University have developed an incubator (an artificial womb) in which spontaneously aborted fetuses have been maintained for up to forty-eight hours. A further type of ectogenesis exists involving individual organs, as opposed to cells, but to date without apparent application to childbearing as such.

The aspect of this research into artificial wombs which most directly impinges on women is reflected in a 1986 newspaper story, "Technology Exists to Make Men Pregnant":

> Male pregnancy would involve fertilizing a donated egg with sperm outside the body. The embryo would be implanted into the bowel area, where it could attach itself to a major organ. The baby would be delivered by Caesarean section.[34]

This image can be understood as the culmination of all reproductive technology, as it robs women of any role at all in reproduction. Let us speculate for a moment. Were this particular kind of ectogenesis to become popular, where would that leave women? Male conception and pregnancy would undeniably alter child-bearing drastically. Finally in possession of the secret that myth, history, and psychology all suggest men have so long coveted, what would men do? Would they become nurturing, caretaking, gentle folk? Male conception could end patriarchy once and for all, healing the underlying cause for the historical polarization of "superior" males dominating "inferior" females. For all this seeming outlandishness, as with technologized reproduction in general, male conception and pregnancy are highly ambivalent images and as such deserve serious attention.

Finally, the broadest and best known of all the new reproductive technologies is in vitro fertilization, a term that covers any conception occurring outside a woman's body in an artificial environment. While this procedure necessarily involves either AID or AIH, the reverse is not necessarily true. Either AIH or AID can involve immediate implantation with conception occurring inside a woman's body.

In vitro fertilization is not as new as headlines in the 1980s suggested. Attempts to fertilize a rabbit actually date back to 1878, although the first was not reported until 1959, when M. C. Chang confirmed his success. Ten years later, Edwards et al. reported the first successful in vitro fertilization of human eggs. On July 25, 1978, Edwards and Steptoe achieved their great breakthrough, the live birth of Louise Brown.

The purpose of in vitro fertilization is to help women whose infertility results from a malfunctioning oviduct. Such malfunction means that despite a normal uterus and ovaries, a woman is nonetheless sterile because her oviduct is blocked, preventing free movement of egg and sperm. Unless egg and sperm can meet, fertilization cannot occur. Surgical repair is difficult, but fertilization outside the woman's body can overcome her sterility. The process takes place like this: First, a healthy egg must be removed from the woman and kept alive outside her body. Simultaneously, a healthy sperm must be obtained from the father. Then the egg and the sperm must be successfully united. Once united, the egg and sperm, now known as the conceptus, must be kept alive outside the mother's body until they develop sufficiently to be safely implanted in her uterus. Most textbooks now carry what can only be called "recipes" for creating life by in vitro methods:

> Procedure:
> Insemination, Sperm Washing and Flushing Media:
> 1. Add 92.65 ml of Ham's F-10 stock to a 100 ml graduated cylinder.
> 2. Add 7.5 ml of patient serum. Mix well.
> 3. Filter 45 ml of medium through a 0.22 mm filter into a sterile flask (Falcon3013) labeled INSEMINATION I and cap tightly.[35]

This recipe continues for more than a page. Common sense says that to be doable, procedures must be set down in sequence. Nonetheless, it is difficult to reconcile a recipe with what has always existed beneath all the images described above: A sacred process. The reduction of impregnation to a quantifiable, step-by-step procedure diminishes reproduction. Now evidently anyone with a few laboratory instruments, some sperm, and some eggs can create life.

Yet once again, an important question must be asked: Is it the *technology* that causes this problem, or is it the manner of its presentation? Consider how the story changes when the same steps appear in the words of a childless woman seeking to become pregnant. This moving account by Gwen Davis in the *New York Times Magazine*[36] begins with a description of the setting: "The I.V.F. clinic represents the end of the road for most of the women here: each of us has a long history of disappointment verging on despair. Our pain is private; we keep it to ourselves." In Davis's case, low fertility resulted from problems with the Dalkon Shield, a situation she describes before expanding on her compelling desire, shared with her husband, to try for a child. Knowing the odds, however, she finds that even so supposedly simple an act as writing for information on fertility programs is almost more than she can bear. Once she is able to do so, she thinks, "Maybe, just maybe, the mother pictured in the brochure, breast-feeding her baby, could be me" (p. 108). But at approximately five thousand dollars per try, with four attempts needed for a fifty percent success rate, the procedure is costly in dollars as well as emotion. She deliberates for eight months before deciding to try. Carefully, Davis details each visit to the I.V.F. center: the initial consultation with the medical, psychological, and financial counselors; the comprehensive physical exam; the medication, both oral and self-injected, to be taken at the proper point of her cycle; the nine days in a motel near the center required for daily blood tests; the daily checks of her estrogen level; the ups and downs of her emotions; the despair that makes her nearly drop out; the ultrasound on day 11 to reveal whether enough eggs are developing in sufficiently healthy sacs to make continuation possible. Each detail contributes to the suspense. Davis's response to her less than optimal, but still potentially usable, test results shows her ambivalence:

> I spend the afternoon in the tyranny of irresolution. I lie for a while face down upon my bed. I close my eyes and rub my face back and forth across my arm. For a brief moment, I can feel the soft, sweet skin of a baby—my baby. Then its phantom warmth evaporates, and I'm stifled by this tactile fantasy—the fantasy of every woman who wants to have a child. Once again, it's brought home to me: I might never give birth. (p. 121)

Finally she does decide to go through with it, describing the transfer of the embryo as

> somewhat like a pelvic exam. After my cervix has been swabbed, the doctor calls out to the embryologist, "Two minutes." "Sounds like the two-minute warning in football," I say to my husband. The "two-minute" call in embryo transfer indicates the amount of time the embryologist has to remove the embryos from the incubator and transfer them to the uterus. The embryologist enters with a tiny, strawlike tube at the end of a syringe that holds our two embryos—our girls, I think.
>
> The doctor takes the syringe and inserts the tube through the cervix and into the uterus. I am asked if I feel the twinge of the tube against a uterine wall. I do. Then the doctor pushes the plunger at the end of the syringe, releasing the embryos and their fluid home of the last 24 hours into my uterus. I squeeze my

husband's hand. I am expected to lie perfectly still for the next two hours—a small price to pay. Finally, I have inside me all the elements it takes for pregnancy. Tomorrow is Thanksgiving: I give thanks. (p. 121)

Then comes the climax: Davis's transferred embryos do not hold. As a result, she writes:

I trust nothing. I'm numbed by the pain, amazed that I'm so fragile. I never thought I could be emotionally crippled by anything. I want to be a mother, plain and simple. What's just as plain and simple, though more difficult to accept, is the fact that I will never be a mother. (p. 121)

What emerges so clearly in this account is the human dimension—not the impersonal laboratory element. Here is a tragedy with no apparent resolution. How is a woman to cope with this situation? Is there any possible model for what she must endure? In Davis's case, a partial answer surfaces from her own words. Describing her reaction when she is told, at an earlier stage, that both her eggs had fertilized, she says, "I'm stunned as I turn to my husband; no matter what happens, I say, we'll have created something together" (p. 121). Whether that brief moment of shared creativity can possibly sustain Davis or any other woman in her situation we cannot know, because the article ends without telling us. Certainly for women who struggle to overcome low fertility but never reach that stage despite repeatedly going through the days of medication, testing, bloodtaking, and so on, that image never even comes into play. In their cases, what image possibly *can* sustain?

This question deserves our attention. One possible answer discards traditional patriarchal imagery, particularly as it has developed in the West. It is an answer that emerges out of situations in which repeated actions yield no visible results in contrast to heroic gestures that typically show achievement against extreme odds, as in the struggle of David against Goliath, or defeat on a grand scale, as in any battle to the death. In the latter case, the defeated member(s) of the fight are "heroes." They die with great honor for their cause, whatever that cause may be. In contrast, a woman who repeatedly attempts, unsuccessfully, to create and carry new life within her body has no ready model at hand. In her case, two words, both generally considered negative, immediately come to mind. One is *failure,* the other *death.* While failure followed eventually by success is typical of patriarchal heroes, and death can be, and historically often has been, interpreted as heroic (epics abound with such instances), death and failure combined are traditionally anathema.

Yet in some contemporary works, such as those of novelists Anne Beatty or Bobbie Ann Mason, "meaninglessness" in the form of repeated death-oriented "failure" is common. In Mason's coming-of-age novel *In Country,* for example, the female protagonist, a young woman ambiguously named Sam, searches for her own identity. In so doing she tries to find meaning in her father's death in Vietnam and in the love that she imagines existed between her father, Dwayne, and her mother, Irene:

Sam had wanted to believe there was something magic between them that had created her and validated their love. But teen-age romances weren't very significant she realized now. . . . Sam had been told so often what a miracle it was that she came along to compensate for the loss of Dwayne. She knew she had been making too much out of the brief time her parents were married before he went overseas. During that month, she had originated. She didn't know why the moment of origin mattered. Scientists were trying to locate the moment of origin of the universe. They wanted to know exactly when it happened, and how, and whether it happened with a big bang or some other way. Maybe the universe originated quietly, without fireworks, the way human life started, with two people who were simply having a good time in bed, or in the back seat of a car. Making a baby had nothing to do with love, or anything mystical, or what they said in church. It was just fucking.[37]

Ironically, the contrast between a totally desacralized view of conception such as Sam's and the intense, agonizing struggle of women such as Gwen Davis to conceive in a manner that does not even allow the luxury of just "fucking" to create a child highlights a kind of meaning: The struggle of women like Davis, regardless of outcome, exists on a level for which we lack appropriate language. Within traditional patriarchal cultures we would call that struggle (if it were a man's) "heroic," seeing its goal as hubristic, its outcome ultimately "futile." But in this context this is not a man's struggle (although many men suffer similarly from sterility), nor is patriarchal culture the appropriate "place" for a relevant language to emerge. Incapacity to conceive children far transcends the failure that a postindustrial patriarchal world makes it out to be. Such incapacity requires new, or at least different, words. Those who suffer from it are women who willingly sacrifice major portions of themselves and their professions (for these procedures require immense quantities of time) in the often vain hope of conceiving new life. These are the women for whom we need a whole new vocabulary reflective of their intense struggle.

3 Miraculous Conceptions

To a degree, all images of childbearing, like those of any other action or event, are fictive. Elements of a purely imaginary nature creep in, raising the difficult issue of what is fact and what is fantasy. Most of us, however, in order to function, acknowledge a scale of fictiveness such that we call "fictive" the stories we read in novels, "factual" the fall that makes us break a leg. Although the novel may contain, or be based on, factual events, and the meaning we attach to the broken bones may well be imagined—as when one insists, "My leg was broken because I defied the odds and walked under a ladder on Friday the 13th, instead of staying home all day"—the divide between the two is nonetheless generally acknowledged, if only for convenience, in contemporary cultures. In the sense implied by this conventional distinction between something called "fact" and something called "fiction," the images in this section are all more clearly fictive than their counterparts in the rest of the book. This category includes pseudocyesis, couvade, and adoption. Both pseudocyesis and couvade are physiological states in which a woman or a man, respectively, exhibits symptoms of pregnancy without actually being pregnant. These equally bizarre somatic conditions not only reflect, in differing ways, prevailing patriarchal attitudes toward childbearing, they also suggest ways of "reconceiving" it.

An even more promising, but very different, fictive version of childbearing is the universal practice of adoption. In this case, the actual childbearing mother sometimes creates the fiction that no pregnancy has ever occurred. By contrast, the adoptive mother may fictively enact it. An adoptive family demonstrates the importance of childbearing by acting as if the adoptee were, in fact, of their own blood, often to the point of hiding its "true" parentage. Thus, while one woman may deny her childbirth experience, another may fabricate hers.

"Fictions" of childbirth share a common foundational belief: Childbearing is so important that either its presence or its absence necessitates the creation of diverse fictions to variously negate, create, or replace it. Thus, even when it is fictionalized, the power of life creation once attributed exclusively to women cannot truly be minimized despite the best efforts of patriarchal cultures to do so. Images of pseudocyesis, couvade, and adoption, by virtue of their obvious fictitiousness, reveal most clearly the power of imagination to either deconstruct or reconceive childbirth for all of us. Thus, despite the apparent bizarreness of two of them, collectively these fictive images of childbearing illustrate one of the strongest means by which women—and by extension, men—have historically experienced the sacrality of childbirth.

PSEUDOCYESIS (FALSE PREGNANCY)

Fictive pregnancies are both fascinating and puzzling. Do they reflect patriarchal injunctions carried to an extreme? Do they instead grant a woman respite from patriarchy, a means for exercising her reproductive power even when it is physiologically unavailable to her? Or do they reflect a more ambiguous blending of patriarchal desiderata with gynecocentric possibilities? In whatever way, fictive pregnancies strain the imagination.

But sometimes, rather than providing a healthy antidote to negative patriarchal attitudes, fantasy simply promulgates them. Such fantasy can become so convincing, its fulfillment so desired, that it assumes a life of its own. In extreme cases it even functions in place of an actual child, as it does for the characters George and Martha in Edward Albee's play *Who's Afraid of Virginia Woolf?*[1] Between them, George and Martha elaborate their "son's" birth with details of teddy bears, transparent floating goldfish, croup tents, and nightmares. But this son is a complete fiction, shared throughout most of their barren marriage, a fantasy child grown out of all proportion to the need that created him. Rather than helping George and Martha escape from the negative images of conception and childbearing so common to patriarchal thinking, this fantasized son ensnares them more deeply. The fantasy labor is difficult, according to George; Martha disagrees. From "conception" their visions clash. Furthermore, the child is "conceived," not for its own sake, but to further its parents' own ends—to function, as so many actual children do, as a pawn. Eventually, George sacrifices this "abused" fantasy child when indulging the fantasy no longer suits his purpose.

Today a fantasy child such as the one created in the minds of George and Martha can actually be had by anyone! According to an article published on the front page of the *Wall Street Journal,* 24 November 1987, "For $19.95, and just 13 minutes out of your busy day, you can have 'the full, rich experience of parenthood without the mess and inconvenience of the real thing.' It's called Video Baby. Let's slip it into the VCR and see, Why, it's a girl. Look at those little fingers. Isn't she adorable?" Seemingly an innocuous kind of adult version of a Cabbage Patch doll, this fictive child actually falls into a familiar patriarchal pattern: It deforms women's reproductive power so much that it vanishes, "humorously" subsumed by a banal yuppie game.

Trivial as this adult "doll playing" is, at the opposite end of the spectrum of fictive childbearing is a kind of fantasy that sometimes approaches tragedy, sometimes epitomizes imaginative conception. This is the bizarre phenomenon known as pseudocyesis. The word, from the Greek *pseudes,* false, and *kyesis,* pregnancy, refers to a condition wherein a woman experiences such symptoms of pregnancy as menstrual disturbances, womb and abdominal enlargement, breast changes, fetal movements, softening of the cervix, nausea, vomiting, constipation, and weight gain. Visually she appears pregnant, although no conception has actually occurred. So convincing is the condition that one major medical study revealed that physicians misdiagnosed 161 of 444 cases as pregnancies![2] Elevated urinary levels of the hormone gonadotropin and a high incidence of false positives with a common pregnancy test contribute to the difficulty of discriminating a fictive pregnancy from its genuine counterpart. Even animals will exhibit symptoms of false pregnancy when various interventions—hormonal, electrical, chemical—are performed on them. Although such studies suggest a purely physiological cause, not all scientists agree that false pregnancy is strictly a biological anomaly, particularly given the close interconnection between hormonal and psychological states. They do admit, however, that pseudocyesis often occurs during the three to six months' depression common after abortion, after sterilization, prior to confirmed diagnosis of pelvic cancer, or after menopause.[3] Surely such connections are not all physiological.

Of the many potentially tragic elements in pseudocyesis, one of the most devastating is its interchangeability with pelvic cancer. In Thomas Mann's short story "The Black Swan," the main character, Rosalie von Tummler, initially mistakes her vaginal bleeding for the return of menstruation. This brings her intense joy, for she is romantically involved with a young American man. That it should be cancer and death which await her rather than infant and renewed life is, of course, the ironic climax of the story.

One psychological explanation of such pregnancy fantasies considers them a "fantasy of function" such that "the childbearing function can be visualized as part of the body image from a theoretical standpoint."[4] In other words, some women visualize their body-selves not as slim and svelte, the "norm" of contemporary Western advertising, but as pregnant. Any woman whose self-image requires her to be pregnant will consequently feel she is not herself when she is not pregnant. The tragedy of this situation is apparent: When she is not pregnant, she will feel as alienated from her "self" as those women who find pregnancy self-alienating feel when they are pregnant. Much like a person who feels compelled to eat, drink, or smoke constantly, she must contrive somehow to be perpetually pregnant. But she may have to imagine pregnancy; pseudocyesis may be the only way she can actualize her potential self as she envisions it. Thus, pseudocyesis may be interpreted as either a sad delusion or a marvelous psychic creation.

Yet, paradoxically, pseudocyesis can also work in exactly the opposite way. For a woman who fears pregnancy or feels ambivalent about it, fictive pregnancy may punish her, fulfilling her worst nightmares. The following case history graphically describes this strange phenomenon in a thirty-six-year-old Catholic mother of four who fears that she will become pregnant following a tubal ligation.

> [She] had a delayed menstrual period, following an incident in which she lifted a heavy object; and she felt a strange pelvic sensation. This led her to believe that the "tubes had come untied." She immediately called her gynecologist, who reassured her that she was not pregnant. "For a year it seemed very strange to me that I wouldn't have any more children, and I couldn't really believe it, but gradually I got used to the idea."[5]

For this woman, freedom from further childbearing does not have its expected happy outcome. An internalized image of religiously mandated reproduction so dominates her thinking that her body "punishes" her with false symptoms. Although actually free now to enjoy a sexual relationship with her husband, unrestricted by possible pregnancy, something in her strongly resists this freedom, which violates entrenched patriarchal norms.

Incredible as such fantasized pregnancies seem, for many women pregnancy is central, and not just for those whom it is easy to label "unusual" or "extreme." Here is a description of just such an "ordinary" woman—not one who goes so far as to exhibit signs of pregnancy, but one whose desire for just one more child nonetheless leads her sufficiently close to show that pseudocyesis is not all that removed from "normalcy":

> Sally, the mother of four children . . . has two complete generations of them: two daughters in their early 20s by her first marriage, and two sons from her second marriage, both in preschool. And though she's 44, has gone back to school and her life is full and good, she was hoping for one more baby. Even after the miscarriage, when her doctor told her she was too old to successfully carry a fetus to term, she had to try again. It's only now, after six months of daily, nearly non-stop grieving, that she's been able to make peace with the idea that there won't be another baby.[6]

While this woman is not going so far as to create an entirely fictive pregnancy or a make-believe baby, she approaches it. Such longing for a baby, so intense that a woman creates a child in fantasy, raises this question: Does the biological urge to reproduce so strongly motivate some women that they resort to fantasized motherhood? Although this question is unacceptable to many contemporary feminists, it cannot and should not be ignored. A recent development in the saga of the renowned experimental gorilla Koko suggests that indeed biology does motivate women's reproductive urges. According to a newspaper account from April 1988,

> Koko, the Woodside gorilla who gained international recognition through her use of sign language, . . . has issued a pressing message:
> "Want gorilla baby," she signs, her arms making a cradle-rocking motion. At other times, she lifts her gorilla baby doll and points to her nipples. "Drink there," she signs.[7]

However one interprets longings for a baby so intense that they lead a gorilla to sign her reproductive urge or a woman to create fictive pregnancies, births, and babies, these longings clearly show how central pregnancy and childbirth are to many women, especially those who are willing to be ridiculed, even labeled "crazy" by becoming falsely pregnant. Are these simply women who are indelibly imprinted with patriarchal images of what a woman "should" do—bear and raise children? Or are these women for whom pregnancy and childbirth matter so much that both these reproductive stages retain their original prepatriarchal sacredness?

Such desire for pregnancy cannot simply be labeled abnormal or dismissed as antifeminist. Fictive pregnancy must be considered a significant image of child-birth, one of the few which may, in some instances, actually reflect a woman's own need rather than superficial patriarchal imperatives. As such, despite its strangeness, women's fictive pregnancy suggests a powerful image in which body language tells us something that counters much prevailing, antiessentialist feminist ideology. It tells us that for at least some women, carrying and bearing children is so important—either negatively or positively—that in the absence of real preg-nancies, their bodies will create fictive counterparts. Only those who discredit all meaning can dismiss this phenomenon as meaningless. Those who trust body lan-guage will surely see this condition as a nonverbal image by which imaginative powers, not just of the mind but also of the body, convey a situation that seems factually impossible. And it is partly through the ability of the imagination to create counterfactual situations that reconceptions of the meaning and importance of childbearing will arise.

COUVADE

"Born Pregnant . . . 6-Yr-Old Boy Gives Birth"
So reads the inch-high headline of the July 26, 1988, issue of the *Sun*. Buried deep inside this tabloid between "Ghosts Aboard Haunted Ship Tell Psychic about Their Past" and "Bank Charges Widow $2—to Change a $20 Bill," the second headline appears: "Boy, 6, Gives Birth . . . to His Own Twin!" What is so astonishing about these headlines is not the fact that a male gave birth—he did not. (For the curious: he had a tumor that contained cells of a never fully devel-oped twin.) What is surprising is that this idea should be so universally pervasive that it has persisted from prehistory to the present. The dream of male childbirth is the male counterpart of pseudocyesis. As such, it reveals intense male longing. Whether this longing is to usurp women's reproductive power or to share in child-birth must be examined closely. Either way, such longing unquestionably reveals just how powerful the condition of pregnancy really is.

Just as mind-boggling to those unfamiliar with it as pseudocyesis, this phe-nomenon wherein a man ritually or emotionally participates in or mimics his mate's pregnancy is known technically as couvade. Interpretations of couvade vary greatly, but its existence strongly supports the thesis that males do, in fact, envy women's powers to carry and give birth to children.[8]

Most men, if asked directly, vehemently deny harboring any desire to carry and bear children. Yet evidence to the contrary exists. For example, Freud, who was scarcely disposed to credit males with womb envy, uncovered overt evidence in the wish of his patient "Little Hans":

> I: "You'd like to have a little girl."
> Hans: "*Yes, next year. I'm going to have one,* and she'll be called Hanna [after his little sister] too."[9]

Although the idea of males giving birth may startle adults unaware of the Couvade Syndrome, many children besides Little Hans find the idea logical. Freud said that children, lacking reproductive and anatomically correct knowledge, often arrive at the theory of couvade on their own:

> . . . through an accidental observation, one of my . . . patients happened upon the theory of the "Couvade." . . . A rather eccentric uncle of this patient's stayed at home for days after the birth of his child and received visitors in his dressing-gown, from which she concluded that both parents took part in the birth of their children and had to go to bed.[10]

Recognized from at least as far back as ancient Greece, couvade is not actually known to have been so named until Charles de Rochefort used the term in print in 1665.[11] In medieval French the word means "to sit on" or "to brood over," as a hen does with her eggs. Thus, it implies that the man actually takes to his bed, as if awaiting delivery. Such an extreme form of couvade is not practiced in most cultures; yet, in some form, male participation in childbirth is common.

Historical references date from as early as the first century B.C.E.[12] In the medieval period, Marco Polo notes the practice, saying of the men he encountered on his travels in a province of China that "when one of their wives has been delivered of a child, the husband takes to bed with the child by his side, and so keeps his bed for forty days."[13] Equally common are literary references variously found in such seventeenth-century British dramas as Dekker and Webster's *Westward Ho,* Thomas Middleton's *The Widdow* and his *Women Beware Women,* and in the anonymous *Aucassin and Nicolete* in the person of the King, who says, "I am brought to bed/Of a fair son."[14]

Anthropologists have observed and analyzed this custom of couvade in various cultures. Typically, the man adheres to certain food taboos and alters his traditional work pattern in the pre- and postpartum periods. Sometimes he is ritually secluded for a stated time, either with his wife in their own house or separately in the men's house or even in a special hut. Among the Black Carib, for instance, couvade practices vary widely in length of time, sometimes being as short as two days or as long as a full year. Work taboos and interdictions against sexual intercourse play a major role for them, although food taboos, often central to couvade in other cultures, do not.

While it is tempting, from a Western feminist perspective, to view couvade simply as one more attempt by males to steal women's reproductive powers, such an interpretation must be considered carefully. Many cultures that now practice some form of couvade or did so in the past are non-Western. To place Western interpretations on non-Western practices is not only academically irresponsible but also risks violating the essence of an alien culture by highlighting elements believed inconsequential in that culture's context and downplaying others that matter critically. Furthermore, various practices of couvade overtly serve not to usurp the childbearing woman's powers but to legitimate those of the father. Thus, for example, among the Malays,

Pantang beranak refers to minute regulations to be observed from the seventh month of pregnancy to the 44th day after parturition. What might be done or not, during pantang beranak—which kinds of food might be eaten and which not—what were the proper and necessary purifications and washings—these were . . . regarded as matters of the highest importance to the father as well as to the mother.[15]

Such *shared* ritual participation in childbirth is surely a desideratum for both women and men. Given the enormous difficulty, until blood-typing (itself not foolproof) and the recent development of DNA fingerprinting, of absolutely identifying the biological father of any child, various forms of socially integrating the (presumed) father were critical for completing a man's transformation into fatherhood. Couvade practices played an essential role in that process.

Far more difficult to understand than ritual practices recorded by ethnographers or portrayed by poets and dramatists is the unusual medical phenomenon known as the Couvade Syndrome. A dramatic illustration appears in this case history:

A twenty-six-year-old soldier on active service developed a markedly swollen abdomen which persisted for twenty-two months, until he returned home on leave and saw his wife and child for the first time since the birth. It was reported that this tumefaction disappeared when he was anaesthetized and reappeared as he regained consciousness.[16]

As with ritualized forms of couvade, this medical variant raises serious questions. Is this man so empathically concerned for his wife that his body tries to lift some of her burden by mimicry? Or is this perhaps a case of a husband trying to usurp his wife's childbearing function? Then again, is this man merely trying desperately to extend his own part in the process of creating new life? Undeniably, whatever his reasons, any man who presents such startling symptoms will gain a great deal of attention. He is certainly doing something "special" when he so closely imitates a pregnant woman.

This phenomenon of fictive male pregnancy and childbearing raises intriguing questions. Would countless men jump at the opportunity to become pregnant? If so, what would this do to women? Would women then be denied our natural capability if suddenly it were valued by patriarchal cultures? Or would women sigh with relief and willingly hand pregnancy and childbearing over to men? Would women whose mates elected to bear children then view them with the same sort of disdain or ridicule that men have long accorded women? Or does this phenomenon indicate how central childbearing really is to both sexes? Rather than seeing couvade as evidence of men's attempt to usurp women's role, a positive view may understand it as a wistful desire to more fully share it.

However we respond to the image of male pregnancy, it is unquestionably a significant fantasy, not just for the presumably rather small number of men who engage in it but for humanity in general. If both women and men could understand couvade not in a literal form but as an embodied image of largely unspoken male desires, then childbearing might finally achieve its potential as a supremely sacred symbol.

ADOPTION

Childbirth by adoption is as "miraculous," in its own way, as pseudocyesis or couvade but so common that it scarcely seems "fictive." Yet adoption often fictively implies that pregnancy and childbirth have not occurred at all. It may so thoroughly ignore the birth-giving mother that, to all intents and purposes, she ceases to exist. Additionally, much like pseudocyesis, adoption creates a fiction that a physiologically nonpregnant woman has "given birth." This woman then raises the child. Of various "miraculous conceptions" by which childbearing fictively occurs, adoption is the most realistic reconstruction for both women and men.

Adoption fantasies are extremely common. As psychologist Otto Rank points out,[17] numerous stories depict heroes early separated from their mothers and raised in totally different families. The biblical story of Moses exemplifies this pattern. After Pharaoh commands that all Hebrew sons be thrown into the river, Moses' mother hides him until, fearing discovery, she places him in an ark of bulrushes. After Pharaoh's daughter rescues him, Moses' birth mother is hired to nurse him. Moses is then reared as though he were higher born than she, being given ruling-class status while his blood mother is treated as a servant. As with other fictive pregnancies, one way to interpret this adoptive elevation of the son over the biological mother is to see it as yet another patriarchal diminishment of the childbearing mother. It is equally possible to see it from the reverse perspective—as a childbearing mother's ultimate sacrifice for her child.

The first view receives confirmation from Otto Rank's observation that adoption of the hero into a "better" family than his own represents a common childhood dream. This fantasy allows children imaginatively to transform their given situations at the expense of their biological mothers. By fictively altering their births they negate both their biological mother and her childbearing. Such a fantasy therefore often reflects strong rejection of both childbearer and childbirth.

But adoption is far more than a common childhood fantasy. An extremely fluid concept, it probably still connotes adoption agencies and unwanted children to most of us. Various new technologies, however, now preclude rapid and easy definition, particularly surrogate motherhood, which may involve "adopting" a conceptus. Furthermore, as anthropologists are quick to point out, a definition that works for white, middle-class members of Western societies does not fit most peoples of the world. Perhaps the most straightforward broadly considers adoption "any customary and optional procedure for taking as one's own a child of other parents."[18] This definition highlights the fictive heart of the procedure.

However defined, adoption enormously affects the mothers involved. Yet even here ambiguity prevails: Who or what is a mother? Anthropologist Ward H. Goodenough helps clarify this term by distinguishing three types of motherhood—physical or natural, psychic, and jural.[19] Although physical motherhood used to be clear-cut, new technologies now make even that category questionable. Is a woman with the eggs of another woman implanted in her uterus the "natural mother" of the resulting infant? Equally ambiguous are the natures of the other two kinds of mother. The psychic mother principally nurtures the child, developing close bonds with it from birth. Can a child not then have more than one psychic mother? And what about a child raised in an all-male household? Can the men involved in rearing it be considered its psychic mothers? Is the nurturing animal mother in myths of abandoned children such as Romulus and Remus a psychic mother?

As for jural motherhood, this, too, is complicated. Some societies prohibit certain women, such as those imprisoned, unmarried, or enslaved, from bearing and keeping children. Ordinarily, however, "jural motherhood consists of the rights and duties in relation to a child to which a woman has claim by virtue of her having borne it." [20]

Furthermore, rather than clarifying the concept of motherhood, adoption often obscures it by ignoring the physiological acts of conception, pregnancy, and delivery. As suggested by these words of a woman who gave up her baby over thirty years ago, childbearing that leads to adoption may not even exist for the natural mother: "We weren't allowed to hold, or even see, our babies. My baby was just sort of spirited away. . . . A few days after giving birth I was hustled off as if nothing had happened. In a way nothing had, because there was nothing to show for my labor pains." [21]

Such fictive "nonoccurrence" of childbirth typifies cultures that value virginity and condemn out-of-wedlock births, as was generally true of most Western cultures before sixties activism, feminism, and the pill loosened sexual mores. The lengths to which parents would go in maintaining the fiction of a virginal daughter were often ludicrous. They might include surgery for "severe illness" or "an extended out-of-town visit with Aunt Tilley." Sometimes, seemingly unrelated to the visit, "Aunt Tilley" would suddenly have a new baby herself, a fiction given a bizarre twist in the following account by a woman whose pregnancy prevented her from graduating in 1918 as valedictorian of her high school class:

> I couldn't marry the child's father because he'd moved on somewhere, and I didn't really know his last name. . . . My parents knew they'd have to send me away and that I would have to give up the child, but my mother decided she wanted to raise another baby. So she sent me to visit my aunt . . . and while I was gone she kept stuffing pillows and things over her stomach to make people believe *she* was pregnant. When it came time for me to deliver, she came to Indianapolis. I had the baby and she went back home without all the pillows and raised my son as her own. [22]

Balancing the fiction that no childbirth has occurred for the natural mother is its *actual* nonoccurrence for the adoptive mother. While adoption provides a desired child, it does so without the preliminaries intimately involving a woman with her fetus for nine months. For the adoptive mother, childbirth more closely resembles such colorful, child-oriented explanations as the stork or cabbage patch stories than it does the biological process itself. To help counter this fictive quality, in some cultures a ritual "childbearing" cements the adoption: "Passing through a woman's underpants or bloomers, as an adoptive ritual, is encountered . . . in the Near East, wherein the mother takes the child against her bare skin, and then brings it out from between her legs, as if she had given birth to it.''[23] This ritual imitation suggests that some adoptions, like some biological birthings, denigrate the blood mother but paradoxically elevate the *process* of childbearing, a situation repeatedly implied by ingenious male attempts to appropriate childbearing. Such ritual enactment strongly suggests that no matter how dismissive patriarchal attitudes toward childbearing often appear, childbirth actually matters so much that only its fictive recreation can sanction an adoptive mother's status.

What makes adoption potentially promising for reinterpreting childbirth is precisely its lack of reliance on biological birth giving. As long as childbearing is understood solely as the province of women—and only fertile women at that—then jealousy from those unable to conceive—infertile women as well as men—may be inevitable. But when biological childbearing is transformed by various fictions enlarging the concept of biological motherhood to include multiple reproductive options, then underlying distortions, denials, appropriations, and denigrations of childbearing may disappear. When that happens, childbirth can truly be recreated.

4 Misconceptions

Not all conceptions, whether accidental, indifferent, or lovingly and consciously enacted, succeed in generating new life. Those that fail through miscarriage may cause a woman deep pain, and the grief she feels may be made even more unbearable because of patriarchally inculcated responses of guilt and blame. Learning to cope with her loss in an appropriately gynecocentric way is essential if she is to reframe her miscarriage in any positive manner.

Abortion lies at the opposite end of the spectrum of misconception. In contrast to the woman who longs to give birth but miscarries instead, the woman who aborts would give anything not to conceive and carry. Furthermore, although in most cases (rape and incest being notable exceptions) erotic feelings brought about her condition, she does not experience pregnancy erotically. Instead, she is left in the awkward situation of harboring inside herself an alien, unwanted potential being. The painful decision to terminate pregnancy often leads a woman to deny the entire experience. To reframe this particularly difficult and highly controversial procedure, it is necessary for women to face it squarely, placing it in the larger context of Nature's cycles.

MISCARRIAGE

Pregnancy gone awry is one of the most painful experiences a woman can face. To make her pain even worse, her loss is often accentuated by responses of indifference on the part of friends and acquaintances. Frequently those not directly involved, perhaps trying to "be nice," will say, "Oh, don't worry, you can always have another." Or, "Aren't you lucky it was only a fetus and not a child you had already grown to know and love," as if miscarriage were no more than losing an appendix. Carried to extremes, this indifference becomes outright denial that any "child" ever existed:

> The first two days I was drugged. . . . My husband arranged for a friend of ours, a minister, to conduct the funeral service. Later, he told us, "I have buried old people; I have buried sick people; I have never buried a newborn."

It was as though he didn't think a funeral was necessary, or appropriate. He said he had almost suggested that we not hold a service. . . .

In filling out our tax return, I asked my husband, "Did we have a baby or not?" . . . The IRS wasn't sure what to do. After four phone calls, they finally said that, if there was a birth certificate, there was a baby. We called the doctor and he said that the fetal death certificate *is* the birth certificate. I guess that if someone dies, she must have lived.[1]

The fact that this woman even had a baby, moribund though it was, is initially ignored—by minister, government, and friends alike. Her pain is significantly compounded by their collective refusal to acknowledge her experience. Although her husband convinced a minister to perform a funeral service, many women are less fortunate. For women unable to counter cultural biases against recognizing miscarriage as death, no ritualized grieving mechanisms have existed until recently. It took until May 15, 1992, for example, for the United Methodist church to vote affirmatively on a "Service of Hope" to ritually acknowledge loss of a miscarried child.[2] In the absence of formal rituals, women must somehow cope all alone. In the past, even expectant fathers often failed to understand how deeply miscarriage can affect women:

We lost a pregnancy at about twelve weeks, and I can remember I was a medical intern, and I can remember my wife aborting in the toilet. It was a little glob, you know. And at that time, I can remember saying, "Well, gee, honey. You're not having any problems." She didn't have to go to the hospital. I can remember that she was really devastated. I didn't remember feeling anything and I didn't at that point in my life really understand what her feelings were, and why she was so bothered by it.[3]

In addition to suffering such cultural nonrecognition of her grief, a woman who miscarries may inadvertently deepen her pain by creating punishing inner images: "I keep dreaming that my baby is lost and I'm searching for him, but I can't find him. I look all over the house and through the streets and I know he's there somewhere. I just can't find him."[4] This fruitless search for a baby that will not die in its mother's imagination epitomizes the punishment women typically internalize whenever childbearing goes wrong. Even when it is not explicitly defined as our fault, centuries of patriarchal images connecting fault to woman, epitomized by Eve, exacerbate our guilt and self-blame. The enormous unfairness of this response is patent. When childbirth goes well, patriarchal thought frequently takes credit, dismisses it, or alters it. When a pregnancy fails, however, often a woman is blamed or guiltily blames herself, as in the case of this woman who miscarried twice: "I kept thinking about anything wrong I'd done in the past that was the reason for all this."[5] While grief is unrelated to patriarchal assumptions, guilt and self-blame are not. Both reflect patriarchal teachings about women's "sinful" nature.

Accounts of miscarriage unequivocally demonstrate an implicit patriarchal double standard. Whereas patriarchal thought glorifies death incurred by traditional masculine pursuits such as war, hunting, and athletics, miscarriage is viewed very differently. Pity is often the most positive response women can expect, and often even that is not forthcoming; more frequently women's loss is glossed over. And frequently, as some of the previous accounts illustrate, women feel guilty. But there is an alternative to patriarchal reactions in cultures that all too often punish still-living mothers in a shocking display of blaming the victim. A gynecocentric response can accord both dignity and acceptance, as indicated by this moving example from a woman named May:

> I . . . walked out to a field behind the house and looked at a big purple cabbage with dewdrops on it. It was so beautiful and full of life-force that I started crying. I felt a lot of love and a little sad but I basically knew that everything was all right.[6]

The need for a woman herself to initiate memorial action is even more evident in the following example. Thirty-year-old Melissa lost two children just before their anticipated birth, but never ritually acknowledged them. Then she successfully bore a son before miscarrying again: "This time, however, she held her son. He was very beautiful to her. She thought of her other children, whom she had imagined as defective and malformed. She saw them in her mind as beautiful. She named her son."[7] After holding a funeral for the third miscarried child, Melissa continued her self-initiated process of recreating her loss by obtaining the medical records of her first two "lost children" and arranging funerals for them as well. Melissa's example, like that of May, shows women coming to terms with their culturally unacknowledged grief. In this way they are reframing a significantly underacknowledged aspect of childbearing—miscarriage—in positive ways.

ABORTION

Far removed from pregnancy so desired that its involuntary termination causes grief is pregnancy so threatening that it leads to abortion. *Abortion.* The very word is so fraught with emotions that any writer deals with it at her peril. It is an issue in which the rights of two claimants, seemingly equally just, come into irreconcilable conflict. I say this as a firmly pro-choice advocate, who believes that pro-choice arguments are not always heard as standing for full choice. It is within this very particularized context that I focus the following discussion, which is purposely limited to one very specific aspect of the entire vexed issue.

When a woman chooses to abort, she may feel that her body houses something intolerable. How she defines that "something" relates directly to the way she handles her abortion. Some women, not visualizing that "something" as anything at all, prefer to treat their abortions as if nothing were happening, an impression readily apparent in this example from the *Wall Street Journal*. A seventeen-year-old takes "her chewing gum out of her mouth, carefully wrap[ping] it" and says: 'I don't feel bad about the abortion. . . . . I'll have kids, but later on. Right now I'm just too young to have kids. I'm not a grown woman myself. I'm still under my mother's care, so how am I supposed to care for someone else?' "[8] The insouciance of this young woman's words and behavior do little to further the cause of pro-choice advocates. Yet, given the opprobrium cast on abortion by patriarchal cultures, what choice does such a young woman really have? The tragedy of her situation is doubled by the fact that she must not only do something that is morally ambiguous for most people but she must then deny its importance. No matter how cavalier some women may appear when they downplay or even deny their abortions, something major is taking place inside their bodies whenever one is performed. However they choose to deal with it, most women feel some qualms.

Believing reproductive choice is every woman's right, a belief that seems undeniably correct in the abstract, is very different from deciding that "*I* must have an abortion." The distinction between this abstract "right" and the personal agony of its actual employment epitomizes the problem that abortion poses from a gynecocentric perspective, no matter what patriarchal religions and laws may require. Very often the emotional pain caused by an abortion is so intense that only denial allows a woman to survive. A vivid literary example of what the young woman quoted above and others like her may eventually feel occurs in Margaret Atwood's moving novel *Surfacing*. In this work, the nameless protagonist returns to her hometown in a remote area of Canada as a thirtyish adult after years of absence and total estrangement from her parents. Ostensibly she has come, accompanied by her lover and another couple, in response to a neighbor's letter describing her father's alarmingly prolonged absence. In actuality, her quest for her father turns out to be a quest for both parents and, ultimately, for herself. Her lost selfhood hinges largely on her denial of a teenage abortion: "I couldn't accept it, that mutilation, ruin I'd made, I needed a different version. I pieced it together the best way I could . . . they had planted death in me like a seed."[9] Before acknowledging what actually happened, the speaker has lived with a fantasy of a husband and child and her own abandonment of both. Only the visions and memories triggered by her strange "homecoming" bring to the surface the actual event for which she has suffered so many years of self-paralyzing guilt.

In this case, denying aborted childbirth appears unconnected with patriarchal thefts of childbearing. In the context of this entire book, however, a major conflict centers around the opposition of patriarchal to gynecocentric culture. Only as Atwood's protagonist comes to fully accept herself in a setting where she reverts so fully to nature as to briefly become virtually feral can she accept her abortion. In this wilderness, the imagery suggests primordial, anti- or prepatriarchal Mother Nature. Thus, even in this instance of repressed abortion, internalized patriarchal ideas rob this woman of her own experience until she finally reaches a level existing far beneath them.

This same theme of abortion, treated as if it were not even happening, informs these words of a thirty-three-year-old married mother of three:

> My husband doesn't know that I am here. Maybe I'm not being fair in not telling him because he does love the three children that we have now, and he's a good father when he's there. But he is not there much. And the circumstances at home are such I just couldn't bring another baby in. Money always entered into it

because the money was always spent for what he wanted with his drinking and this type of thing. . . . I don't want anybody, like my bosses, to know I was pregnant and came for an abortion. It's nothing shameful, there's nothing the matter with it, and I wish that we had the laws in my state. It's not that I think it's shameful, it's your outlook, I guess. I'm conscious of what people think of me. You know how the rest of the world is, and they may hold it against you for the rest of your life like you killed somebody. I know how I felt when I had my cat spayed when she was pregnant and I didn't know it. It really upset me. "Mrs. Douglas, did you know that your cat was pregnant?" "No, I didn't." "Another two weeks and it would have been too late." I was really upset, because like I told him I would have let her have the kittens and then had her taken care of.

Maybe I didn't think about the abortion long enough. Sometimes I feel like it is murder.[10]

This woman's attitude toward what she is doing is unmistakably ambivalent. Unlike the protagonist of Atwood's book, she is not repressing her sense that what she is doing is murder. She therefore suffers in a somewhat different fashion from Atwood's protagonist. What makes abortion especially difficult for this woman is the double loss she is experiencing. First, she must somehow cope with the loss of her child. That is traumatic enough. But, on top of that, she must then find some means of conceptualizing it, some "story" to account for what she has chosen to do. In a patriarchal culture that repeatedly attempts to control a woman's right to her own body, she cannot even admit openly that what she has done may, in fact, be considered murder. In order to argue for continued legalization of abortion, the possibility that any "person" exists to be murdered cannot even be raised. Thus, for a woman who does truly feel it is murder, the horror of the situation is compounded. Not only must she do what she inwardly feels is wrong, she must then pretend to herself and others that it was *not* wrong, it was not "murder." This she *must* do to cover her deed in a patriarchally disapproving culture.

A parallel case exists for men forced to serve in their country's armed forces who must then justify their "murder" of the enemy, calling it anything but murder. In both instances, the original horror at something or someone being destroyed increases afterwards as the destructive act is repressed or falsely glorified. In both instances, patriarchal standards require a fiction which, by its very creation, variously robs mother and soldier of what may be her or his own subjective experience. The two situations diverge drastically, however, for whereas the soldier is urged, even expected, to cover up what he perceives to be murder by glorifying the deed, the woman who aborts and believes her act is murder must either deny it or risk castigation. While both cover-ups are equally unhealthy psychologically, one at least is given the psychological sanction of patriarchal tradition.

This is in no sense a plea to justify "murder." But it is a plea to readers to understand the terrible quandary of unwanted pregnancy. From a woman-centered perspective, it seems absolutely clear that a woman being forced against her will to endure an unchosen pregnancy is akin to a man being forced to fight a war he doesn't support or to suffer, defenseless, from unprovoked attack. Few men can really know, empathically, how devastating it is for a woman to find herself in this situation. If it were simply a matter of nine months of possible psychological anguish and physical discomfort, the issue might be different. But unwanted pregnancy presents a lifelong challenge to a woman's entire being. Does her life not count? Often those who label themselves ''pro-life''—as though only those who oppose abortion favor life—neglect this aspect. Who is going to raise this child? A caring woman cannot simply have a child and then give it up for adoption without enormous pain, as cases like Baby M illustrate. To believe otherwise is to ignore the realities of pregnancy and childbearing. It is precisely because the potential life is so important that deciding whether to bear it at a particular time matters so intensely. Were childbearing not a sacred experience with ramifications extending throughout the child's and the mother's lives, the right to choose abortion would be less pressing. A woman could simply have an unwanted child and leave it for someone else to raise without concern. But of what possible advantage is it to either baby or mother to force a conceptus into life when it is not wanted? Our country is full of people suffering from low self-esteem. Why add to the misery? The arguments are too familiar to rehearse. But the question that does need to be asked is this: Why does a barely potential life merit concern, whereas that of an already existing woman does not? That paradox is baffling.

Only if the issue of unwanted pregnancy is examined squarely, as being analogous to unprovoked attack or enforced conscription of an antiwar protester, is the full horror likely to be understood. Then perhaps this most difficult of all childbearing issues can be reframed.

One step toward reframing could be allowing women to fully experience and name their actions in a fashion that feels authentic to them even if that name should happen to be as ugly as ''murder.'' Surely this is preferable to pretending it is something ''good'' or denying its very existence if neither of those alternatives feels right. While not all false namings are equally destructive, to whatever extent they help us to hide from ourselves and our experiences, they undeniably wound us. A choice in the names we use should be every individual's prerogative. As with any other psychologically traumatic event, to accurately name abortion can be a first step in dealing with it responsibly. Conversely, to not name it is to deny a part of ourselves, to push it aside as if it simply did not exist. No matter how painful the act of naming is, abortion must be acknowledged in some fashion before a woman who has experienced it can truly reconstruct her life. And no matter what circumlocutions we use, whether in the case of a woman facing abortion or of a soldier facing an enemy, the termination of a living Other is never accomplished without pain to any perpetrator who is not so sociopathic as to be incapable of feeling. At the same time, as vegetarians so adamantly insist, no life can exist without the killing of some other lives. Yet even vegetarians may be said to sanction the killing of the vegetables they eat. The point is that we all kill. How we name that killing, or even if we choose to name it at all, is the central issue as I have chosen to frame it here. Yet this is an issue which patriarchal cultures (the only cultures we know experientially) have almost always chosen to ignore through assorted false namings. As a possible second step for coming to terms with abortion, why not consider the somewhat analogous arguments frequently made for a "just war." Why do no similar arguments exist for a "just abortion"? Painful as it may be, that step could be critical for helping some women (and men) deal with the deeply troubling issue of abortion.

5 Pregnancy: A Natural Initiation Process

Pregnancy often forces a woman to confront and evaluate herself. In most premodern cultures, menarche serves a similar function, marking a young woman's readiness for marriage and reproduction. But in contemporary Western cultures, not only has onset of menstruation typically moved back until it begins at age eleven, instead of between fifteen and seventeen, but young women marry later as well. Consequently, while menarche still separates childhood from adolescence, a far more significant life passage is marked for many contemporary women by pregnancy. Changes merely potential in menarche become actualized at this time. Furthermore, pregnancy, especially a first one, severely tests a woman's identity. Consequently, it functions naturally much like a socially constructed initiation rite. As religionist Mircea Eliade says, "Initiation is equivalent to a basic change in existential condition; the novice emerges from his *[sic]* ordeal endowed with a totally different being from that which he possessed before his initiation; he has become *another*."[1] Similarly, it is a rare woman who does not experience some fundamental alteration of her core being during pregnancy.

This chapter explores five stages of pregnancy from several points of view, always working against a patriarchal and toward a gynecocentric perspective. Early in pregnancy, when a woman is trying to adjust to her drastically changed condition, particularly in the face of patriarchal messages, she commonly experiences two closely interconnected conditions—self-loss and transformation. As pregnancy progresses, fears and fantasies may occupy her as she alternates between fearing her baby will be monstrous and hoping it will be exceptional. Although both fears and fantasies are warranted, in their extreme manifestations they may reflect divergent patriarchal influences. Of the more obviously gynecocentric images that also characterize pregnancy, one particularly in need of reframing is "woman as vessel." This often maligned image is actually a deeply positive symbol of feminine transformation useful to women seeking to understand themselves and the sacred dimensions of pregnancy.

SELF-LOSS

When a woman first suspects pregnancy, she may deny it. This response is especially common in unmarried women who often think, "It can't happen to me." No woman, however, is immune. As one mother told me: "We had only been married two months. The day I missed my period we were moving. My husband said, 'Oh, it's just the excitement of the move. It will come in a few days.' But it didn't. After a week I began thinking it must be a tumor. It just didn't seem possible that I could be *pregnant*—I had too many things to do first—like finish college."

Once a woman actually believes in her pregnancy, her next challenge is to integrate that belief into her self-image. This is a difficult task that can easily threaten a woman's very identity. Part of the threat comes from her often-conflicting inner voices, some patriarchal, others authentically her own. Sometimes, as researcher Reva Rubin explains, the growing fetus does not seem a fetus so much as an internal body part: "In the present, ongoing experience of being pregnant, the image of the fetus is of an inner organ, a part of the vital self, without separable physical boundaries but differentiated by its own movement and mass.[2] To imagine "losing" this organ through "delivery" may conjure up images of losing selfhood, rather than adding to it by creating a new individual. That makes childbirth seem rather like an operation to extract an inner organ. While such loss is not the same as having an extremity such as an arm or leg amputated, it nonetheless represents removal of *part* of a woman; in that sense, bearing a baby will not necessarily feel positive. Instead, thoughts of giving birth may make a woman fear that less of her will subsequently exist.

Somewhat akin to the impending sense of body organ loss that a woman may experience as a negative aspect of pregnancy is a shift in body sense whereby her ordinary experience of an intact body may give way in a highly unsettling manner:

> In the third trimester . . . there is a remarkable thinning of the abdominal wall in all women except those who are obese . . . [creating] "an increased protective response of the hands and arms at this time . . . ." [and] a sense of fragility of the self . . . from [which] a woman perceives the world around her at this time.[3]

Those who have never been pregnant but have experienced abdominal surgery may recall from their own postsurgical vulnerability fears of invasion and body loss similar to those felt by some pregnant women.

Different pregnancy-induced threats to a woman's selfhood can occur if she interprets her pregnancy not as bodily vulnerability but as fatness. Perceived as gross distortion of body shape, fatness triggers intense fear and repulsion in many people. In mainstream contemporary American culture, associations of fatness with pregnancy are negative for another reason as well: fatness commonly connotes lower-class status. Given such negatives, a pregnant woman's altered sense of identity as her body swells becomes understandable.

Considering contemporary emphases on physical appearance in the United States, it is scarcely surprising that some women should experience self-loss because of pregnancy-induced body distortion. Although it is easy to place a value judgment on such a response, labeling it shallow and narcissistic, such judgment misses the point: Part of who we are relates to body image, a fact well understood in many premodern cultures where body mutilation often forms an important part of initiation rites. According to anthropologist Bruce Lincoln, in women's initiation practices, the initiate's body "is taken as the locus of her very being, and the transformation desired for her is effected on her physical self. Such action is, of course, suggested by the events of puberty, whereby the body transforms itself, and bodily mutilation does seem to be practiced primarily by those among whom the performance of women's initiation is signaled by menarche."[4] Elaborating the Navaho practice of "molding" an initiate into womanhood, Lincoln quotes a Navaho informant:

> The woman molds the girl to press her into a good figure and shape her body. At that time and period she is soft and can be pressed into certain forms. You shape her so she will have a good figure. If it is not done, she will probably have a belly like a nanny goat's. The present day has things such as beauty contests; there, girls are judged by the shape of their bodies.[5]

While it is easy to claim this as one more example of patriarchal thinking, the Navaho (as Native Americans in general) do not actually consider themselves patriarchal. Some claim they are the only matriarchal groups in existence, although not all scholars agree with this assessment.[6] Lincoln's words make clear the import of his informant's statement: "It is not the girl's body that is transformed, but the girl herself."[7]

Similarly, some women experiencing the physical alterations of pregnancy will simultaneously feel a symbolic loss of self taking place. This is because sense of self very closely relates to the kind of bodies we have and the way we can move them in space. To say otherwise, positing some "inner" self as the "real" one, is to perpetuate traditional Western dualisms that separate body and soul. A woman who suddenly feels heavy and awkward if she has always been lithe and supple is bound to be a partially different self, if only for a few months. Not all women, of course, will experience this difference as loss.

An additional physical factor contributing to self-loss in pregnancy may occur if a woman's self-image has always been more masculine than feminine. In her case, the jolt to her identity may take one of two courses. It may be overwhelming if she wishes she were a man. Conversely, it can be extremely reassuring if she has secretly feared that she is "too masculine." For a woman whose primary sense of self reads like a list of "typical" male traits—success oriented, aggressive, athletic, competitive, goal oriented, and so on—the physical changes of pregnancy are often shockingly disorienting as the following case history indicates:

> Before I began to menstruate, I was one of [the boys]. Everything I did I loved. I felt strong, immortal and secure. No disease could touch me. Then one day on

the handball court, while I was beating the pants off this guy—suddenly this damned cousin yells, "Hey, you're bleeding." I got panicky, then hateful, then angry. I could have killed someone. I thought I would never "fall off the roof." Suddenly, I realized I can't do what I want. Now it was to be monthlies and pads, marriage and babies. No more ball-playing, no more kidding around. . . .

Womanhood means pain, blood, pads and perfume, diaphragms. Pregnancy is a duty, a disfigurement and a way of getting ungrateful brats. That's what mother and her fancy ladies taught me. I could never use diaphragms; I couldn't touch that disgusting part of me. I could take the first pregnancy—it was a boy; but the second was a nightmare. I vomited and felt like killing it.[8]

Among the challenges to selfhood that many pregnant women must face is "morning sickness," an ordeal characterized by nausea, sometimes to the point of severe and frequent vomiting. While this affliction is not limited to women whose self-identity is severely challenged by pregnancy, many studies strongly correlate it with negative reactions to pregnancy, often specifically to rejection of the fetus. Yet the studies by no means all agree. "Two propositions have been advanced: hyperemesis [vomiting] is a sign of 'rejection' of the foetus or, alternatively, lack of nausea is an indication of denial of the pregnancy.[9] Consequently, a pregnant woman may be caught in a double bind. If she does not experience nausea, then she is rejecting her pregnancy; yet if she does experience it, she is rejecting her fetus! As with almost all facets of pregnancy and childbearing in a patriarchal context, she seems doomed to "lose" no matter what she does.

Physician Grantly Dick-Read suggests that morning sickness may be largely self-induced through expectations that it will occur:

Pregnancy means morning sickness to some . . . [and] having heard that it is one of the signs of pregnancy, they believe it to be a necessary accompaniment. . . . On two occasions women whose menstruation was overdue consulted me about their pregnancy because of morning sickness, nausea, and loss of appetite and weight. Neither was pregnant, and their symptoms cleared up as soon as they knew for certain that that was so! Conversely, it is frequently observed that the girl who does not know that she is going to have a baby does not have any of these symptoms.[10]

Nonetheless, Dick-Read is quick to point out that chemical changes in pregnant women's bodies do cause actual physical symptoms for some. Any woman who does suffer intensely from morning sickness experiences self-loss in a particularly devastating way. In the words of one of my colleagues:

Every day, day after day, for up to several hours, I was so sick I could not do anything. This kind of continuous nausea is devastating. It nearly ruined my life for three months. I couldn't work; I couldn't read. I could barely even watch TV. All I did was retch over the toilet. It was as if *I* didn't exist any more—just some automaton in my place.

As these words suggest, the loss of self occasioned by morning sickness can alter a woman's life so totally that she scarcely feels that she *has* a life of her own.

Other psychological factors are potentially threatening as well. A woman uncomfortable in her relationship with her own mother may discover that pregnancy feels wrong, like a trap that will turn her into a replica of her mother. The sexual nature of pregnancy may also cause distress. A woman raised in a puritanical household may find pregnancy provokes anxiety. Here is the unavoidably visible sign, for all the world to see, that she "did" it. Sexual shame is uncommon now, but not long ago pregnant teachers and students were forbidden to remain in public schools. And before that, pregnant women were confined to their houses until after delivery. How could a woman possibly feel she was the "same" self if the world declared her unfit to be seen? Conversely, once a child is born, it visibly sanctions a woman's sexual activity. For a woman pleased with her sexuality, a child indicates her "accomplishment," signaling her transformation from girl into woman. How then should we characterize these various alterations of self-identity that pregnancy and childbearing occasion?

If feelings of self-loss dominate a woman's pregnancy, they may overwhelm her; she may believe that she is no longer a self at all. Feeling denuded of identity in the absence of all the "props" associated with her previous world, especially if it was one of paid work, she may panic. Instead of knowing who she is and experiencing a stable core, she may lose her sense of self. Her individuality becomes swallowed up by the biological role into which she has been thrust:

> The review in memory of who and what she has been is a self-initiated process of disengagement from the self and from ideal imagery which is no longer relevant or compatible with becoming a mother. During pregnancy, the process, a form of grief work . . . is tentative and is expressed in the past imperfect tense: "I used to . . . ," "I always thought . . . ," "I was. . . ." In the pragmatic and conservational style of the pregnant woman, actual disengagement and release from an earlier identity is contingent on a successful delivery.[11]

Negative as these experiences of self-loss may seem, they are a natural and inevitable part of pregnancy. The pain a woman may feel at this time parallels the pain typically experienced by initiates in cultures that socially construct rites of passage. As the next section indicates, understanding the necessity for these changes and reinterpreting them positively can help women reconceptualize negative associations of pregnancy. When that occurs, self-loss is experienced as self-transformation instead.

TRANSFORMATION

Pregnancy: some women experience it as self-loss, others as positive self-transformation. While one woman feels her selfhood drained away by the fetus inside, another feels enriched by its presence. Childbirth professional Reba Rubin refers to this relational aspect of pregnancy as the I-You relationship. This is an obvious, but unacknowledged, borrowing from religious scholar Martin Buber, whose book *I-Thou* examines the profound difference between an I-Thou and an I-It relationship. To explain this difference, Buber uses the example of an individual and a tree. One can variously approach the tree, seeing it as a picture, an element to classify, a movement, and so on. In all these relationships, however, the "I" remains a detached observer of an objectified tree; thus, all three exemplify an I-It relationship. But as Buber says, "It can . . . also come about if I have both will and grace, that in considering the tree I become bound up in relation to it. The tree is now no longer *It*." [12] Ideally this same shift from It to Thou also occurs in pregnancy. When it does, a woman experiences the unavoidable changes of pregnancy positively.

In pregnancy a woman loses her accustomed awareness that nothing fills her body cavity except internal organs and body fluids. Slowly, she notices a fetal presence. Sonography corroborates her suspicions, providing visual evidence early on, enabling her to "bind-in" the child to her self-image. [13] Once the preborn becomes "real," the mother may feel ambivalent, alternately experiencing the fetus as "It" and "Thou." Both ways, this awareness of another self inside her significantly marks the first stage of her nine-month initiation process.

When a pregnant woman relates to her fetus in an I-Thou fashion, her self-concept begins altering positively. This creates "motherselfhood," a binary unity simultaneously two and one, its parts consisting of mother and child in varying degrees of relationship to each other. Reva Rubin describes this developing relationship like this:

> There is a cognitive mapping of the "I" and the "you" and a constant reaffirmation of the "I" in relation to the concept of "you." This mapping is the predominant behaviour during pregnancy and continues through the neomaternal/natal period until the identity of this child and the reciprocal maternal identity are fully constructed. The conceptual interweaving of the reciprocal and instrumental self in relation to the stage of identity of the child binds the woman into this unique relationship mentally as well as biologically. [14]

Despite her abstruse language, Rubin makes an excellent point. During pregnancy, a woman is discovering who she is relative to the developing self embedded within her. The task of determining who is who strongly characterizes the whole initiatory process. Ideally, it also continues long after pregnancy, for the issue of "where Mommy leaves off and I begin" structures every individual's necessary development into a separate self. Thus, a pregnant woman graphically represents the ongoing, generational nature of this centrally important psychological process. On the one hand, she herself has had to separate from her own mother. On the other, she must now bind-in to this newly developing person who, in its turn, will have to separate from her and slowly individuate her- or himself. It is a daunting task that manifests the power of every woman to safely enclose the developing selfhood of another potentially separate human being.

Paradoxically, however, this very power has been twisted in patriarchal thinking. Freud's influence is particularly striking in this regard. Consider, for example, this heavily Freudian passage from Nancy Friday's popular *My Mother/My Self* about young women's developing sexuality: "The real thing, the penis inside, for many women never does lives up to that early substitute: security. And tight security—control—is the antithesis of orgasm—letting go." [15] These words, from a gynecocentric perspective, are backwards! Why is the penis the "real" thing? This is, of course, a classic example of Freud's view that a doll or a baby is a woman's substitute for the penis! But from the perspective of a woman who has gestated and given birth, it seems self-evident that the child inside is the primary "thing," not the penis.

For a pregnant woman, it is extremely important to experience her fetus gynecocentrically. If she can only experience it through patriarchally acculturated eyes, she will feel loss, for the fetal presence causes her to "lose" a self defined and previously experienced through an androcentric norm. That self is a physically unitary self—the only self a male knows experientially—for this is what self automatically is in patriarchal understanding. But *that* self radically departs from the symbiotic relationship of motherselfhood occasioned by pregnancy and maternity. To appreciate motherselfhood positively necessitates reframing "self" to accord with gynecocentric experience. How then is a woman, especially one educated to career and fast-track goals, or one who feels unmaternal and dislikes pregnancy, to bridge this gap?

Fortunately, over the past decade and a half, childbirth education has come into its own in the United States. Classes are no longer limited, as they were through the early 1960s, to preparing women (and their mates) for labor and delivery. Now courses also help women negotiate the often-difficult initiatory process of pregnancy. Some are conducted by midwives, others by childbirth educators of various sorts, usually nurses, psychologists, or social workers. [16]

Common to the practice of many childbirth educators are certain specific techniques for positively transforming selfhood during pregnancy. Particularly popular is visualization, a healing method originally aimed at cancer patients when it was developed in the 1970s by Carl and Stephanie Simonton. [17] Childbirth expert Claudia Panuthos defines this now popular self-hypnosis technique as "an indirect relaxation and integration technique . . . an exercise in enlisting all available positive resources for the purpose of a positive childbirth experience." [18] Visualization is used in many ways. Childbirth educator Gayle Peterson often uses it to help clients accept previous unsatisfactory birthing experiences. For instance, she tells of one woman reliving a repressed birth of a child long since adopted out:

> In a relaxed state she was able to visualize and remember the labor, her feelings
> of shame and inadequacy, and her guilt about her son. As she worked through
> the experience, she was able to create change in her visualization, to give herself
> the right to hold and touch her baby, to say good-by to her son. [19]

Potential for positive transformation is built right into this process: "She was able to create change." In this case, the current pregnancy becomes the venue for healing an emotionally painful previous childbearing experience. Visualization is thus serving the dual function of restructuring the earlier experience, then allowing the current pregnancy to proceed positively in light of the newly reframed original. *Both* pregnancies could have been experiences of self-loss; both together now effect positive self-transformation. Visualization, used this way, breaks what would otherwise be a recapitulation of old trauma, allowing new stories to emerge instead.

In her use of visualization in *Birthing Normally*, Claudia Panuthos speaks of "creating an inner sanctuary of psychic resources for birthing, enlisting support, and focusing on positive outcomes" (p. 109). In a sample visualization, she begins by directing her client to find a comfortable spot in the room, guiding her by possible, not absolute, suggestions such as "You *could be*." This nondirective technique departs markedly from the authoritarian mode common to patriarchal instruction, especially that associated with medical practitioners. Thus, Panuthos's method matches feminist principle as well as satisfying current populist desires for empowerment of lay people. Such nondirective visualization also allows for the greatest possible creativity on the part of the visualizer. Unlike a specifically focused directive, this kind suggests only possible options: "You could be lying down on the floor, sitting against the wall, or up in a chair" (p. 109). The one being guided need not restrict her choices in any way. Whatever suits *her* needs and fancy is okay. Also characteristic is the way Panuthos intersperses encouraging words such as a single "Good." How greatly this differs from no feedback or, worse, a negative evaluation. The way the visualization is conducted is as important as its content.

Panuthos's representative sample proceeds with a fairly standard relaxation exercise format, sprinkled with suggestions for appropriate breathing followed by hints to relax and focus on pleasant memories. Then Panuthos says, "Now, without thinking or reasoning, look around and feel with your heart if this atmosphere would be one in which you could choose to birth a child" (p. 109). She asks the visualizer to consider sensory as well as technical capacities and then moves on: "Take a moment to affirm your ability to create now inside of yourself an ideal and sacred place within your heart for a child to be born—a place where guilt and inadequacy are unknown and support is abundant" (p. 110). This section of her book typifies the remainder of Panuthos's fairly lengthy sample visualization. Several features are noteworthy. First, it blurs customary professional lines: Is this a psychotherapist speaking? A New Age guru? A priest or minister? A witch or priestess? This blurring of roles matters enormously in this context of pregnancy and childbearing because both are so often dominated by medical-technological models based on a mind/body split. The childbirth professional is clearly challenging our accustomed classification system. If mind/body is understood as one, then those who minister holistically cannot themselves be separated out as specifically "this" or "that."

From the perspective of anyone drawn to the spiritual dimension of childbearing, the nature of Panuthos's visualization process is compelling for another reason. Here is a visualization guide *invoking* a response. Ordinarily invocation is reserved for religious settings. It is usually couched in the second person singular, as is implicitly the case throughout the entire sample visualization. More important, invocation is usually specifically addressed to deity (or spirits) in an attempt to secure their presence. Here, what is invoked is slightly different—a vision, but one specifically designed to sacralize the pregnant woman's womb. Thus, although no deity is overtly called, the intent is precisely the same: to sacralize a particular place.

Obviously a technique of this sort can only work if a woman accepts it in the spirit in which it is intended. Unfortunately, nowadays visualization has become so common as to be nearly routine. But if its overuse can be overlooked, its original healing intent may be regained. Then the related idea of a pregnant woman's womb being a sacred place can be understood as a meaningful symbol of self-transformation.

Understanding the womb as a sacred place also relates it to various rituals of goddess worship. Consider, for example, imagery from the Villa of Mysteries at Pompeii of "the god Dionysus, voluptuously spent, reclining on the lap of a woman." Jungian therapist Patricia Reis discusses this imagery:

> The story encoded in this image of Ariadne and Dionysus is one particular type of female initiation. . . . The transformation is a process of sexual magnification, wherein the woman experiences herself in a body that is authentic, ensouled, and fully female. . . . [It is] a process of a woman coming into her own powers, through contact with her own divine life-force.[20]

Whether one chooses to name this process in terms of the Greek deities Ariadne and Dionysus, or whether one thinks of it as a "sacralization of the womb," it seems absolutely clear that any woman who experiences herself as transformed positively during pregnancy is experiencing "her own life-force." And to attain awareness of this force is to recreate pregnancy from a gynecocentric, life-affirming perspective.

FEARS AND FANTASIES: MONSTERS AND PARAGONS

An integral part of the initiatory aspect of pregnancy is the sometimes terrifying, sometimes exhilarating play of the imagination at this time. Often this play occurs in tandem with quickening in the second trimester. Now the self-concern common to a woman in early pregnancy merges with concern for her baby. Exciting and wondrous as is this sign of life, which suddenly makes the infant inside seem "real, " it also inevitably triggers intense fears. Once she has felt life, a pregnant woman cannot help but worry whenever her baby stills. Considering the uncertain outcome of any pregnancy and the long history of truly monstrous progeny of myth and fairy tale, no wonder so many women are bedeviled by nightmare images "of monsters, of limbless cripples, brainless vegetables, lipless, earless, blind, deaf, . . . cosmic jokes on the daring of the rational human being to reproduce . . . dreams of chicken heads squawking on dog bodies . . . months of attention to the kicks that signaled life was still there."[21]

Added to such hideous fears for the fate of her baby is a self-concern different from her earlier fears of self-loss. Because woman and Nature are historically identified, genetic accidents automatically lead many people to blame the woman whenever they occur. Consequently, a pregnant woman may find her original fantasized fear needlessly compounded.

Such blame is implicit in the Greek myth in which Gaia, Mother Earth, and Ouranos, Father Sky, produce the three monstrous Cyclopes—Steropes, Brontes, and Arges. Each hideous child possesses but a single eye, right in the center of his forehead. Here Mother Nature, personified as Gaia, has gone completely berserk, making Ouranos appear the victim of her "evil" action.

In addition to fear and guilt, horror and fascination surround the idea of "monstrous birth," as brisk sales of tabloids with their lurid tales of two-headed babies and grandmothers reborn as their own grandchildren attest. For a woman to even suspect such an aberration capable of emerging from *her* body is unbearable. What would such a birth say about *her?* How could she possibly respond to it? Would she react like the Japanese creator gods Izanagi and Izanami when they first mated: "The child of this union was born without legs and could not stand (it was a so-called leech-child). They refused to accept it as their own, and cast it adrift in a reed boat." [22] Could a woman who produced such a child even look at it, much less love it? How could she bear the stares and questions of others?

Inherited patriarchal fears tell her that such a child represents God's judgment against her, a view epitomized in these words from Governor Winthrop in 1638, condemning as a witch the bearer of a "monster":

> I heard since of a monstrous and prodigious birth which [Mrs. Hunkington] should discover amongst you; and also that she should retracte her confession of acknowledgemente of those errours, before she went away. . . . If your leisure would permite, I should be much beholden unto you, to certifie me in a word or two, of the trueth and forme of that monster. [23]

Nor is this idea of monstrous birth divinely punishing a woman limited to biblically influenced cultures. Navajo myth, for instance, tells of monsters resulting when women "sin" by giving birth parthenogenetically: "The Holy People were at that time being exterminated by monsters conceived by masturbating women: 'a women who masturbated with an elk's horn produced a horned monster, one who used a feather gave birth to a monstrous eagle, and so forth.' "[24] Besides fantasies about physically deformed children, fears of carrying an abnormally destructive child also haunt some pregnant women. Consider such modern images as *Rosemary's Baby* or *The Bad Seed*. The bearer of such a monster, believed to be the chosen conduit for unholy powers, is often labeled "demonic" herself. Whatever the nature of her child, no "monster-producing" mother's self-image remains unscathed.

Such monstrous fantasies of pregnancy and childbirth often include the mythic connection of birth and death. Almost every woman fears carrying a dead fetus, an image particularly disturbing because it violates two fundamental tenets of consensual reality—that birth brings new life, and that mothers give and sustain that life. Any woman who violates these tenets by actually producing some kind of "monster" suffers the punishments such violation of these commonly held images demands.

This violation and punishment currently stigmatize all AIDS babies as "monstrous," the way syphilis once scourged infant victims and their mothers. Such "monstrous" outcomes of demonized diseases justify underlying patriarchal fears about the inherent witchlike powers of women to harm innocent victims. Other fearful fancies of childbirth made "monstrous" and death-oriented rather than "normal" and life-connected seize on potential genetic defects capable of producing disease and deformity. Anencephalic babies whose lack of brain renders their human classification somewhat problematic and oddities known as hydidaform moles—benign growths which early in pregnancy replace or deform the embryo, leaving for eventual "delivery" a bizarre tumor instead of the anticipated fetus—strain the divide between human and something that no words can adequately describe. These deformities can also reinforce notions that pregnancy is somehow "freakish" as well.

What woman living in a Judeo-Christian influenced culture can possibly not connect such "monstrous" fears to punishment for sexual "sins"? Everything in our culture reinforces this notion. If her worst fears come true, her child will be marked for all the world to see with the signs of her own "depravity." It would be her baby who would pay for actions in which it played no part. Even without the guilt-inducing apparatus of biblical attitudes, a pregnant woman can scarcely escape these images.

Today, however, a woman has recourse to external interventions such as amniocentesis and ultrasound to help allay such fears. No longer must she suffer so intensely the worry of producing an "untoward result." This frees her to some extent from deep psychological fears that her innermost sins will be revealed in monstrous form. Yet such interventions are themselves a mixed blessing; they may make her feel better in one way while making her suffer in quite another. Consider, for example, these words addressed by Phyllis Chesler to her fetus as she undergoes amniocentesis:

> What if you're a Mongoloid? I lie on the table, look at the ceiling, hide my fear with scientific questions. . . . There you are: my baby, in me. The sonogram screen is filled with this tiny, oh so tiny creature, floating, turning, always moving inside my womb, alive on the three-dimensional gridded screen, alive for seventeen weeks now. I am seized with sadness! Here you are, yet to be born, yet to live, and you're being watched by so many strangers. It seems like a gross invasion of privacy. . . . I lie on the operating table, my belly exposed. When the doctors find the right spot to enter with their long reverse-syringe needle, I see, *and they see*, that this baby, you, quickly move to the exact chosen spot—as if you're playing with us, as if you want no invasion.[25]

As Chesler's words reveal, this intrusive procedure often seems abhorrent, simultaneously violating a woman's bodily integrity and the privacy, hence the developing selfhood, of her fetus. Yes, amniocentesis can undeniably reassure a pregnant woman and her mate, alleviating potential fears of dark, "divine punishments," but in the process, it raises other issues.

Because the test exists, for a woman at risk not to use it seems irresponsible. Yet using it is not an easy decision. Either choice may feel wrong for different reasons. To refuse it and later discover something wrong would be devastating. But to go through with it reluctantly may induce Chesler's reaction—discontent at violating something sacred, the privacy and selfhood of her own child—making a woman feel that she, like the ultrasound specialist and the physician who inserts the needle, is guilty of voyeurism on a scale far larger than any heretofore known.

The problems raised by amniocentesis are even more graphic for many women in the case of ultrasound scanning. Just as destructive of previously experienced bodily integrity and imagined privacy as amniocentesis, this nonsurgical procedure, which is akin to sonar detection of submarines, can evaluate a fetus at almost any stage of development:

> At first, it is hard to make sense of the swirling, unstable patterns of light and dark, but when the fetus is still, one can soon distinguish its head and then, a little less clearly, its torso. I . . . was unprepared to see that figure emerge from the initially unintelligible swirls, unprepared for the knowledge that I was looking at my baby specifically as it was at that very moment. The picture shocked me, as though I had broken a taboo, thrilled me for the extension of my powers, surprised me by its concrete actuality, frightened me by bringing me closer than I am accustomed to being to the nothingness out of which we all come.[26]

These words reveal just how shocking this prebirth visual encounter with the fetus still inside the body can be—as if one were peering into the very heart of creation itself. Particularly disorienting is the way this glimpse alters the accustomed gestational relationship. Instead of the almost unconscious unity of the baby invisibly resting inside the body, this is a sudden dislocation. Now what has seemed part of one's self, albeit a new part, is suddenly "other," separate, before its natural time for separation. It is difficult enough to deal with this seeming bifurcation of self when delivery forces it; dealing with it beforehand may greatly intensify maternal fears of body loss and future separation. And both procedures also seem likely to activate negative imagery which, as I discuss later in "The 'Birth Trauma,'" some hypnotically regressed subjects claim to recall from their own uterine existence.

On the other hand, according to some medical advocates, sonography is

> a great opportunity for [a woman] to meet her child socially and in this way, one hopes, to view him [sic] as a companion aboard rather than as a parasite. . . . Doctors and technicians scanning mothers have a great opportunity to enable mothers to form an early affectionate bond to their child by demonstrating the child to the mother. This should help mothers to behave concernedly towards the fetus.[27]

Read with suspicion, this statement yields some ominous implications. Why do some medical advocates assume that mothers, who, after all, have existed for many years without such fetal monitors, need this artificial means of "meeting" our infants and establishing an early bond? This sentiment sounds a familiar note.

Here are some physicians, still mainly male, trying to tell women what is best for us and our children. The intimate bond that develops *naturally* while an infant gestates is simply ignored. Only what the doctor can observe counts. Yet read another way these words suggest that the ultrasound scan might hasten one of childbearing's most sacred components, the bonding of mother and child, for women who do not otherwise feel this closeness.

The ethical issues raised by such medical interventions are not easy to decide, particularly given their newness. It is too soon to know yet what psychological harm such seemingly benign, even undeniably helpful prebirth intrusions may wreak on the fetuses to whom they are applied, or what lasting negative effects they may have on women's sense of selfhood. Fortunately, however, for any woman who feels uncomfortable with the ambiguity of using them, who does not choose to prebond or allay her fears of infant deformity through artificial means, a natural counterbalance exists.

In contrast to a pregnant woman's fears, there are many positive fantasies a pregnant woman can indulge while waiting for her baby to arrive. To carry a baby and *not* imagine what it will be like is nearly impossible for most women, according to pediatricians Marshall H. Klaus and John H. Kennell, experts renowned for their work on bonding:

> Mothers in the West dream of the expected infant. The mental portrait in the mother's mind before birth often includes specific hair color, sex, and so forth, but the real baby is never like the infant the mother has pictured, and during the first days after birth the mother must adjust the mental portrait to match the actual baby.[28]

Their findings indicate that women who do not indulge such fantasies bond less often and less successfully with their babies when they do arrive. Built right into pregnancy is the capacity to fantasize positively. This serves as a valuable antidote to negative fears, which receive much more emphasis in received patriarchal thought. This antidote specifically enhances the mother-child bond even before the child leaves the womb.

Such positive fantasizing also allows a woman to heighten or transform the reality of her patriarchal culture any way she chooses, even to envision a baby who will be raised as no other baby has ever been:

> I thought of how I would hold the baby, the new soft skin against by breast. My nipples would be the center of the baby's life, and my arms folding around the infant would fold around myself, holding the two of us together. Never would I allow a Gretchen to touch my child. Never would other hands wash or clean or cut the fingernails of my child. Never would I allow my baby to cry out in the middle of the night and see a stranger appear at the bedside. Never would I, like my mother, go to parties or shopping, never would I leave the child to reach out its arms for the reassuring touch that had disappeared. Never would my child wait outside my door for me to finish a nap, a phone conversation, a card game. I would undo, I would redo my childhood. I would do for my child what had never been done for me.[29]

Happily, utopian pregnancy fantasies such as this one are nearly as common as their nightmarish counterparts. They allow a woman to indulge herself by relishing her own power. Such fantasies, held in perspective, function as healthy vehicles for change, as the words "I would undo, I would redo my childhood" suggest. A woman who suffered abuse in her own childhood, for instance, can consciously determine never to repeat that same devastating pattern: While fantasy alone will not save her from such problems, positive fantasizing helps create new patterns in her mind. To whatever extent she subsequently actualizes her dreams, she may be able to counter prevailing patriarchal attitudes and create new, gynecocentric ones. Here, in this critical stage of a woman's initiation into motherselfhood, is an opportunity for each woman to create through fantasy her own personal vision of childbirthing.

WOMAN AS VESSEL

It is easy to understand how a woman who fantasizes negatively and experiences pregnancy primarily as self-loss may envision herself as merely a vessel. Although basically the vessel symbolizes feminine sacrality, the image is commonly twisted by patriarchal thought so that its original connotations are all but lost now. Construed negatively, vessel imagery associated with women both dehumanizes and objectifies us. Vessel imagery also has serious implications for contemporary maternal/fetal legal issues.

One way the vessel image dehumanizes and objectifies women is by analogy. With a growing fetus inside her, a woman appears like a vessel containing objects or fluid. Superficially, that likeness appears innocuous. But how readily this likeness is used to diminish a woman! The analogy of woman and vessel employs the rhetorical devices of synecdoche and metonymy.

Synecdoche involves using a part to refer to a whole, as in the common contemporary usage of *suits* to refer to professional men. The vessel, which reduces a woman by analogy to her womb, is but one of many similar reductions of women to various body parts—legs, hands, suggestive decolletes, and so forth. In a patriarchal context, speaking of a professional man as a "suit" emphasizes his power, whereas associating a woman with her womb reduces hers, rendering her nothing but a reproductive or sexual commodity. Furthermore, in a patriarchal context of pregnancy and childbearing, such part-for-whole thinking is common to medical thinking, which often makes the uterus, which carries the child, supersede the unavoidably attached woman.

Metonymy refers to one thing in terms of another commonly associated with it. For example, most reporters say "the White House says," not "the president says." In this case the image resonates power because of what the White House stands for. But when a woman is being imaged as a vessel, this is not necessarily the case. Sometimes if the contents of the vessel are valued, then the vessel is, too, as when women are valued because of our sexual and reproductive apparatus. In that case, however, we can as readily degenerate into the stereotypical, devalued "whore" as the glorified "mother," depending on where the emphasis is placed. At other times, as I discuss in my section on "Displacement" (Chapter IX), the content of the vessel—the child—is valued, but the vessel itself—the mother—is ignored. In that case, as anthropologist Robbie Davis-Floyd puts it, "The most desirable end product of the birth process is the new social member, the baby; the new mother is a secondary by-product." [30]

In the worst case, this valuation is reversed, again to the detriment of the mother. Because of anatomical proximity, "woman" thought of as a vessel for sperm may become "woman" as a vessel for urine and feces as well. In this way, vessel imagery often reinforces negative associations occasioned by the similarity of childbirth to various excretory functions. As Freud says, when discussing children's common confusion on this point, "The child cannot guess that another substance besides urine is excreted from the male sexual organ, and occasionally an 'innocent' girl on her wedding night is still indignant at her husband 'urinating' into her." [31] Such images not only defile women, they may lead to physical harm as well, and by extension they may also devalue and harm the children inside our wombs. This disturbing point is exemplified by an American Medical Association report stating that "the rate of domestic violence against pregnant women is . . . one of every six." [32]

Because vessel imagery has been twisted and used by men against women for so long, its original positive import is often difficult to retrieve. But stripping away negative accretions is essential for women trying to value pregnancy fully. Nowhere is this need more evident than in the area of women's rights to eat, drink, and drug as we choose when pregnant. Are we merely vessels? Or do we have rights apart from those of the infants we gestate? As long as the image of woman-as-vessel appears only negative, then pregnant women will understandably rebel when asked to curb ingestion of drugs and alcohol, a major issue in several 1990s court cases. Such self-constraint superficially appears to ignore the selfhood of the woman. Can women rediscover in the vessel image the gynecocentric power originally attached to it and, in so doing, find a way of overcoming the contemporary fetal versus maternal rights impasse?

By turning to myth, we learn that the vessel, as cauldron, has long symbolized the creativity of the cosmic womb of the Great Mother Goddess. This is a potent image. Furthermore, many traditions tell of vessel-borne, magical ambrosias and potions that confer immortality, salvation, or special creative power. Teutonic mythology, for example, speaks of the god Odin's theft of mead from an underground cauldron guarded by giants, which provides its owner with limitless creative power. Welsh mythology features a cauldron of regeneration, representing the womb of the goddess, which revivifies any corpse placed there for the night. Subsequent legends identify this cauldron with the much sought after Holy Grail, reputedly used by Jesus at the Last Supper and saved by Joseph of Arimathea after he caught the crucified Christ's blood.

Furthermore, far from being unique, the Grail is but one of many inexhaustible mythic vessels which, like the horn of plenty and the endless pitcher, provide unlimited sustenance to their owners. Real world possession of an inexhaustible object is granted but twice: to the fetus in utero and to the infant at breast. The mother is the model, providing all necessary nutriments for fetus and newborn.

Viewed in this way, the vessel is undeniably a priceless "object" to be sought and stolen by those who, like men, do not themselves naturally possess it. Unfortunately, not all fertile women fully appreciate their vessel-like gifts. But, by fully understanding the "secret" of the vessel, women can reframe its significance as a powerful woman-centered image for childbearing.

The "secret" of the vessel is incarnation, the ability to embody new life. Although we are all embodied, most of us know relatively little about our bodies. Like men, women "have" or "are" bodies, depending on whether we separate or identify "selfhood" with body.[33] And like men, we too have been inside our mother's body. But unlike men, we can also carry within ourselves another's body. Thus, most women experience three variations on the theme of embodiment: from inside a maternal body, through embodiment in the world, and through gestating a fetal body. It is our ability to carry within ourselves another body that most significantly differentiates us from men.

Often the word *incarnation* implies some preexistent, nonphysical essence—soul, spirit, self, life-force, breath, or even deity. Understood that way, as in the case of many other images that deny woman's creative role in reproduction, the incarnational aspect of the vessel grants reproductive power to some "other" source. By becoming embodied, some preexistent, nonphysical essence animates a particular body. In Western cultures, this phenomenon is frequently associated with Jesus, in whose person humanity and divinity are believed to unite. But the idea of a god incarnating himself to benefit humanity is not uniquely Christian. It also occurs, for example, in the Hindu concept of avatars and in some versions of Buddhism.

But from a gynecocentric perspective, such a view of incarnation feels backward. Emphasizing the one being incarnated rather than the one doing the incarnating reflects birth from a male point of view. Consequently, it makes a masculine principle the ground of being. The question is, Does one emphasize the vessel or its contents?

On the level of lived experience, the answer is clear: It is the vessel. After all, the mother's womb—as the word *matrix* so aptly denotes—is every individual's ground of being. Positing some other preexistent state automatically displaces this original physical state of being and makes the original inferior to some purely imagined condition.

For a woman, in whose womb these natural but still miraculous events of conception, pregnancy, labor, and delivery occur, incarnation is more appropriately understood as a process occurring within the vessel, her own body. During pregnancy, her body, with its protective coverings and its nutritive fluids, allows incarnation to take place. And as this happens, a woman's own sense of embodiment intensifies. The gradual expansion of her belly and the baby's movements within allow her to feel incarnation as it actually happens. Simultaneously, her own body changes, making her more conscious of herself as body. Thus, she knows what it is to incarnate a body within herself at the same time that she experiences herself as body. She is then doubly participating in life creation, that of her own body-self unfolding in time and that of her developing embryo. Faced with such an enormous gift of female life giving, it is scarcely surprising that men have struggled so long and so ingeniously either to downplay its significance or to appropriate it for themselves. If women can see incarnation this way, then perhaps we can retrieve it for ourselves, valuing it as it deserves.

Unquestionably, the secret of the vessel—incarnation—shows how potent the vessel is. But for full reinterpretation of the vessel image it helps to envision the vessel appropriately. First of all, as anyone knows who has inadvertently poured water into a purely decorative vase, many vessels, especially those made of un-fired clay, are extremely permeable. As indicated by researchers at the Kaiser-Permanente Medical Care Program in Oakland, California, in a report released to the general news media on 5 June 1988, a permeable vessel image is highly ap-propriate for pregnant women: "Women in first trimester pregnancy who use video display terminals for more than twenty hours a week suffer nearly twice as many miscarriages as women engaged in other kinds of office work." [34] Further evi-dence of maternal "vessel" permeability comes from some rather startling find-ings that a fetus can actually "see" light:

> An unborn child's vision develops . . . slowly, for obvious reasons: A womb, although not totally dark, is not exactly the ideal place to practice seeing. That doesn't mean a fetus can't see. From the sixteenth week in utero, he is very sensitive to light. He can tell when his mother is sunbathing from the rays that reach him. And while that usually does not disturb him, shining a light directly on his mother's stomach does. He often looks the other way and even if he does not, the light startles him. [35]

Sound also permeates the barrier of the womb, although science has been slow to substantiate this ancient idea, which appears in Luke 1:44, when Elizabeth exclaims, "For lo as soon as the voice of thy salvation sounded in my ears, the babe in my womb leaped for joy." Infant responses to sound even force some women to stop listening to extremely loud music. Some actually report leaving rock concerts because fetal kicking becomes unbearable. [36]

According to physician Thomas Verny, a somewhat unexpected offshoot of such sound permeation of the uterine vessel involves fathers:

> A child hears his father's voice in utero, and there is solid evidence that hearing that voice makes a big emotional difference. In cases where a man talked to his child in utero using short soothing words, the newborn was able to pick out his father's voice in a room even in the first hour or two of life. More than pick it out, he responds to it emotionally. If he's crying, for instance, he'll stop. That familiar, soothing sound tells him he is safe. [37]

Paternal influence on the fetus in the permeable uterine vessel includes more disturbing elements as well:

> During these months, a woman is her baby's conduit to the world. Everything that affects her, affects him. And nothing affects her as deeply or hits with such lacerating impact as worries about her husband (or partner). Because of that, few things are more dangerous to a child, emotionally and physically, than a

father who abuses or neglects his pregnant wife. Virtually everyone who has studied the expectant father's role—and, sadly, so far, only a handful of researchers have—has found that his support is absolutely essential to her and, thus, to their child's well-being.[38]

This passage makes clear the enormous impact of vessel permeability in yet another way—its ability to conduct emotional as well as physical stimuli to influence fetal development. But the vessel image needs further amplification, for permeability in and of itself is insufficient to characterize it.

Whether permeable or not, vessels are commonly assumed to be passive. This idea needs correction, as any cook knows who has tried to prepare tomatoes in a reactive pan. Not only does the leaching of the reactive metal discolor the food unpleasantly, it also endangers health. Envisioning the vessel-womb as both permeable and reactive greatly changes the nature of the image, illustrating its enormous interactive, transformative power for both harm and good.

Finally, an even more powerful reinterpretation of the vessel image occurs if its shape is revisioned. Borrowing from the world of advanced math, it is possible to envision the vessel as a Klein bottle. This is a kind of three-dimensional glass mobius-strip, the mouth of which bends down to penetrate its own body. In a Klein bottle, it is impossible to determine where inside and outside begin or end. This image perfectly captures the ambiguity of the mother/fetus relationship, for who can say where one begins and the other ends?

Through all these ways—looking to myth, examining the incarnational "secret" of the vessel, envisioning the vessel as permeable, reactive, and relational—women can reinterpret this important image of women's sacred potential. In so doing, perhaps those women who chafe at pregnancy "restrictions" on their intake of substances may be able to reframe their understanding of this increasingly prominent legal issue as well. A potential problem, as the next chapter suggests, is that women do not always feel strongly enough to do so in a patriarchal context.

6 Models of Labor and Delivery

Once a woman becomes pregnant, she typically begins thinking about how she wants her childbirthing to take place. Most women find that just researching and preparing for labor and delivery require much work. This is particularly so in contemporary Western cultures that offer an enormous array of choices. Should you have your baby in a hospital? a birthing center? at home? Do you want anesthesia or "natural" childbirth? Will your mate be present? your other children? your friends? While such abundant choices represent an enormous gain in women's attempts to reframe childbirth, the often ambiguous nature of these choices makes further reconstruction necessary.

Modern medical techniques create one of the most ambivalent models of childbearing. Yet, despite many negative effects of medicalized childbearing, women who exercise their own judgments often find it possible to resacralize childbearing in meaningful ways.

But some women strongly oppose a medical model, seeing in it the worst excesses of patriarchal and technological domination. For them, important alternatives emerge when they embrace consumerism. A consumerist approach to labor and delivery permits a woman to take direct action in changing current practices. But sometimes a power struggle erupts, and desacralization of childbirth results. Reframing childbearing as a consumer event is fraught with potential dangers.

Several closely interrelated models for labor and delivery emerge from the consumer model. One is a midwifery model. Of various possible choices of birth attendants, midwives have become increasingly popular in the United States since the 1960s. Midwifery includes some of the most overtly religious attitudes toward childbirthing found in any of the relevant literature. The location chosen for childbirth provides another model. Whether a woman opts for a hospital, birthing center, her own bedroom, or some form of underwater birth, she is generally concerned with feeling comfortably "at home." Finally, there are diverse "natural" childbirth models, many of which give men an equivalent role and thus permit a possible truce in the longstanding competition between the sexes. While not without perils of their own, these emphases on male-inclusive rituals augur well for the way women experience childbirth and men value it.

THE MEDICAL MODEL

Some women seeking to connect with the sacred dimension of childbearing reject images of medicalized labor and delivery, believing them too innately patriarchal to accept. As sociologist Barbara Katz puts it, "The 'medical model' shows us pregnancy and birth through the perspective of technological society, and from men's eyes." [1] This ideology dominates most childbirthing books written during the 1970s and 1980s, such as Suzanne Arms's *Immaculate Deception: A New Look at Women and Childbirth in America* and Margot Edwards and Mary Waldorf's *Reclaiming Birth: History and Heroines of American Childbirth Reform*. These books emphasize both a lack of personal meaning for women and antiwoman biases in medicalized childbirth. Their stance is understandable, given the sterility of many medical procedures and continuing patriarchal attitudes in many fields. But a more promising viewpoint for reframing medicalized childbirth is less overtly adversarial: It finds merit in medical techniques while stressing the need for applying them carefully. When a proper balance is struck, some women find sacrality even in the rather unlikely venue of a hospital setting.

One aspect of the medical model that arouses antagonism originated with Louis XIV, the French king who perversely liked to watch, hidden, while his mistresses gave birth. Finding it difficult to see well because laboring women typically squatted on birthing stools, he persuaded his court physician to use a high table. Soon fashionable women clamored for this table delivery, and their attending physicians discovered, like Louis, that they too could observe childbirth far better this way. Table delivery rapidly became standard medical practice. Thus was "born" the custom of birthing as voyeuristic "sport," with woman the object of the male gaze. But a supine position is totally inappropriate for childbearing. Neither women nor newborns were built to fight gravity. In so doing, women must push too hard for the good of both infant and mother.

A second medical development negatively significant for women and preborns was the invention of obstetrical forceps around 1600 by the barber-surgeon Peter Chamberlain. When the secret of their design, which remained within Chamberlain's family for the next hundred years, became public, midwives were strictly forbidden to use them, a stricture with enormous consequences. The traditional midwife soon became a much less acceptable attendant. Increasingly she was viewed as ill-educated, dirty, and incompetent by physicians. Eventually she was forbidden to practice in the United States and Canada. Consequently, childbirth in the West, most particularly in North America, became more and more male-dominated, and what little status a woman once had had in childbirth was lost.

A third pertinent medical development was the creation of maternity hospitals in Europe in the early nineteenth century. Because of their high incidence of childbed fever, entering them was tantamount to death for mother and child. Not until Semmelweiss discovered that careful handwashing could prevent infection did this scourge abate, and even then, aseptic practices were slow to catch on.

A fourth development with mixed significance was the application of anaesthesia. Chloroform, first introduced for childbearing by British physician James Simpson, grew increasingly popular after Queen Victoria used it for her sixth delivery. This medical procedure, which alleviated pain, also drastically limited the ability of women to experience their own labors.

All these medical "advances" contribute to another major drawback of medicalized childbirth. Typically, the physician's practice of obstetrics is elevated over the mother's act of giving birth. Often, when a physician dominates childbirth, his or her presence makes it an experience of illness rather than a natural physiological process. When a woman is admitted to the hospital, usually through an emergency ward because of the unscheduled nature of labor's onset, she becomes a "patient," and to be a "patient" is automatically to be something other than, or in addition to, a mother-to-be. Unless she consciously works against it, patienthood may make a woman subservient to her attending physician, because by definition a "patient" requires medical expertise. She cannot produce this child on her own: the physician must help. As "patient," she may be prevented from controlling her own experience. As in many traditional male-female relationships, the doctor as authority figure (regardless of sex) plays a heroic role; the laboring woman, defined as needing help, then must become a passive heroine. The following personal account from a thirty-seven-year-old French woman delivering her first child in 1955 illustrates this once common, but now vanishing, pattern: "I hardly dare to speak of the delivery. The doctor did all the work. He used two big spoons that looked like a fruit-salad server. Then I pushed and he managed to catch my baby. It is wonderful and moving to see the doctor make your baby come into the world, give it to you and say whether it is a boy or girl."[2] This new mother willingly plays heroine in need of "delivery" to her physician "savior," her words dramatizing the position he plays: "It is wonderful and moving to see the doctor make your baby come into the world." Yet her words are also highly ambivalent. It is not the mother through whom childbirth takes place as was the case in ancient prepatriarchal images of parthenogenesis; nor is there even a fiction of male deity to whom credit goes. Instead, it is a physician who is elevated, as a perpetually popular medical school one-liner has it, to the level of "M. Deity." Here, indeed, are both patriarchal appropriation and desacralization in operation.

This is certainly one way to read the situation, but such a reading ignores the woman's positive words, "wonderful" and "moving." It also ignores the partnership her words indicate she feels was created between her and her attending physician for the duration of the event: "Then I pushed and he managed to catch my baby." Thus, her words support two divergent positions as she simultaneously elevates her physician, thereby diminishing her own efforts, and expresses her awe at this event. To ignore what she says because of postmodern psychological awareness that she is largely projecting her own feat onto her physician is unfair to *her* perceptions as she understood them.

A further complication once common to medical models was the traditional refusal to allow partners to share labor and delivery. The rare partner allowed entry to the delivery room was made nearly as subservient as his wife. Even the clothing forced on a prospective father lucky enough to be admitted served to isolate him:

> Protective garments play a ritual role, denoting status in the hierarchy; the lower down the hierarchy, the more protective clothing must be worn. Some hospitals insist on gowns, masks, caps and overshoes for husbands. Others do not make partners wear *any* of this paraphernalia. A great amount of protective clothing seems to produce a barrier between husband and wife. The mask, above all, means that they cannot kiss each other. It has been found that the mask used for longer than 15 minutes is no longer sterile, and hence fails in its protective function. . . . It should be possible in hospitals for husbands to be more familiar figures to their wives, and to appear in their normal rather than a "medicalized" identity.[3]

But as with so many models of childbirth, the medical model is open to differing interpretations. For some women, hospitals do not conjure up negative associations but function positively. A colleague told me:

> I found being in the hospital—on a special maternity ward, attended to by nurses, learning from them about nursing, bathing the baby, changing diapers, etc. (and with my second, having five days freed of all family responsibilities and being alone with my infant son), in some sense sacred. I even thought of the floor my room was on as a sacred space and the time I was there as a sacred time.

This counterview clearly shows how some women may connect, within a mainstream contemporary medical milieu, to sacrality. Once again, the issue is interpretive. Though many people consider hospitals "sterile" places devoid of positive meanings or, worse, places horrifyingly demonic, others feel contented and secure as patients.

Furthermore, in some cases, a woman or her baby actually is sick. These women welcome medical intervention. Just knowing that a problem could arise is enough to make some birthgivers choose the hospital. It is important, though, to recognize when intervention is appropriate and when it simply reflects the reaction of medical practitioners trained to intervene rather than to wait and see. Consequently, some women who choose hospital-based delivery may nonetheless balk at various procedures advocated by their attending medical practitioners.

Cesareans are good examples of such procedures. Many women feel they are performed more often than necessary. Unquestionably, many circumstances legitimately warrant cesarean delivery, among them fetal distress; malpresentation of the fetus, such as transverse or breech presentations; cephalopelvic disproportion (a situation in which the fetal head is too large to go through the mother's pelvic area); fetal abnormalities; placenta previa; and toxemia. But the old rule that "once a cesarean, always a cesarean" has long been superseded.

How does such intervention affect a mother's experience? From one point of view, a cesarean drastically changes a "normal" delivery into the epitome of desacralization presumed characteristic of all medicalized childbirths. The fear most people associate with operations may so distort childbirth that a woman takes no joy in it. Indeed, fear is the dominant response reported by a number of women who were told in advance that they must deliver by cesarean. Here is a representative account:

> Do you know how really scared I was? For a time, I actually thought I might die. The night before the cesarean was a really long one with many moments of thinking I might not make it. I even made some preparations, just in case it really did happen. . . . I know how morbid this might sound to you now, but at the time I didn't feel like I could take any chances in case "it" did happen.[4]

Other women find that guilt, more than fear, dominates, as indicated by these words of a woman for whom an unanticipated cesarean came as a great shock:

> I had trained myself in the psychoprophylactic method with the aid of a record and books. The baby was to be born at home, and I had explained what I was learning to my doctor and midwife, who were quite sympathetic. Unfortunately, both were away on the night when my labor began and I was left temporarily in the care of a pupil midwife. This girl made a mistake in determining full dilation, and having used the Lamaze techniques extremely successfully up to this point, I was made to push on an incompletely dilated cervix for nearly three hours. This, of course, resulted in an obstetrical emergency, and I was taken to the hospital not understanding at all what had gone wrong—and I was criticized by the doctor on duty for not having been sedated at the beginning of labor and told that this had delayed the birth and endangered the baby's life! . . . I was very deeply affected indeed by this childbirth, and it was many months before I regained my self-confidence. I used to wake in the night screaming for many weeks afterwards.[5]

As happens in many negative childbirth experiences, this woman feels *guilty,* as if she had done something *wrong,* when she has simply tried to give birth naturally. Worse, the blame directed at her masks the initial unavailability of her physician and midwife. She is also confused, knowing something is wrong but hearing no explanation. She not only loses control over her own body but she also fails to achieve the sense of accomplishment voiced by many women who deliver vaginally. Instead, hers is a negative, disempowering birthing experience.

Given its unexpectedness and truly urgent character, this particular example represents the negative end of the spectrum. But even fully anticipated cesareans often raise issues that nonsurgical childbirth does not. Neither avoiding anaesthesia—although it may be local in some instances—nor fully controlling the birthing process is possible in a cesarean birth. It is therefore difficult for a woman not to feel that this is something being *done to her,* rather than something she herself *is doing.* How is a cesarean-delivered woman to handle this situation, which she may feel devastatingly reenacts familiar patterns of dominant males (or females) "delivering" helpless females? By what mechanism can she transform this negative pattern into one of strength and power?

One possibility involves self-sacrifice, but not the traditional self-sacrifice of a male hero. When faced with a cesarean, a woman can reframe her impending "operation" as a necessary sacrifice of her own potential experience, made in the interests of her unborn child. Such reframing can give positive meaning to an otherwise numbing alteration of an experience that she had rightfully anticipated.

Often, however, childbearing experience must be "sacrificed" because of a woman's health rather than her preborn's. This means she must somehow reframe the equation of pregnancy, labor, and delivery with illness. Forewarned that a cesarean is her best hope for success, a woman may mourn her loss of vaginal delivery but nonetheless celebrate her ability to give birth at all, in the belief that facilitating new life is well worth sacrificing personal experience. In fact, if a preexistent condition such as diabetes or heart trouble puts her at risk, even purposely to conceive involves soul searching. Thus, like her more fortunate sisters who can deliver vaginally, she may feel in control, having intimately involved herself all along in decision making.

By contrast, a woman faced with a last-minute cesarean must find different means to sustain her. For her, a more appropriate model may come from the very different universe of sudden death, as when a fatal accident leaves unprepared survivors stunned. Overt mourning helps. Acknowledging her loss of an anticipated life-experience even as she welcomes her new infant is an important first step for integrating her loss into her life. Using her own words, a cesarean-delivered mother can tell herself and others her story; she need not remain alienated from her experience by medical terminology that reflects an unknown world. Such renaming is one means that most women, even those not forced to cope with extremes like unexpected cesareans, can use to make their medicalized childbearing experiences their own.

THE CONSUMER MODEL

Over the past two decades many women, unhappy with a medical model of childbirth, have looked for alternatives. One relatively new one, childbirth construed as a consumer event, reflects attitudes characteristic of postindustrialized cultures. But as a consumer event, childbirth becomes predominantly an economic relationship between the mother-to-be and her birth attendants. Satisfying the "purchasing" needs of the parents in terms of both "product" and service becomes paramount. Like images of medicalized labor and delivery, childbirth as a consumer event can as often elicit automatic negative responses as positive ones. Yet, like many other models, this, too, can be construed as a life-affirming, sacred understanding of childbirth.

Many women find consumerism the most viable attempt to date for recovering childbirth from what they consider the negative impact of medicalized childbirth. Certainly it represents a major step in the struggle to make childbirth once again truly sacred, not just for women but for their partners as well. Childbirth consumerism emerged during the second wave of feminism in the late 1960s to counter physician-dominated models. As women became more aware, a major area of concern was our bodies, especially as related to childbirth and health care.

A good example of childbirth viewed as consumer event is the Patient's Bill of Rights, an elaboration of five points, all variants of the first:

> 1. The Pregnant Patient has the right, prior to the administration of any drug or procedure, to be informed by the health professional caring for her of any potential direct or indirect effects, risks, or hazards to herself or her unborn or newborn infant which may result from the use of a drug or procedure prescribed for or administered to her during pregnancy, labor, birth or lactation.[6]

This Bill of Rights exemplifies women's heightened awareness of various options and responsibilities. Besides promoting safer childbirth, it is intended to restore personal involvement in our own reproductive processes. A major aspect of such involvement is a drastically altered attitude now common to many women as they enter labor. When a physician stars in the drama of childbirth, a woman often hesitates to assert herself. More commonly she gives in rather than oppose her doctor. Nowadays, however, several factors including feminism, the consumer movement, more women physicians, and increased cultural resistance to authoritarianism have made that authoritarian model increasingly obsolete.

Despite its power for precipitating positive changes in childbearing experiences for both women and men, a very real danger lurks. Childbirth may become so consumer oriented that it will be primarily an adversarial relationship between "consuming" childbearer and "purveying" physician. Then the focus, as in the medicalized situations it seeks to correct, may once again cease to be the childbirth experience itself. If that happens, childbirth as a consumer event simply perpetuates modernist and patriarchal tendencies to deflect attention from childbearing onto something else—in this case, a contest pitting a woman's expectations against her physician's:

> Women approached the health team with a chip on their shoulders because of their stereotyped picture of the inflexible medical establishment. Doctors and nurses reacted to their own stereotype of demanding and unreasonable patient. It was confrontation rather than communication. Instead of the enemy being the potential hazards of childbirth, those who should have been the allies became the antagonists.[7]

The importance of the consumer movement for reframing childbirth is undeniable. But women seeking to exercise their consumer rights must bear in mind that these same rights inevitably change the context of childbirth. To be a "consumer" is automatically to be a purchaser. As such, a woman may shift her concerns imperceptibly from the personal significance of childbearing to attaining her money's worth. If that happens, her baby subtly becomes a "product" rather than a human being. The consequences of this shift are enormous. Once perceived as a product, the baby must be perfect. After all, few of us unprotestingly accept defective merchandise from a store. Why, then, should we accept less than perfect babies?

A serious implication follows. If a baby is not perfect, why should its parents accept it? It is frighteningly easy for this thought to trigger a snowball effect. If tests exist, and they do (amniocentesis and sonography, for example), to determine common birth defects such as Down Syndrome and spina bifida, then they should be performed. By this same logic, if a defect is discovered, this particular baby's life should then be terminated.

At this point the combined weight of medical and consumer models places the "consumer" in a difficult position. The "logical" option is abortion, as exemplified in the following exchange between anthropologist Rayna Rapp and the father of a fetus aborted following diagnosis of a sex chromosome abnormality by amniocentesis. The father first says that the fetus, if brought to term, might have been slow, and he was going to be aggressive. "I didn't know how to handle a kid like that. When he got moody and difficult, could I be a committed parent, or would I have thrown up my hands, thinking, 'It's in his genes'?" Rapp then asks the question that triggers the "snowballing" logic: "What if you hadn't known through prenatal diagnosis?" The would-have-been father replies, "I'm sure if it had just happened we would have handled it. But once you know, you're forced to make a choice." [8] How clearly these words illustrate the problem. What sounds positive on the surface suddenly opens up to reveal a very complex situation underneath.

As the father's words so dramatically reveal, extremely important interpretive issues result from the seeming logic of a consumer model of childbearing. Can abortion of "imperfect" fetuses simply be allowed as the "right" of every woman? Is abortion in this consumer context necessarily the same as abortion performed without knowledge of the baby's physical and mental status? Or does the shifted emphasis change its meaning? Does abortion chosen by a woman because she feels that she cannot become a mother at this particular time in her life involve one kind of decision making, whereas abortion chosen because one or both parents cannot accept a less than perfect baby involves a different kind? At issue in the latter consumer context is this question: What constitutes an acceptable baby? It may be easy to sympathize with any parent who chooses not to continue a pregnancy when the fetus is known to be severely retarded. Yet consider these words told to me by the mother of a Down Syndrome child:

> Without Jimmy, our lives would have been much less full. He is so warm and loving. It almost seems like a miracle that we had him. I wouldn't trade him for any other child, no matter how intellectually gifted. I shudder every time I think that we came so close to aborting him.

These words are echoed so often by parents of Down Syndrome children that they cannot be dismissed as exceptional. Yet a strictly consumerist perspective makes it logical to refuse such children life. Only if that perspective is set aside does it become clear that a human life cannot be evaluated the same way an automobile can. Nonetheless, the truly anguishing issues connected with less-than-perfect babies often involve desires for perfection. Severe cases such as anencephalic infants may strike some people as less ethically disturbing because such children, lacking brains, may seem scarcely human, but even such a borderline example is difficult to judge. That anomaly aside, what about the cases of Down Syndrome, spina bifida, and cerebral palsy? Or cleft palate, hare lip, or missing digits? Here the worry is that the "norm" of acceptability will change, making progressively less severe defects reason enough for abortion. Where does one draw the line? And what message do relatively new technological "advances" convey to disabled persons about their worth?

Closely interrelated with this concern about "perfect" babies are the legal rights of everyone involved—from baby and parents to attendants and hospital administrators. Once childbirth is placed in a consumer context, then the idea of fault necessarily arises. If a less-than-perfect baby results at delivery, somebody must be held accountable:

> My baby didn't have to die! The thought of suing became an obsession. No matter how much it would take of my time and energy, I owed it to that baby to make sure that this terrible mistake would never happen again. And the doctor owed us something too. We could use the money for our other children.[9]

Before childbirth was framed on a consumer model, parents rarely blamed, let alone sued, their doctors. Ironically, when physicians had fewer techniques to offer, they were often classed along with "men of God" or, in premodern societies, as God himself. Examples abound. In China Pao-Sheng Ta-Ti, originally a human doctor, was elevated after his death to god of medicine and healing. In Japan, even today, faithful Buddhists assure health by keeping images of the King of Medicines, the Buddha Yakushi, in their homes. And in Western cultures, the best-known example is Asklepios, the ancient Greek god of healing and medicine, whose staff of intertwined sacred snakes, the caduceus, symbolizes the medical profession to this day. As a god, or agent of God, the physician was unlikely to be held accountable by patients. A "defective" baby would therefore not be his "fault" but an act of God—a tragic situation that could happen for no discernible reason. But in the wake of generally heightened consumer awareness, belief that some situations are truly beyond human control has almost disappeared. Now when something goes wrong, a culprit must be found.

Once the idea of "fault" is accepted, all notions of mystery, deity, or Nature with a capital N vanish. Childbirth then becomes one of many consumer events within the power of humans to control, and it loses all vestiges of the deep spiritual and personal meaning it can hold for women. To stop with this image of childbirth is counterproductive. What women gain in the process is but a pale imitation of the rich experience we really seek: awareness, enactment, and celebration of life-creation, which is what childbirth is potentially all about. Can this model be reframed constructively?

Trying to answer this question points up an important irony. The consumer model raises a problem familiar from earlier chapters, but with the traditional positions reversed. Whereas women have repeatedly been victimized in other images of childbearing, in the consumer model it is more often the doctor who is, turning physician into *pharmakos,* an ancient Greek term for scapegoat. Some of the same language, imagery, and conceptual issues that historically apply to women apply here as well. Thus, in making the consumer model of childbearing work, it is critical to consider how physicians, as well as childbearing women, want to be seen. Do they want to be viewed primarily as business persons, the logical players in a "consumer" model? as technocrats? as scapegoats? If none of the above, what then?

Close critical reading of the consumer model helps us determine how we can reframe the model positively. What the consumer model contains as subtext is a tangle of issues involving control, power, anger, and antiauthoritarianism. But as with attacks made by some women against men as a class, this subtext of the consumer model is not based on holistic thinking. It merely attacks and transforms the medical model into a business analog, and in so doing, it reverses the power positions of the two major players. That reversal may make some women feel better, but it misses the point of truly gaining access to the potential sacrality of childbearing. No recourse to a court of law can satisfy the need for a full, rich childbearing experience.

Close reading also reminds us that to "consume" is to "possess." In a negative sense, the model can therefore suggest greed and materialism. Yet, positively, "possession" is an apt metaphor, for what is desired is possession or repossession of childbearing. If this cry for ownership is misunderstood by any of the parties, however, then it risks the kind of degeneration I have just depicted. But if its underlying cry for full and active participation in childbearing is heard correctly, then the consumer model of childbearing can be understood not as a cry for vengeance and scapegoating but as a cry for mutual cooperation among all the participants in the drama of childbirth.

THE MIDWIFERY MODEL

An extremely promising result of heightened childbirth consumerism is choice of birth attendants. Of the various kinds—obstetrician, family practitioner, monitrice (an R.N. who provides labor support), nurse practitioner, general practitioner, nurse midwife, lay midwife, and lay birth attendant—the midwife most fully symbolizes women's retrieval of the sacred gynecocentric dimension of childbirth. This is true for several reasons.

The first reason is implicit in the word *midwife* itself, from the Anglo-Saxon *medwyf* meaning "with woman" or "wife." Thus, she is *with* the laboring woman, not against or in place of her. This "withness" is a critical feature of the midwife's role.

Furthermore, most midwives have themselves borne children, in contrast to most obstetricians, who, until the recent surge of women into the field, had not.

That automatically places midwives in a far better position to explain what child-bearing is like. They can tell women what labor *feels* like at different phases, not just what it is like from an outsider's abstract point of view.

Another reason the midwife so obviously symbolizes women's reconstruction of the sacred, gynecocentric dimension of childbirth relates to her history. Almost all cultures tell of various goddesses, and sometimes gods, presiding at childbirth. In ancient Egypt, the cat- or lion-headed goddess variously called Bast, BuBastet, or Pasht watched over the process as a whole; the god Bes protected laboring women; and Sevenfold Hathor, goddess of midwifery, gave each infant its seven souls. Such mythical figures provided important models for actual birth attendants. They also serve nowadays to anchor midwifery in a long and mostly honorable past.

Although the specifics of midwifery necessarily differ, in most traditional cultures older women, often including a laboring woman's own mother, perform this task. One of countless examples appears in cuneiform-inscribed tablets from the Hittites, a people who dominated Asia Minor in the second millennium B.C.E. Their legitimating myth tells how the moon god, looking out from Heaven and seeing a cow grazing in a meadow, was smitten and mated with her. When the cow's time came, her cries so moved him that he sent the mother goddesses to attend and soothe her. So successful were they that midwives have ever after attended women in childbirth.

These same tablets indicate that birth occurred in a ritually purified inner chamber. A midwife would place cushions on two facing wooden stools, apparently ordinary items of furniture rather than pieces exclusive to childbirth. She would then sit on one, facing the mother on the other, a cushion on the floor between them to catch the baby when it emerged. References to ritual objects and surgical implements, presumably for use by the midwife, are unclear because of difficulties in translation. One tablet, for example, mentions a bronze knife and four bronze pegs, the exact use of which is unknown. Sometimes two midwives attended. In that case one primarily tended the child, as the following personal testimony found on one tablet indicates:

> I . . . wash his head. Then the Queen [this is a royal birth, therefore unlikely to be the norm] dresses him, and I take away from her, her own [child], [and] I place the child on [the father's] knees.

Elsewhere, the text states that before taking the child to its father, the midwives "lift the baby, turn it upside down, and then place it at the mother's breast." [10]

That the midwife who tended the infant was also a magical healer of the sort eventually called a witch is suggested in the details of a ritual performed on behalf of a bewitched child: "And upon him his clothes are bound. . . . How shall we act when we perform the incantation?" The answer, evidently from the Birth Goddess to whom the question was addressed, is, "Go! Fetch the Hasa(u)was woman, and let her incant for him, over the skull." [11] The healing incantation was uttered in conjunction with the sacrifice of a goat, which was first pressed against the child, then dismembered and burned.

This ancient connection linking midwifery and magical healing practices has persisted throughout history, often to the detriment of midwives. According to a medieval English witchhunter,

> by witches we understand not only those which kill and torment, but all Diviners, Charmers, Jugglers, all Wizards . . . commonly called wise men and wise women . . . and in the same number we reckon all good witches, which do no hurt but good, which do not spoil and destroy, but save and deliver. . . . It were a thousand times better for the land if all witches, but especially the blessing witch, might suffer death.[12]

Barbara Ehrenreich and Deidre English argue provocatively in *Witches, Midwives, and Nurses: A History of Women Healers* that this systematic persecution of midwives was not really the attack on magic that the Church claimed but a war against women's control of healing and birth giving. Over the centuries, the role of midwives steadily diminished in Western cultures, particularly in the United States from the late nineteenth century. Renewed interest in feminism in the 1960s brought midwifery back into fashion, particularly among countercultural women.

In contrast to their low status in many contemporary Western cultures (far less the case in Europe than the United States), midwives in traditional societies often enjoy equivalent status with priests and shamans. For example, the Senai of Malay still consider all midwives holy. Each functions as a kind of godmother with spiritual ties to every child she brings into the world. Mexican peasants also believe in the magical powers of the *partera,* who is part witch, performing complicated knot-magic when she binds umbilical cords, and part diviner, casting spells to determine babies' fates. Like shamans, midwives are frequently believed to be called to their practice. Such is the case for Juana, a contemporary midwife who initially fought her vocation but now practices in her Zutuhil (Mayan) community in San Pedro la Leguna in highland Guatemala:

> In her dreams Juana was visited by big, fat women, all in radiant white, who told her that she was sick and that her children had died because she was not going to help the women in childbirth. These were the spirits of dead midwives. When she tried to sleep, the spirits would appear. They would grab her ears and scold her, tell her that she would die and her husband would die if she did not exercise her calling. They reminded her that she had already lost six children. You were punished, they said, because you did not pay attention to those who gave you the *virtud* ["a curiously shaped white bone about nine inches long," which appeared in a dream as a sign of her calling]. Now, if you continue to hesitate your other children will also die. Remember, they reminded her, that your mother died because you did not obey God's call.[13]

This same emphasis on midwifery as a spiritual calling prominently marks the words of contemporary American midwives, even to the point of forming the title of an influential book on the subject, *Spiritual Midwifery* by Ina May Gaskin.[14] This is a fascinating account of childbearing experiences on a rural Tennessee commune known as The Farm. It is very much a woman's book, as Gaskin makes clear in her Preface: "The information in this book is almost exclusively derived from women by women. . . . Here, the culture surrounding pregnancy and child-birth was put together by the women who were still having babies. The care system was designed by those who were using it" (p. 8).

The spiritual dimension of childbearing comes through consistently. The com-mune itself is explicitly organized around the Book of Acts (2:44–45): "And all who believed were together and had all things in common; and they sold their possessions and goods and distributed them to all, as they had need." Gaskin states that "we are not just a community. We are a church" (p. 17). In her instructions to midwives, drawing from her observations of more than seventeen hundred birthings, she says, "Every birth is Holy. I think that a midwife must be religious, because the energy she is dealing with is Holy. She needs to know that other people's energy is sacred" (p. 277). Speaking of the miracle of birth and the consequent holiness of the midwife's role, Gaskin stresses the importance of grace:

> For this touch to carry the power that it must, the midwife must keep herself in a state of grace. She has to take spiritual vows just the same as a yogi or a monk or a nun takes inner vows that deal with how they carry out every aspect of their life. (p. 277)

Gaskin vividly dramatizes the notion of "laying on of hands." Thus, she simul-taneously emphasizes three critical elements of midwifery: grace, communication, and healing in the sense of making whole.

This wholeness is itself twofold. It is the wholeness of self, stressed repeatedly by various childbirth professionals, brought about by the initiatory stages of preg-nancy and childbirth, and it is also the wholeness of women as a community stretching back in time:

> We are the perfect flower of eons of experiment—every single person alive today has a perfectly unbroken line of ancestors who were able to have babies naturally, back for several millions of years. We are the hand-selected best at it. The spiritual midwife, therefore, is never without the real tools of her trade. She uses the millennia-old, God-given insights and intuitions as her tools—in addition to, but often in place of, the hospital's technology, drugs, and equip-ment. (p. 277)

Thus, Gaskin presents a dual linkage of women over time—one as childbearers, the other as midwives. The image of these two intertwining circles of women provides a strong metaphor for women's spirituality.

But it is perhaps in Gaskin's renaming of the word *contraction* that she most fully combines feminism and spirituality. She says, "I like to use the term 'rush' in place of 'contraction' because I think it describes better how to flow with the birthing energy" (p. 25). The difference this change makes in conceptualizing labor is startling. *Contraction,* after all, has long been used to designate child-bearing movements associated with pain. Consequently, it connotes neither joy nor anticipation, but rather a diminishment. *Rush,* by contrast, suggests power, as in a surge or dash. Such renaming of women's experience has long been called for by feminist thinkers such as Mary Daly, Susan Griffin, and Monique Wittig. What makes this particular renaming so significant, however, is the way it emerges directly from women's lived experience rather than being consciously crafted to fulfill a theorized need, as seems to be the case with some feminist academic writers.

Another contemporary American midwife whose spiritually oriented work has proved influential is Elizabeth Davis. Her concerns for the religious, communitarian nature of her calling are particularly evident in her discussion of the way that midwifery can overflow into one's home and family life. She cites a midwife named Tina, a mother of five practicing in rural Hawaii, who told Davis of a last-minute situation with which she had to cope. A stranger called Tina two days after her due date, asking to see the midwife because she felt unprepared for a hospital birth. "There she was on my doorstep. . . . I . . . made some tea, sat down with the woman and felt out the situation. She looked pretty tense, had been having contractions all night, but didn't want to go to the hospital. She didn't even know if she wanted to keep the child."[15] Before Tina could make arrangements for the woman, however, labor began. Tina's calling to midwifery is evident in her detailed description of unexpectedly delivering this unattached, homeless woman's baby. Tina delivered the woman, then hosted her and the baby for several weeks. Such nurturance of others, while admired by many, is rarely actualized this fully. As this story implies, the "healing" associated with the midwife's art may assume a dimension in which distinctions between body and soul, childbearing and socioeconomic status are obliterated. This blurring of commonly accepted distinctions is the exact opposite of the mechanical separations that often accompany medical-technological models of childbearing.

Another prominent contemporary midwife whose spiritual attitude toward her calling deserves mention is Rahima Baldwin. Near the beginning of her book *Special Delivery,*[16] she explains:

> I first became involved with childbirth in the Spring of 1972. We had been on a spiritual search that had taken us as far as India. Sitting on a bus in Bombay just after leaving the ashram of a very holy man, I received the guidance that I was to be involved with birth and should write a book about the spiritual aspects of childbirth. At the time, I knew nothing about having a baby. (p. 29)

Like Gaskin and Davis, Baldwin stresses people rather than technology. "Any birth carried out with this awareness [that birth is a natural process for which couples themselves remain ultimately responsible], with the focus on the people rather than on the technology, on the process rather than the goal, is a special delivery" (p. vii).

Of these three midwives, Baldwin is most militantly against hospitals and for home birthing. Her language is filled with "revolutionary" imagery: "As is the case with all revolutions in consciousness, the people are changing faster than the institutions, and there are more couples involved with the new homebirth than there are medical people prepared to help them" (p. 3). In *Special Delivery,* Baldwin thus overtly places midwifery and homebirthing in a context of revolutionary social change, her emphases being equally divided between a populist notion of self-reliance and a feminist "need to reclaim birth as [women's] own and to ask for, and insist on being treated with respect for themselves and the birthing process" (p. 8).

All three of these representative midwives see their calling as a holistic process in which the whole woman, not just an isolated part of her, must be considered. A woman's selfhood must be evaluated, as well as her homelife and social setting. A key word in this process is *community*—the community to which the childbearing woman belongs and the community that the midwife creates with her, for the relationship that develops between a laboring woman and her birth attendant is often astonishingly close. This is particularly so when it is another woman who performs the function, suggesting that in addition to everything else childbirth involves, it can also create community at a very deep level:

> Body to body, skin to skin, a midwife will rely on touching and holding a woman, rather than speaking to her. When she does speak, she will use simple words, words a young child could understand. This ideal communion does not exclude a degree of firmness in certain situations. For instance, if a woman in labor feels sleepy just before the last two or three contractions, the attendant should encourage her to remain active. It's important then to say something like, "It's too late to postpone the birth, it's time . . ." Words, however, are usually irrelevant at times like this.[17]

These words emphasize how intensely community may be created when the proper birth attendant presides. Communion at its holiest, this sharing of the creation of new life clearly manifests the sacred dimension of childbearing. It is a very important gynecocentric vision of childbirth.

PLACE-CENTERED MODELS

Just as many women find choice of a sympathetic birth attendant central to recreating appropriately gynecocentric childbirth, many also consider freedom to select an appropriate setting just as critical. One of the positive results of consumerism is that newly expanded possibilities for birthplaces do now exist. Both birthing centers and private homes have become increasingly popular in the United States since the 1960s. The comparative intimacy of both strongly contrasts with the bleakness of most hospitals, a bleakness starkly evident in the following passage from Marilyn French's *The Women's Room:*

> The nurses were cold and brusque. They sat her down and asked for information: father's name, mother's name, address, religion, Blue Cross number. Then they gave her a hospital gown and told her to get undressed in a cold damp room that looked and smelled like the locker room of a gym. She was in some pain now and the very air of the place irritated her as it brushed against her skin. They

ordered her to get up on a table, and they shaved her pubic hair. The water was warm but it got cold as soon as they put it on her body, which was already shivering. Then they gave her an enema: it drove her insane, she couldn't believe they were doing this to her. Her belly and abdomen were aching worse and worse, as if part of her insides were pulling away from the rest and wrenching the organs with it and pounding down on her pelvic bones like a steady hammer. There was no letup, no rest, it just kept happening. At the same time, they were pumping warm water into her backside. It pulsed upward in a different rhythm, then bent her double with a different cramp. When it was over, they told her to get up on the table again, and they wheeled her into a different room. It was bare and functional: white walls and four beds, two against each wall, foot to head. They put her feet up into stirrups and laid a cloth over her knees. Every so often a nurse or an orderly would come into the room, lift the cloth, and peer in. Out in the hall, beds on wheels were lined up waiting to enter the delivery room.[18]

Such a hospital experience, horrifying in many respects, would be dissatisfying on sensory grounds alone. Who could possibly respond positively to stirrups, beds on wheels, and bare white walls?

At least one contemporary doctor champions the need to emphasize the aesthetic component of childbearing: Michel Odent, mentioned in the preceding section. Odent's former hospital in Pithiviers, France, contained only one traditional birthing room. It featured instead what he called a *salle sauvage,* a "primitive room," with a low, foam-covered platform and a wooden birthing chair, and another room, all in shades of soothing blue, with a round pool seventeen millimeters deep for women to relax in during labor.

Adding to the soothing, pleasing effect at Pithiviers, the lights were habitually kept low, and voices, when used at all, were hushed. The importance of such muting is emphasized in these words, written by a physician not connected with Pithiviers, who had always been accustomed to traditional hospital practices:

> There really was a sensational change in the atmosphere of the delivery room when the lights were turned down. We are all so accustomed to "lights, camera, action," to the swinging electrical doors, intercoms going off, basins clanging . . . it's hard to imagine *how much* noise there is until it stops. With all the commotion, all the instrumentation, the emotional content of the moment for the woman and her husband could be virtually ignored. As soon as the lights were dimmed, however, all eyes were automatically directed toward the birthing process.[19]

For an institution, Odent's clinic offered women an amazing setting in which to experience one of the most sacred events in life.

Still more amazing, however, are births in which the setting of choice is water. This is a practice especially championed by the Russians, who have been experimenting with underwater birthing for several decades now. Igor Charkovsky, a major researcher in this area, believes that in moving from water to land we, like all land animals, began a fateful battle with gravity that has led our species to an impasse.[20] Because water is the cradle of life, birthing in it will greatly aid human development. Charkovsky asserts that water-born, water-trained babies are more intelligent and better developed physically. Parents who choose water as their birthing medium must train for months because the entire labor and delivery take place in a tank. Birth attendants include nurse midwives and "sensitives"—people with parapsychological abilities. Underwater childbirthing may take place either in a birthing center or in a couple's own home.[21]

While underwater birthing remains a great rarity in the United States, a larger number of women—approximately one percent—choose home delivery. Generally speaking, these births are attended by midwives, most physicians being reluctant, for fear of possible complications, to deliver outside a hospital or community birthing center. In addition to the aesthetically pleasing components a woman's home ordinarily displays, at least from her point of view, it also offers familiarity and intimacy.

> Susie gave birth to Leila . . . but Mary helped. I suppose there were twenty-five present . . . mostly women. Two children wandered in and out among us. . . . Three-year-old Blake said, "She popped out." Sabra, Leila's sister, asked "Is she my baby?" . . . Three women nurses or midwives were there. . . . Joe breathed with Susie through her contractions. . . . Joe cut the cord. Leila cried some more. In an hour or so Susie got up and sat in a rocker in the sunshine with Leila. . . . Friends went out and cooked the biggest dinner of all that night. . . . It seemed that Leila had come to all of us. Later we talked of the overwhelming awe. The birth was life-giving.[22]

A very few homebirths are not attended at all. These few, however, represent one of the most interesting attempts on the part of the few women who risk them to recreate childbirthing. The principle advocate of unattended childbirths in the United States is Marilyn Moran, a self-published author and mother of ten, who has devoted much time to researching and writing on the topic. Moran bases her advocacy on the idea, discussed briefly below in "The Erotic Dimensions of Childbearing," that all aspects of childbirth from conception through lactation are erotic. She argues that not only should men therefore not be excluded from childbirth but they should be present to share this culmination of lovemaking in private.

Although Moran's advocacy of husbands (she always uses the word *husband*, never *mate*) functioning as midwives will strike many as extreme, her ideas nonetheless deserve consideration for the way they recreate childbearing. Despite a superficially countercultural stance, Moran espouses very traditional ideas about marriage and sees childbirth and conception as a man's gift to his wife, with childbirth being her return gift:

> When the love relationship is finalized in marriage, and the young man bestows his most precious gift, his sperm, and conception results . . . the appropriate response is for her to mirror his action and to personally give to him her most precious gift at the moment of childbirth. . . . Childbirth is not the time for a woman to get a baby but rather the time for her to give a baby to her beloved, bringing full circle that action which he had initiated nine months earlier.[23]

In spite of its curiously old-fashioned language, ideology, and admonishment, what Moran is advocating holds important implications for feminist thinking about childbearing, especially in light of the words of feminist Dorothy Dinnerstein: "The deepest root of our acquiescence to the maiming and mutual imprisonment of men and women lies in a monolithic fact of human childhood: under the arrangements that now prevail, a woman is the parental person who is every infant's first love, first witness, first boss, the person who presides over the infant's first encounters with the natural surround and who exists for the infant as the first representative of the flesh."[24] One implication of Moran's populist approach to childbirth is that having fathers share it so totally will effect precisely the rearrangement of sexual arrangements that Dinnerstein, in her far more abstract fashion, is advocating. Physician William Hazlett, who supports Moran's work, emphasizes a slightly different aspect of this same point when he says, "Birth is qualitatively different when the husband participates in the natural birth, in contrast to the time before if he waited outside. Separately their bodies and minds unite. . . . The husband as midwife simply goes one step farther to complete a unity."[25]

When Hazlett and Moran stress the need to cement the family bonds from the moment of birth, they intend something far more than simply bonding father and child. Theirs is a vision truly recreative of childbearing, for it recognizes the full personhood of all three players. If the importance of any one of these players is downplayed, then a very different outcome occurs. But by integrating the three into and within a forcefield of love, a mutually positive orientation to the world is created along with the birth of the child. This is truly the birth of a family, and with it comes a possibility for changing the current status of sexual arrangements that Dinnerstein, among others, so strongly laments.

The implications of viewing childbirth as a truly shared, loving, bonding event are enormous. First of all, in such a circumstance, the father is not left out, and so, logically, neither womb envy nor feelings of being displaced by the child should occur. Second, the mother should logically feel closer not only to her child but also to her husband. For her, feelings of being forced into an unwanted role by either mate or child should be greatly reduced. Furthermore, by being immediately bonded and welcomed into a loving relationship, the baby presumably should not grow up being hampered by the many negatives so frequently cited by today's army of walking wounded. It does not seem entirely impossible to think that Moran's insights could be adapted—although she herself would probably cringe at the idea—to childbirthing centers or hospital settings. If lovers can enjoy lovemaking in hotels, surely some of the same intimacy can also be created in non-home settings. Despite very real safety concerns, the potential for intimacy and family bonding in private birthing represents a genuine recreation of childbearing. It is one more example of the way a consumerist model is helping women to reconceive childbirth and the settings in which they give birth in widely divergent ways.

"NATURAL" CHILDBIRTH MODELS

Consumer demands for choice in birth attendants and birth locations extend also to methods of childbirth. The most popular methods are lumped together rather imprecisely as "natural childbirth," although some educators reject this term, claiming that all birth is "natural." Here is a representative description of a hospital-based "natural" childbirth:

> Mother and father wash their hands with ordinary soap and water. He dons a scrub suit, then helps adjust the pillows at the head of the delivery bed, which has already been tilted up about 45 degrees. She stares down at the immense surface of her abdomen, now gaily tinted "antiseptic orange." Then the lights are dimmed and voices in the room are stilled, waiting. . . .
> "Push," the delivery-room nurse whispers close to her ear. "Push."
> The baby's head and shoulders emerge. "Would you like to help?" asks the obstetrician. Gratefully, the mother nods between pushes. Reaching down, she grasps her baby as the doctor gently pulls him up and places him face down onto the bare skin of her belly.
> When the mother is allowed to complete the delivery herself in this way, she feels an enormous sense of relief. "It's as though," Grover [an obstetrician prominent for his encouragement of woman- and family-centered birthing] says, "a psychological link is forged between the fetus she has carried for nine months and the warm and wet infant resting snugly against her body." Not only does this simple act prevent the onset of an "empty womb" syndrome, but many parents have described it as the most meaningful moment in the entire delivery.[26]

Such "natural" childbirth evolved out of an early twentieth-century mix of ideas propounded by various physicians, nurses, and midwives, traceable to the groundbreaking work of medical giants Grantly Dick-Read, Fernand Lamaze, and Robert Bradley and childbirth educator Sheila Kitzinger.

British physician Grantly Dick-Read was deeply impressed when a woman he attended in a slum tenement during World War I refused anaesthesia. Much surprised, he afterwards asked her why. "It didn't hurt," she responded. "It wasn't meant to, was it, doctor?"[27] That interchange led Dick-Read to devote his professional life to fighting the biblically inspired view that pain is an inevitable, God-ordained part of childbirth. Building on his observations and his reading of Pavlovian psychology, he developed his theory: Fear, not something inherent in childbirth itself, causes the pain. Because women have been culturally conditioned to expect pain, they do, in fact, feel it. In anticipation, they tighten up exactly those pelvic muscles which they should relax.

Dick-Read's two books, *Natural Childbirth* (1933) and *Childbirth without Fear* (1944), started the trend away from childbirth as a strictly medical event. Dick-Read believed that women properly prepared, both mentally and physically, would not suffer in childbirth. Therefore, he instituted a program to teach relaxation and breathing. But he was not doctrinaire. Anaesthetics were readily available for women who wanted them, although many "prepared" women unfortunately equated their use with failure. Furthermore, many *did* need them, some because their preparation (or their deconditioning from societally imposed fears) was insufficient. However, despite some early setbacks for this reason, the Dick-Read method remains highly influential.

Another physician important to developing attitudes that can facilitate retrieval of childbirth is Fernand Lamaze. More consciously Pavlovian than Dick-Read, Lamaze developed the psychoprophylactic method, as it is now commonly called, which teaches a woman to respond to verbal cues with controlled exercises. These she practices during pregnancy, the idea being that they will become so automatic that she will not even have to think about them during labor. Lamaze espoused these principles in his book *Painless Childbirth* (1956).

Unlike Dick-Read, Lamaze and his followers consider childbirth innately painful. The whole point of the Lamaze exercises, which involve panting, effleurage (abdominal massage), and a concentration point, is to divert attention from the experience, not to deepen it. In 1960, physiotherapist Elisabeth Bing helped found ASPO, the American Society for Psychoprophylaxis in Obstetrics, to teach the Lamaze method using the term *prepared* rather than *natural* childbirth. The shift in wording resulted from some of the earlier unfortunate results for women not able to carry out the natural method. To be insufficiently prepared was less threatening than to be "unnatural."

Along with prepared childbirth came couple-oriented, family-centered childbirth, first strongly advocated by American physician Robert Bradley, author of *Husband-coached Childbirth* (1965). Some of Bradley's writing, however, raises the disturbing issue of just how sympathetic to women some proponents of "father-inclusive" childbirth actually are. Consider, for example, the tone of the following:

> It behooves you as a husband, then, to have a good idea of how your big-tummied wife *positions* herself at home in her own bed while asleep. . . . Try not to awaken her as you come in late from that long poker party with the boys, and carefully study her while she sleeps. She then presents the identical picture we want you as a labor coach to help her assume now in the hospital, by your careful guidance during her uterine contractions.[28]

Even more overt is Bradley's comment that women are "nuttier than a fruitcake."[29] Such disturbing instances of male chauvinism also occur in other writings devoted to including husbands as equal partners in childbirth. For example, Nathan Cabot Hale, in his 1979 book, *Birth of a Family*, addresses the father this way:

> So you see, the creation of this new kind of family actually depends very much upon you in the end. If you learn how to handle the childbirth situation, no doctor, midwife, nurse, or hospital can give your wife or newborn child the special kind of support and love that you can. No one but you will have the necessary motivations, emotional needs, and basis for contact with them.
>
> Though birth is the most important event of life, without your participation,

medical technology can make it a sort of production-line process. Doctors and nurses do have feelings of reverence for birth, but they have to get on to the next job, and because of this, it can never be the big event for them that it is for you. But they will help you and your wife to have the most meaningful experience of your lives if you show them that you have done your homework. . . . You will learn, through participating in the birth process, a greater and deeper respect for what a woman is and, while this occurs, you will become more defined as a male and more naturally manly.[30]

It is difficult to ignore the "manly" father who once again stars in this drama of childbirth.

Along with Dick-Read, Lamaze, and Bradley, the work of English childbirth educator Sheila Kitzinger ranks as ground breaking. An expert in cross-cultural childbirth preparation and styles, a prolific author, and a strong advocate for patients' rights, Kitzinger is particularly noted for her view that childbirth is

part of a woman's whole psychosexual life—not simply . . . an isolated occurrence at one end of her body—[This view] must not only permeate all the teaching and affect the verbal imagery used and the way in which it is put over but should involve sensitivity to difficulties that a woman may be confronting in her marriage, in the way she sees herself as a woman, in her attitudes to motherhood, even in her relations with her own parents.[31]

To help prospective parents integrate pregnancy and childbearing into their psychosexual lives, Kitzinger has developed a large number of techniques that have greatly influenced other childbirth educators already discussed here, such as Claudia Panuthos and Gayle Peterson and midwives such as Rahima Baldwin and Elizabeth Davis.

What sets Kitzinger apart is her emphasis on openness—"There is no 'right' way to teach expectant mothers"[32]—and her insistence that different women respond in different ways. Indicative of the far-ranging nature of her influence is the growth of childbirth education classes that enhance pregnant women's self-esteem by teaching them to work with their own bodies rather than feeling alienated from them. This now-familiar approach marks a significant step forward, making Kitzinger's contribution to recreating childbirth in a gynecocentric mode truly extraordinary.

In addition to important approaches which focus on both parents is one pioneered by the French physician Frederick Leboyer, who emphasizes humane treatment for the child. Leboyer directs his attention primarily to the child. Like Bradley, he often sounds suspiciously antiwoman:

one day the baby finds itself . . . a prisoner. And in such a prison! The cell so small that the prisoner's body touches the walls—all of them—at once. Walls that draw nearer all the time. To the point when one day, the infant's back and the mother's uterus seem to be fused together. . . . Then, one day the prison comes to life. No longer content merely to keep the infant huddled in submission, it begins, like some octopus, to hug and crush. . . . One day labor starts.

The delivery has begun. An intransigent force—wild, out of control—has gripped
the infant. . . . The prison has gone berserk, demanding its prisoner's death.
. . . These things are all one: the mother![33]

Despite this antiwoman bias and an almost exclusive concern for the child, the
rituals that accompany Leboyer's myth nonetheless create an atmosphere condu-
cive to furthering women's interests. In this regard, his method differs greatly
from those associated with the Lamaze or Dick-Read methods. The latter occasionally sound more like extremely difficult athletic events than they do childbirth,
as this excerpt from a follower of the Lamaze method indicates:

> there was a wild encouraging cheering section, dedicated to spurring me on. I
> felt like a football star, headed for a touchdown. My fans on the sidelines, Dr.
> Lamaze, Mme. Cohen, the midwife, the nurse, all exhorted me, "POUSSEZ!
> POUSSEZ! POUSSEZ! POUSSEZ! CONTINUEZ! CONTINUEZ! CONTIN-
> UEZ! ENCORE! ENCORE!" When I ran out of breath, Mme. Cohen reminded
> me to exhale, inhale, and hold again. When the contraction was over, the cheer-
> ing stopped. Each time a new contraction began and I started to push again, the
> cheering section burst forth. It was fantastically exhilarating; it made me push
> harder and harder. Then, finally . . . the head crowned.[34]

By contrast, in a Leboyer childbirth, the lights are dimmed to avoid traumatizing
the newborn with bright lights after its nine months of near darkness. Furthermore, the room is kept quiet, not so much for the sake of the mother (who requires quiet to maintain her necessary concentration) but, again, to avoid disturbing the newborn.

   Another important step in the Leboyer procedure involves the doctor's placing
the baby in a fetal position and gently massaging it. This differs markedly from
the emphasis in the Kitzinger/modified Lamaze approach of placing the newborn
on its mother's stomach and allowing time for mother-infant bonding to take place.
Once the infant's spine has been slowly straightened out for the first time, the
final Leboyer step is to bathe the newborn to relax him again.

   Far more attuned than Leboyer birth to the mother's needs is childbirth as
practiced by French surgeon, Michel Odent. When his clinic in Pithiviers was
operative,[35] neither medications nor the routine IVs of the traditional medical model
of childbirth were used; the goal was to help women utilize such natural capabilities as their own hormones. Generally, unless the mother (or father) wished otherwise, the woman's mate participated throughout. Typically he would stand behind her, holding her under her arms while she maintained a comfortable position,
generally half standing, half squatting. But unlike many male physicians, Odent
was highly attuned to the potential dangers of allowing women's mates equal
access to childbirth:

> A particularly overprotective and possessive man can . . . have a negative ef-
> fect on labor. He continuously massages, caresses, and holds *his* woman, who
> belongs to *him*. He anticipates her demands rather than responds to them. The
> woman in labor requires calm, but he can provide only stimulation. Men some-

times find it hard to observe, accept, and understand a woman's instinctive behavior during childbirth. Instead, they often try to keep her from slipping out of
a rational, self-controlled state. It is not mere coincidence that in all traditional
societies, women in labor are assisted not by men, but by other women who
have had children themselves.[36]

What happened in the soothing setting at Pithiviers allowed childbirth to become a highly charged sacred event, as the personal accounts of women who gave
birth there attest. This mother from Leeds, who starts out detailing the course of
her experience in a very matter-of-fact way, epitomizes in her conclusion the
profoundly moving nature of childbirth as it was practiced at Pithiviers:

> One push and I feel our baby coming out. The midwife catches her; I think she
> helped turn her slightly. My memory of that second is hazy with excitement.
>   Eddie lowers me and they put the baby in my arms. I am stunned: not a
> word is spoken. The baby cries a bit and starts looking for the nipple. All is so
> peaceful and so intense. The midwife and Dr. Odent are in a corner, available,
> yet making themselves totally unobtrusive. The moment belongs to the three of
> us. Somebody brings a bath. . . . Camille, our daughter, still attached to me,
> unfolds in the water.[37]

Understood in this way as a fully shared event, childbirth not only assumes
the charged qualities commonly associated with religious ritual but allows a woman
to claim it as her own. Even when childbirth is not shared, a prepared mother is
ready to play her role. This experience differs greatly from that of a woman anaesthetized, not through choice but because she is told that this is the way childbirth must be. Whether coached in a psychoprophylactic method or told to tune in
to her own bodily instincts as in the Odent method, the prepared woman either
stars with a very strong supporting cast or else numbers among a team of inter-
dependent players. Either way, she plays a role in which *she* must perform certain
tasks.

What turns this hard work into ritual is not the labor as such but the patterning
of the laboring woman's behavior in certain very specific ways. A central aspect
is rhythm. Because Lamaze practice assumes childbirth is innately painful, it aims
to block out the pain or distract the mother by focusing intensely on something
else, the same principle dentists use when they play music to distract their patients
from the drill. Rather than flowing with childbirth as the Odent method teaches,
here the object is to ritually distract the laboring mother, thus placing her in control.

A chief means of rhythmically patterning a woman's labor is controlled breathing, a practice integral to the psychoprophylactic method. As taught by Lamaze,
controlled breathing resembles the hathayoga practice of Pranayama. Rhythmic
breath control is used to cleanse and aerate the lungs, oxygenate the blood, purify
the nerves, and achieve spiritual release and longevity. But in Lamaze, while the
technique is similar, the function of breath control is quite different: to distract
the laboring woman from her pelvic contractions, a goal more in keeping with
shamanistic out-of-body experiences designed to conquer evil spirits than with

ascetic practices designed to maintain a disembodied state of mystical unity. Lamaze childbirth does not stress being at *one* with the contractions; instead, a laboring woman tries to "get on top of the next wave," controlling and blocking it:

> A contraction . . . has a wavelike shape: it begins gradually, builds in intensity and strength to a peak, then decreases and disappears. Women always refer to the need to "get on top of" a contraction; this is like riding on the crest of an ocean wave. The alternative is to allow the wave to get on top of you, to be drowned in it, *to have no control*. [Emphasis added] [38]

Marjorie Karmel describes just how this breathing is to take place, quoting an early Lamaze birthing coach: "The ribcage is capable of great expansion. . . . Here, and here, at the sides, and here at the top. If you lift your chest—shoulders at rest please—you will find that you have room for a large quantity of air." Then Karmel describes exactly what her birthing coach did to teach her what she would have to do:

> She inhaled slowly through her nose, keeping her lips closed tight. It was astonishing to watch the expansion of her chest: everything below her waist remained perfectly still. Then she slowly blew the air out soundlessly through her mouth, much as if she were blowing up a very fragile balloon. The air entered and left her chest in a slow steady stream. It was tremendously yogi. . . . We will assume that your contractions are coming every four minutes for a duration of fifty seconds. I will tell you when you first see the wave. You will breathe in this manner, evenly and rhythmically until it has passed under you and subsided. [39]

Correct breathing sounds relatively simple, but it taxes many women. Furthermore, as with many rituals, the "correct" way is often debated by specialists. Thus, childbirth advocate Sheila Kitzinger says:

> The pace and depth of the breathing is a matter of very subtle adjustment according to the intensity and duration of the contractions. Only the woman in labor herself can judge the exact speed of respiration which helps her at that time. We have seen that some women tend to "over-breathe"—tackling the whole process so energetically and enthusiastically that they breathe at once too deeply and too quickly, and this may result in an excessive loss of carbon dioxide from the lungs. . . . There are certain women who cope with their labours so intensely and with such deliberation of purpose that they over-play their role in this way. [40]

In addition, many teachers insist that different stages require different kinds of breathing. During transition, when the cervix is dilated about eight centimeters, a new procedure typically begins with a "cleansing breath" at the start of each contraction. Following this, a woman should give four to six pants, followed by blowing out, panting, and blowing out for the duration of the contraction. A final cleansing breath should occur at this point. During this stage, a woman must consciously counter her urge to push by blowing out. Premature pushing fruitlessly exhausts her and may harm her baby by pushing its head against her cervix before it is fully dilated. When the cervix is fully dilated, she must practice a different, precisely worked out pattern of breathing.

Another distractive technique advocated by followers of the psychoprophylactic method is effleurage:

> massage of the area just above the pubic bone, the place where the contractions were likely to be felt most intensely. . . . It was a light stroking, in a circular pattern, that felt as though a butterfly had condescended to brush his wings across my skin. Mme. Cohen [the informant's coach] arranged my hands in a position where they were held up, not resting on my body, just over the pubic bone, the fingers touching the skin ever so lightly. First, though, she sprinkled the area with talc to avoid irritation of the skin. Then she guided my fingers lightly out toward the hip bones on either side, up over the area of the contracted uterus, then down to meet again at the starting place. The sensation sent a shiver of delightful relaxation out over my entire body.[41]

This practice relaxes the cervical muscles, preventing them from tensing during contractions.

In addition to the rhythmic techniques of breath control and effleurage, a practice particularly important to some of these ritualized childbirthing practices is the bath. In an Odent birth, the bath is primarily intended to relax the mother, in a Leboyer birth, to ease the newborn's transition from womb to world:

> Where do we place the child? What must we do to ensure that this separation is not a shock, but a joy? . . . Let us place the infant, replace it rather, into water! For the baby has emerged from water, the maternal waters that have carried it, caressed and cradled it. Made it light as a bird. . . . At the temperature of the body or thereabouts. . . . We place the child in it.[42]

Of all the rituals associated with these diverse methods of childbirth, one of the most innovative was a weekly singing group devised by Dr. Odent at Pithiviers:

> singing provides a simple way for women to exercise their diaphragm muscles and learn to concentrate on breathing out, which can help them relax during labor. Singing also encourages women to feel comfortable, unselfconscious, and expansive. . . . The warmth of these gatherings is difficult to convey. Everyone sings: the midwives sing and so do I. When we all sing together, the usual separation between consumer and professional dissolves, and a new relationship emerges.[43]

This practice fostered community, an element central to most rituals but usually lacking in contemporary childbirths, especially those carried out in any sort of medical setting.

Some of these practices of childbearing may strike potential mothers and their mates as extreme. Others, such as giving birth at Pithiviers, are no longer possible. Nonetheless, they are exciting for several reasons. First, they enormously diversify women's choices. Second, their existence has greatly altered more traditional practices so that hospitals now routinely include spouses and permit choice about anaesthesia. Third, many of them engage women in our own body knowledge. Furthermore, many allow women to experience childbirth as a sacred event. And not to be overlooked, these practices also recognize the danger of excluding men. To reframe childbirth as one of the most significant of all life experiences, it is not enough to orient it just to women; it must be available to men as well. As partners, both must work to counter the age-old antagonism between mothers and fathers as they play out their roles in the drama of childbearing. Whereas in the past women and men have often been polarized because one or the other starred in the childbirth event, contemporary childbirth attitudes, behaviors, and rituals typically equalize the two. Such equalization, historically so counter to the divisions of power in the reproductive drama, sounds one of the most hopeful notes for reframing childbirth as a deeply meaningful, shared experience for both women and men.

7 Phases of Labor

 Regardless what model a woman and her mate choose, actual childbearing may challenge their expectations. With onset of labor comes the beginning of the final and most difficult stage of the transformation begun approximately nine months earlier. At this time, the learning and changes brought about by and during pregnancy are fully tested.

Childbirth is usually divided into three phases: labor, delivery, and delivery of the placenta. Labor is further divided into the early, late, and transition stages, although as sociologist Barbara Roth Katzman points out, these stages are a misleading representation of reality, in the way that norms based on statistical averages always are. By analogy with height, Katzman writes, "A woman of over six feet is a statistical abnormality." Similarly, what is statistically normal in labor is not necessarily normal for every woman. The discrepancy between the two kinds of norm—the individual woman's and the statistical average—would not matter except that, as Rothman says, "statistically abnormal labors are medically treated." That means that a woman whose labor goes on "too long" will be "treated": "Doing something is the cornerstone of medical management," Rothman adds. "Every labor that takes 'too long' and cannot be stimulated by hormones or by breaking the membranes will go on to the next level of medical intervention, cesarean section."[1] Thus, even terminology seemingly as innocuous as "stages or phases of labor" needs reframing if women are truly to recreate childbearing.

For some women, onset of labor is signaled by strong, regular contractions, although it is not always easy to distinguish these from the prelabor movements known as Braxton-Hicks contractions or false labor, another construction that Katzman questions on the grounds that these seemingly "false," early pains may be a "normal" beginning for some women, of a much longer than statistically "normal" labor.[2] For others, labor may begin when the bag of waters breaks or the mucus plugging the cervix loosens and produces a bloody show.

In early labor, the cervix dilates from zero to five centimeters. The time necessary to complete this stage varies considerably, but "statistically" it averages twelve hours for a first-time mother. Many women find this stage comfortable, at least relative to the late stage. When the cervix opens from five to eight centimeters, labor typically moves faster and occasions discomfort because it involves far stronger contractions. Finally, transition, the time it takes the cervix to dilate fully by going from eight to ten centimeters, is the shortest but most difficult part.

As the word *transition* implies, this is the bridge between first and second stage labor, the time when the baby's head normally moves down into the birth canal, followed by its shoulders and the rest of its body. Historically, this time was considered the most difficult for a laboring woman. It was also the time when she was told to work hard and push. For women so instructed, this is, indeed, an arduous period. But thinking has changed drastically on this point. Nowadays, women who have been properly prepared and know how and when to push or hold back often find transition exhilarating. But if a woman experiences a difficult delivery, she may feel herself to be involved in the sort of titanic fight often dramatized by myths, in which a mother/monster struggles with a child/hero. This archetypal fight typically equates childbearing with pain.

Retrieving childbearing from associations of pain presents women with one of our greatest tests. Anaesthesia allows some women to retrieve this image while others find its use turns childbearing into a destructive nonevent. A different kind of destructiveness attaches to a self-sacrificial view of childbirth that some consider sadomasochistic, a theme also evident in pain-associated imagery. This theme, in turn, reinforces the common belief that childbearing is a "dirty" or polluting event. Although seemingly negative, the idea that childbearing is polluting actually reveals the potency of women's reproductive power. Thus, paradoxically, ideas about childbirth pollution provide one avenue for helping women recreate childbirth in a positive way. Most promising of all, however, is a dimension of childbirth closely interconnected with women's "secret" power of incarnation. This is the erotic side of women's childbearing.

PAIN, DANGER, PUNISHMENT, AND SIN

One of our most common inherited patterns of thinking pictures labor as a mixture of pain and danger. This pattern presents women with one of our greatest challenges for retrieval. For women raised in a Christian context, these combined images exert unusually great power because Christian, and to a lesser extent secular, thought closely connects the pain of childbirth with punishment for sin. Without doing so overtly, Simone de Beauvoir provides a dramatic example when she says that

> gestation is a fatiguing task of no individual benefit to the woman . . . often associated in the first months with loss of appetite and vomiting, which are not observed in any female domesticated animal and which signalize the revolt of the organism against the invading species. There is a loss of phosphorous, calcium, and iron—the last difficult to make good later. . . . All that a healthy and well-nourished woman can hope for is to recoup these losses without too much difficulty after childbirth; but frequently serious accidents or at least dangerous disorders mark the course of pregnancy; and if the woman is not strong, if hygienic precautions are not taken, repeated childbearing will make her pre-

maturely old and misshapen, as often among the rural poor. Childbirth itself is
painful and dangerous.[3]

What is particularly disturbing about this excerpt is the way it castigates childbirth as strongly as the biblical original, although it varies the specifics. Note the
plethora of negative words and phrases: "fatiguing," "of no individual benefit to
the woman," "demanding heavy sacrifices," "invading species," "loss," "re-
coup these losses," "dangerous disorder," "prematurely old and misshapen,"
"painful and dangerous." This negative view of childbearing differs from the
biblical model only in its extended message of awfulness and its implied attribu-
tion of that awfulness to nature instead of to God. Otherwise, its message for
women is, if anything, darker.

For women acculturated to believe, as Beauvoir did, that childbirth *is* so painful and dangerous, how is it possible to reframe pain? One way is to see it as
something to conquer, rather than as something threatening to conquer us. That
way, its "meaning," though not necessarily its intensity, may change. For some
women, one potential source for reconstructing childbirth pain could be ascetic
practices, although only certain temperaments are likely to find this source directly
applicable. Such practices as flagellation, donning of hair shirts, walking or sleeping on nails, burning, or laceration are clearly painful. Generally, ascetic practices, especially those involving self-inflicted pain, are penitential, their appeal
being particularly strong in theistic traditions such as Islam and medieval and post-
Reformation Christianity, as well as such nontheistic traditions as Buddhism and
some forms of Hinduism. For instance, the Bhagavadgītā tells of the hero Bhisma
being pinioned by arrows like a butterfly impaled on a pin by an avid collector.
This unpleasant image is supposed to model behavior for those Indian holy men
who employ beds of nails as their preferred ascetic practice. Similarly, some Roman Catholics choose as their model the crucified Christ, seeking essentially to
"become" him through imitating his bodily mutilation. And according to Saint
Paul, all Christians carry within their bodies the mortification of Jesus:

> We are afflicted in every way, but not crushed; perplexed, but not driven to
> despair; persecuted, but not forsaken; struck down, but not destroyed; always
> carrying in the body the death of Jesus, so that the life of Jesus may also be
> manifested in our bodies. For while we live we are always being given up to
> death for Jesus' sake, so that the life of Jesus may be manifested in our mortal
> flesh. (2 Corinthians 4:8–10)

It is not hard to read these words as masochistic, although that is not at all the
terminology Christianity itself uses. Yet, if a woman in our culture were similarly
to glory in her painful childbearing, she would likely be accused of masochism.
If it is acceptable for ascetics to glory in their pain, why has it not been acceptable
for childbearing women in the West to do so also? For a woman who does find
childbirth painful, why is this pain not a badge of spiritual and physical strength
and suffering in the same way that an ascetic's practices of mortification are?

In Western cultures, Christian attitudes toward pain in childbirth are almost unbearably significant. On the one hand, Christian women have been told that the pain of childbirth punishes our original sin of disobedience. On the other hand, we have frequently been shielded from that pain, in which case we cannot possibly judge for ourselves what (or even if) that pain really is. Furthermore, historically, the pain we have been told we will feel when we give birth has been construed as anything but self-transformative. Instead, it has been considered just the opposite, for childbirth pain is understood as miring us further in the material world. Throughout the history of Western thought, with its strong otherworldly inheritance from Plato, the material world has been consistently found lacking, often even interpreted as evil, in contrast to the ideal "other" world somewhere up there "above" us. Against this history, reframing imagery associating childbirth with pain is not easy.

But compelling evidence suggests an alternative way of experiencing childbirth. Consider, for example, the comparative mildness of the "pain" described in this account by Margaret Mead:

> All night I felt as if I were getting an attack of malaria. . . . And I was fascinated to discover that far from being "ten times worse than the worst pain you have ever had" (as our childless woman doctor had told us in college) or "worse than the worst cramps you ever had, but at least you get something out of it" (as my mother had said), the pains of childbirth were altogether different from the enveloping effects of other kinds of pain. These were pains one could follow with one's mind: they were like a fine electric needle outlining one's pelvis.[4]

More startling in its contrast with the ubiquitous image of childbirth as unbearably painful is this account quoted from a letter by Mme. D., age 28, of the delivery of her second child, a boy, nine pounds, fourteen ounces, in October 1954:

> In the end I had absolutely no pain, and I pushed very hard, and it was a very satisfying moment when I felt the baby moving through me. I did not even realize when the head passed, but I think I shall remember all my life the sensation of sweetness and warmth which the baby's body gives as it comes out. The sensation lasts for only a second, but from that moment I felt the child to be mine. Perhaps I have shocked some people by describing this feeling in detail. But it was the climax of my childbirth, and I often think of it now when I am attending to the child. It is also really the end of labour.[5]

Is childbirth painful, or is it not? Definitive answers to this question are not easy to come by. Just as women disagree, so do the practitioners who attend us. Thus, as indicated earlier, two of the physicians who have most influenced birth practices in the twentieth-century Western world, Grantly Dick-Read and Fernand Lamaze, hold divergent views. To Dick-Read, childbirth approached without fear as a natural event is not inherently painful; pain results from fear, which prompts laboring women to tense their muscles. Women trained to relax appropriately will therefore not suffer painful deliveries. By contrast, Lamaze believes that childbirth is innately painful but that the pain can be circumvented if a woman learns proper distractive techniques to block it out.

The impossibility of definitely asserting that childbirth is or is not painful matters critically. Of the many assumptions about childbirth, belief that it is painful most obviously raises the issue of whether it is language, something intrinsic to the experience, or a mixture of the two that shapes the event of childbirth and hence either prevents or permits its becoming a deeply sacred gynecocentric experience. Is it solely inherited patriarchal language that creates the pain many women experience in childbirth? Or would the pain exist if there were no such thing as patriarchy?

The impossibility of definitely asserting that childbirth is or is not painful is also critical because it points to *one* means by which childbirth not only *can* be, but for many women already *has been* reclaimed from pain. To do so requires relying on the view that reality is socially constructed. In this view, childbirth, like any other experience, is no more inherently painful than it is inherently anything else until humans construct its meanings. Rather, its pain comes from received (patriarchal) wisdom. Once a woman realizes this, the logic goes, her labor pains should vanish, deconstructed by her new gynecocentric awareness that labor pains are merely a patriarchal construct. For some women, reclaiming childbirth in this way works, as the success of countless variations on Dick-Read's "natural" childbirth attests. For all those women, natural childbirth with its resulting banishment of pain is truly wonderful. What is troubling, however, is testimony, often muted in the zealous enthusiasm of advocates of unanesthetized childbirth of women who feel their childbirth pain does not result solely from social construction. Consider, by way of illustration, the experience of an acquaintance of mine who fully expected to enjoy a pain-free birth:

> I can only say that having been brought up with no concept of original sin and having been told from everyone I talked to how great an experience childbirth was, that if you breathed correctly it wouldn't be too painful, etc., I was surprised to discover that the pain was *so overpowering.* I could think of nothing but somehow getting through it—knowing that I had no choice—but all thought of delivering without any medication went out the window by the fifth hour of labor. I was ready to take anything.

For women who experience labor like this, and written accounts show that many do, how is childbirth pain to be reinterpreted? Can it be?

Reinterpretation depends first on what is meant by the term *pain*. What one person considers painful, another may only find annoying. And in some cases what one finds painful, another may even enjoy. The following comments by a physician well illustrate what it is that at least some women seem to feel as, or instead of, pain: "The relief of pain for a short period of time has to be weighed against the effects of altering this unique experience in the life of a woman, which under unmodified conditions is reported to be frequently associated with orgasmic sensations and followed by a period of particularly heightened perceptions."[6] An obstetrician who has observed numerous births similarly focuses on the orgasmic quality he has noted for some women, particularly during delivery of the baby's head:

> For years, convinced of the fact that delivery of the head constituted, owing to the perineal distension, the most painful phase of childbirth, we traditionally administered an anaesthetic to the parturient. It is striking to observe that women who have been conditioned by the psychoprophylactic method frequently declare that delivery of the head affords them the most exhilarating moment of the entire event. Indeed, we have frequently observed that the birth of the head, far from producing the usual tearing pain, stimulates an intense thrill, very close to that of orgasm.[7]

Yet so strongly do most patriarchal cultures maintain ignorance about, or inveigh against, any potential for an erotic, orgasmic component of childbirth that it is unsurprising to find such feelings lumped together under the more acceptable heading of pain. The suppression of some women's erotic experience of childbearing extends our culture's general lack of recognition that some women actually find pregnancy erotic. But, unprepared for the possibility of erotic sensations rather than pain at the end of labor, many women find such sensations too shocking to handle, as childbirth expert Sheila Kitzinger describes:

> When the bearing-down reflex is fully established, the urge to push is compelling and irresistable. Some women are horrified at the intensity of the desire to bear down. "It is," as one mother commented afterwards, "a very primitive sort of urge. I was astonished that it was so strong." Women who have been inadequately prepared for the passion they feel welling up in them in labour may try to escape from the sensations. They panic and grip themselves in pain, resisting the urge with all their might.[8]

These comments suggest that some women might find the ability to name their childbearing with words more congruent with their experience to be sufficient to retrieve childbirth from its strong associations with pain.

Another way of retrieving pain is to look at other ways it may be valued, although to do so is complicated. One step is to consider the role that pain plays for men in patriarchal cultures. For them, accepting—even relishing—pain traditionally signals courage. Many male initiation rites, for example, equate withstanding intense pain with manhood, as the ordeal of noninfant circumcision attests. Withstanding pain, however, does not generally form part of a repertoire of "feminine" skills in Western cultures. Quite the contrary. A woman crying and then being comforted by a "big strong man" is a staple of romantic popular culture. Obvious exceptions exist, but in the West, women *as women* are rarely taught to conquer pain as part of our *womanhood*. Consequently, although some women refuse to "give in" to labor pains by crying out, this response is not common to Westerners' approaches to childbirth. Furthermore, while such stoicism may bolster some women, it does so negatively. It is one thing to withstand pain stoically, all alone without guidance, as male initiates must do in ritually changing from boy to man. Enduring childbirth stoically, all alone without guidance, as women facing hospital-based childbirth until the 1970s were forced to do, is quite another:

> When I went into hospital I was relaxed and happy that the day had come, but was horrified to hear that not only could my husband not enter the ward, he even had to leave the hospital—although I sorely needed him with me. I began to feel swamped by the pain. I couldn't speak and what I found most frightening was the utter callousness of the nurses . . . they could hear me gasping, trying to tell them, trying to *contact* them during this awful experience, and they remained utterly unimpressed. It wasn't only the pain, it was the way nobody around seemed to acknowledge it. It was the fact that I couldn't cope alone and in dignity or in the company of caring people with this pain I found so horrifying. I think it was being left alone for so long, very confused and totally humiliated in the way I was behaving. I could not stop crying.[9]

While tales abound of male bravery on playing field or battleground, one seldom hears counterparts in the West for women in childbirth. Instead, one hears terrifying tales, like the following, focused on "how awful it is, how painful": "Even when I was a very little girl I remember hearing how much pain I'd given my mother during birth. Grandma joked that she never wanted to see me because I'd caused my mother so much pain. I figured it must be terribly painful to have a baby for her to say such things."[10] Thus, in Western cultures, emphases for the two sexes are typically reversed. Male stories focus on men's heroism, female lore on women's pain. Consequently, childbirth imaged as painful reinforces traditional patriarchal distinctions between man as active doer and woman as passive object. Yet precedent certainly exists in some other cultures for a far different response to labor pain. For instance, a 1989 anthropological study, *Maternity, Medicine, and Power* by Carolyn Fishel Sargent, makes very clear that a childbearing woman of the African Bariba ethnic group inhabiting northern Benin is expected to respond stoically to her pain:

> Ideally, she will not display to friends or relatives that she is in labor, will deliver alone, and call for help with cutting the umbilical cord. Expressions of pain by the parturient are denigrated, and believed to bring shame to the family of both the woman and her husband. For women, ideal behavior during childbirth is the key example of courage.[11]

In no way does this reaction suggest that these women don't *feel* pain. Rather, the entire culture is infused with the belief that visibly or audibly responding to pain is shameful. Even such minimal responses as saying "wee," clicking one's teeth, or shaking a hand in the air are criticized. "Among women, the mother who delivers her children alone, in silence, is much admired."[12]

In many tribal cultures, expectations of stoicism are such that a woman's giving birth and a man's fighting a battle have been seen as equivalent acts of valor. Both the ancient Aztecs and the Comanche of Texas, for example, honored women who died in childbirth as they honored warriors who died in battle. The tribespeople of the Maikal Hills in India say that "a man fights in the open air with sword and spear; a woman's battle is in the dark, behind shut doors." [13] And the Gbandes of Liberia feel it is essential for birth to be out of doors because they view the process as a birthing woman's war with nature.

For women who are able, philosophically, to set aside qualms about an image equating childbearing and battle, even if the image is reversed to make battle men's surrogate for childbirth, such reconceptualization can yield positive results. First, that particular image is no more final than the one more common to our biblically influenced culture in which pain essentially renders women victims. If a woman can either adopt the warrior image or alter it to suit herself, she may find she can relate positively to it. Thus, a woman athlete might reconceptualize childbearing as a kind of athletic event. In so doing she would see herself as anything but a victim of pain. The potential problem with this reconceptualization, however, is that it connotes control, a state of mind many midwives find antithetical to the "letting go" they find more helpful for childbearing.

Yet another possibility that avoids the trap of victimshood on the one hand, the need to control on the other, is to reconceptualize the act of giving birth as a kind of dance along the lines suggested by William Butler Yeats in his poem "Among School Children," when he asks, "How can we know the dancer from the dance?" Such an image places the childbirthing woman in a very different relational context, quite unlike that in which she is either a victim or a controller of the process.

Yet, for many women, reconceiving the common Western notion that childbearing is necessarily painful simply doesn't work. Trying, and not achieving, pain-free childbirth may make the situation even worse, adding guilt for perceived failure onto the pain. Nor does turning pain into a positive image work for every woman. As the next section shows, for many women, pain so inhibits a sacred experience of childbirth that only its total eradication through drugs or anaesthesia allows a breakthrough into the sacred dimension of childbearing.

NONEVENT

Not every woman finds it possible to withstand the pain associated with childbirth. Some consider it absurd even to try. Anaesthetized relief helps these women feel positive about their childbearing experiences and hence about the babies they bear. It is not without risks, however. In the worst cases, it leads to abuse as bad as the physical pain it is supposed to alleviate. If anaesthesia is applied less to help a laboring woman than to control her, her childbearing experience may become so alien that for her it ceases to exist. Childbearing then becomes a nonevent, and what a woman should have been allowed to experience as a meaningful, sacred experience is denied her. The central issue here is precisely the same as the one that is so ferociously debated about abortion: choice.

Every woman should be free to make her own choice about anaesthesia. Furthermore, she should be as free to choose as to reject it. Sometimes zealotry is as common from natural childbirth advocates arguing against anaesthesia as from physicians and nurses extolling it. But barring some health-related complication,

the choice should be the woman's. For many women, sacrificing conscious awareness of childbearing is a reasonable price to pay for avoiding unbearable pain. For
others, pain is a fair exchange for full awareness of childbearing. But no woman
should be kept in ignorance of her options.

Like members of colonized groups whose experiences are externally decreed,
women anaesthetized without any say in the matter often find themselves cut off
from their own childbearing. Even though we all, as Freud repeatedly indicates,
personally deny painful experiences, externally mandated denial drastically differs
from individual repression. Patriarchally imposed obliteration threatens a laboring
woman's selfhood. Because traditionally we have been defined almost exclusively
by our childbearing capacity, eradicating our childbirth experience destroys precisely the quality by which we have been permitted to define ourselves. For a
woman lacking alternative self-definitions, historically true for most women, denying that one quality opens a horrifying void. Although some would value confronting this void of selfhood, to have it forced on a woman unaware of the issues
involved in the patriarchal construction of selfhood threatens whatever "selfhood" she has.

When anaesthesia is total, it annihilates a woman's consciousness for the duration of her delivery. She goes to sleep with a fetus inside her belly and awakens
with a baby outside herself. If missing labor and delivery this way is not by
choice, it renders a woman's position superfluous. A great event in her life has
taken place, yet she was not allowed to "be there" for it. "When I began labor,
it came fast and hard. Terrible pains. Just before he was born the doctor put a
mask over my face and I went right to sleep. I woke in the morning. . . . I
cried. I'd had my baby and I couldn't see him."[14] Not only has this woman
missed the climax of her own "production"—her actual delivery—afterwards, she
cannot even see her baby until medical personnel allow it. How totally this externally imposed nonexperience of childbirth departs from the wide-awake, prepared
childbirth described in these words:

> And because I was becoming really active, I had the feeling that his arrival
> depended on me alone. It seemed that I was finishing his creation, helping in
> the completion of the work. My strength increased tenfold. I pushed six or seven
> times. I saw the head appear, the shoulders, and I had my baby placed on my
> stomach. It is an unforgettable moment, the greatest joy that a woman can know.
> My husband was beside me, trying to hide his tears. And then we were together
> and happy, admiring our work. Such memories can never be forgotten.[15]

These words vividly highlight the difference between the two experiences.

A woman unconscious during labor and delivery is just as excluded from the
ultimacy of women's mystery as is the man physically barred from the delivery
room, a similarity that arouses suspicion from a gynecocentric perspective. Typically husbands were banished from delivery in most Western hospitals until about
1970, just as they were in most premodern cultures where female midwives have
always been the norm. Being banished, it would not be surprising if, historically,
men chose to downplay childbearing rather than value it positively. How much

fairer if women, too, could be excluded from childbirth! Then neither parent would see, hear, or touch the infant until *after* its birth. Both would then enter parenthood equally deprived of the intimate birthing experience. Could it be that, subconsciously, anaesthesia is sometimes administered less to ease the laboring woman than to alter this inequality?

Not "meeting" her baby until after its birth does not bother every woman, but some want desperately to be conscious of the child throughout delivery. Whichever choice a woman makes, deciding for herself should be *her* prerogative. Choice is especially important. When a mother is not permitted to meet her baby until after anaesthetized delivery, her child may appear to materialize from nowhere, complicating the initial encounter:

> I was helped to walk to the recovery room, where I felt wiped out and sorry for myself. I didn't have a sense of personal failure, since it was the baby's problem and not mine that prevented a natural birth, but I was badly disappointed, and really upset over the episiotomy. I had a certain mourning to do to resolve my feelings about the not-so-little cut. Meanwhile, I felt really unconnected with having given birth.[16]

This particular mother's disconnection from her own childbearing disturbs her tie to sacrality and also alienates her from her own "creation," the baby whom she then mistakenly blames for her disappointing experience. Having not consciously experienced the sacred thread connecting her long months of pregnancy to this now separate, fully formed, miniature human, this woman has lost a part of her own life that she might have preferred to live firsthand.

The surrealistic, dreamlike quality of such nonexperience dissolves the boundaries between "real" and "unreal," waking and sleeping. Instead of being in charge, actively and consciously giving birth, an anaesthetized woman emerges groggily from drugged sleep after "being delivered." Newly awake, she is unsure what has happened: "I remember how I woke up from my first confinement—crying and incapable of taking any interest in the baby, who was already dressed and in a corner. My first thought when I saw him was: 'Why have they brought a baby here?' So little did he seem to belong to me."[17]

Given the nature of some anaesthetics, such as scopolomine, once commonly used in childbirth, a laboring woman may drift in and out of consciousness. In her twilight sleep, as it was often called, she may dream the baby's arrival before its birth. Actual delivery then carries with it a disheartening anticlimactic feeling.

But, rather than feeling that anaesthesia is thrust upon them against their will, many contemporary women actively choose it. Commonly their choice is an epidural, a local, often used in hospital births, which allows full consciousness, while numbing the body. According to the findings of anthropologist Robbie Davis-Floyd, many of the women who choose epidurals are highly successful professionals who strongly believe that "birth is a mechanical process and that there is no intrinsic value in giving birth 'naturally,' because technology is better than nature anyway."[18] The following words from a woman named Liney typify the attitude commonly expressed by these women:

> I read all this stuff that told me I would be a complete asshole to have an
> epidural and I revolted. [The books said that] I would be able to see that it's
> much better for the baby and it's a natural experience, and there's just all this
> pressure. . . . I quit smoking, ate meat, drank milk for months and months—I
> had been such a good girl. A couple of hours of whatever an epidural was going
> to do to me, tough. You can put up with it, kid.[19]

As Davis-Floyd points out, "For this group of women, technology is not only *not*
an enemy, it is a friend, which empowers them. They do not see *themselves* as
being controlled by the medical establishment, but rather as manipulating its technocratic resources to control their own bodily experiences."[20] These women share
the belief that "the mind is more important than the body; that as long as their
minds are aware, they are active participants in the birth process."[21] Thus, the
anaesthesia that signals loss of childbearing experience for some represents
achievement for others. Davis-Floyd found that those who chose anaesthesia hold
very different attitudes toward selfhood, body, and technology from those who
chose homebirthing and/or midwife deliveries. The *meanings* of anaesthetized
childbirth can thus totally oppose one another, depending on a particular birthing
woman's attitudes toward herself, technology, and, implicitly, sacrality.

Anaesthesia undeniably benefits countless women. It helps some to counter
pain they would otherwise find unendurable. And it helps others to feel that they
are in control while their bodies are numb. However, anaesthesia is no panacea.
The childbirth that results, depending on the type of anaesthesia, may take place
without the conscious awareness of the laboring woman, thus obliterating firsthand
experience of one of the most important events in her own life. This obliteration
must be carefully weighed against the nonexperience of childbirth. It is one thing
for a woman to *choose* anaesthesia, feeling that extreme pain will damage her
experience of childbirth and maybe even cause her to resent her newborn; it is
quite another for someone else to arbitrarily decide that she will be anaesthetized.
In choosing anaesthesia, a woman may be reasonably rejecting a manifestation of
sacrality that she either knows nothing about or that feels demonic to her because
its painful dimension overwhelms everything else. Conversely, if anaesthesia is
forced upon her, she must forgo what might turn out to be one of the most illuminating, powerful moments of her life. Only if she can freely choose between
these two circumstances is a woman able to claim the otherwise disempowering
image of childbirth as pain that can so easily turn childbirth from sacred experience into nonevent.

SACRIFICE

Historically, men have often claimed for themselves the childbirth pain that
anaesthesia can obliterate. Male "childbirth," creation, typically equates this kind
of pain with self-sacrifice. Not too surprisingly, this equation is found in some
birth regressions:

Quite frequent are scenes of Pre-Columbian sacrifice rituals, visions of crucifixion or identification with Christ, experiential connection with deities symbolizing death and rebirth, such as Osiris, Dionysus, Attis, Adonis, Persephone, Orpheus, Wotan, or Balder, and sequences involving worship of the terrible goddesses Kali, Coatlicue, Lilith, or Rangda.[22]

Such images of male sacrifice enacted in the name of creation may seem as strange as those of more overt male "birthing." Terms commonly associated with sacrifice—*victim, pain, renunciation, loss*—suggest meanings more frequently attached to women than to men. Yet in myth, sacrifice traditionally connotes power so strong that it governs the entire universe; hence, it is usually associated with males. For example, the creation myth found in the Rgveda, the oldest extant book of Hindu sacred verses (composed between 1500 and 900 B.C.E.), exemplifies an ancient pattern of sacrifice that illustrates its underlying connection to childbirth. According to Hymn 10.90, the "first man," Puruṣa, created the universe out of his own body:

When they divided Puruṣa how many portions did they make?
The Brahman was his mouth, of both his arms was the Rajanya made.
His thighs became the Vaiśya, from his feet the Śūdra was produced,
The moon was gendered from his mind, and from his eye the sun had birth; . . .
Forth from his navel came mid-air; the sky was fashioned from his head;
Earth from his feet.[23]

From a gynecocentric perspective, childbirth obviously provides the model for this image of the primordial man sacrificing himself to create the physical and social worlds. While many myths and rituals include sacrifice of a person or body part to produce new life, in nature only one model actually exists for this process: a female birthing new life from her body. In a world view that considers self-sacrifice the underlying principle of creation, such a death is logical. The view differs, however, depending on whether the sacrificial death is voluntary, as with Jesus, or imposed, as with the mythic mother Tiamat.

Tiamat, mother of the gods, is one of three primordial figures in the Babylonian creation myth, the *Enuma Elish,* probably composed early in the second millennium B.C.E. Her name, signifying the original watery chaos from which everything subsequently evolved, aptly characterizes her. Her mate, Apsu, the father, is a slightly more creative, orderly force who prefers to remain quiescent. The third figure, Mummu, is variously their son, mist, storm wind, cloud, or mentality. The three together represent the original state of chaos with which nearly every cosmogony begins. But that chaos cannot last forever. Tiamat and Apsu's children disrupt it. So boisterous is their play that their parents plot to destroy them. One child, Ea, discovers their plan, however, and kills his father first. This leads Tiamat to rise up in wrath, assembling an army of monsters to battle her own children and grandchildren for control. Her grandson, Marduk, leading the younger generation, agrees to battle Tiamat, on the condition that he be granted supremacy in return. It is his splitting of Tiamat's body after slaying her that so well illustrates the theme of sacrificial creation:

> The lord [Marduk] trod on the legs of Tiamat,
> with his unsparing mace he crushed her skull. . . .
> Then the lord paused to view her dead body,
> That he might divide the monster and do artful works.
> He split her like a shellfish into two parts:
> Half of her he set up and ceiled as sky

From the other half of Tiamat Marduk makes the earth. The enormous importance of this theme of creation out of bodily sacrifice is then underscored by its repetition in the subsequent dismemberment of Tiamat's follower Kingu:

> They bound him holding him before Ea.
> They imposed on him his guilt and severed his blood [vessels].
> Out of his blood they fashioned mankind.[24]

Unlike this Sumerian myth, which explicitly celebrates imposed sacrifice as a key to creation, some women do not consider childbearing to be a sacrifice at all, much less one that is imposed. They believe childbearing is what they are meant to do; therefore, they want to do it. By contrast, women who consider childbearing unambiguously negative may see it as a biologically imposed sacrifice reinforced by patriarchal norms. Still others, accepting this presumed biological imperative, choose or feel that they choose to "sacrifice" themselves to become mothers. Such a self-imposed sacrificial view of childbirth is difficult to accept from a gynecocentric perspective, at least as we ordinarily understand the concept. Looking at Jesus as the epitome of patterns of self-sacrifice helps show why this is so.

Jesus is a misleading model for childbearing women because he is an example of divine self-sacrifice, which by definition no human can possibly match. To follow his example, the human side of a person must "die," just as Jesus did. The human Jesus endured crucifixion to return the divine Jesus back to his original, nonhuman, heavenly form. But this pattern precisely opposes childbirth. To bring new life into this world is to celebrate and affirm *this* world—not to deny it in the name of some other, nonhuman place and condition.

To reconstruct the image of childbirth as self-sacrifice, what is needed is greater clarity about the nature of sacrifice in general. It is obvious why imposed sacrifice does not provide a viable image. What healthy woman wants to be forced to give up her body and her selfhood to become a breeder? But why, apart from the difficulties of knowing if it *is* freely chosen, is the freely chosen model not helpful either?

The problem is complex. Because we think dualistically in Western cultures, we are more comfortable with separation than with blending. No matter how you look at it, if you polarize the concept of sacrifice, it is negative, inherently subtractive, rather than additive. When you sacrifice, you give up something. When you, yourself, are the sacrifice, then you give up yourself in your entirety. Both views of sacrifice suggest death rather than life, because both are a casting off, a losing, a giving up—all of which take something away, making it "die" in the process.

The problem is that sacrifice, viewed as separation, involves splitting; it opposes inclusiveness and is perceived negatively. But unlike Jesus' example, the willing self-sacrifice of a god like the Hindu Puruṣa does provide a viable counterimage. Puruṣa's sacrifice focuses on *this* world, rather than splitting off some "other" world. The difference is enormous. In Christian tradition, God is transcendent: He is totally separate from, and other than, this world. Whereas He is good, *this world,* despite the fact that He created it, contains evil. That is not the fault of God, of course. Rather, it results from Adam and Eve's choice to disobey Him and sin. Because of their original sin, we humans have ever after had to redeem ourselves and this "fallen" world into which we are all born.

How strongly this biblical image of the world departs from that of a tradition which views the world as God's body. Because the world made from Puruṣa's body automatically contains deity, it is innately divine. From a gynecocentric perspective, this second image is an appropriate one for understanding childbirth. In the Puruṣa image, sacrifice does not denigrate this world, it creates it. This sacrifice is not aimed at some place and time to come. It is aimed at the here and now of the material world. It is therefore an image to which any childbearing woman who finds sacrifice a compelling concept can assent. Understanding the creative function of sacrifice like this turns it into a positive image of a concept that Christian tradition has made impossible for flesh-and-blood women to uphold. It also strongly counters thinking that rejects the very idea of sacrifice and allows even this image of childbearing to be reconstructed.

THE POWER OF POLLUTION

More potentially damaging than self-sacrificial images of creation and childbearing are those that associate women's reproductive power with dirt and pollution. The imagery that psychologist Stanislav Grof uses to describe his own regression to what he calls the third perinatal stage of birth is typical:

> I felt surrounded by some indescribably disgusting stuff, drowning in some kind of archetypal cesspool epitomizing biological garbage of all ages. Foul stench seemed to penetrate my whole being; my mouth was full of excrement that was robbing me of my breath. The experience opened repeatedly into scenes of complex labyrinths of the sewage systems of the world.[25]

These extremely negative words epitomize the almost universal androcentric association of childbirth with both dirt and pollution. In a theory he calls "the fetal drama," psychohistorian Lloyd DeMause recasts this idea of birth-pollution in an intriguing way, seeing it as the basis for group affiliations:

> Being emotionally part of a group may be defined as sharing a fantasy of being in a womb, connected to others by umbilicuses, that is, literally by "blood ties," organising one's group around fetal symbols, and acting out cycles of the

fetal drama of growing pollution and purifying rebirth through a battle with a poisonous monster.[26]

DeMause connects the ubiquitous mythical motif of the great serpent of the underworld to what he calls the "poisonous" placenta, examples of which include the Gorgon, numerous great goddess figurines such as the well-known female statuette from Lespugue, and the guardian of the cedar felled by Gilgamesh. DeMause explains that "the only experience in life which corresponds to the group's basic conviction that the world is forever in danger of being swamped by blood pollution is that of fetal life."[27]

But what exactly do Grof and DeMause mean by pollution? According to anthropologist Mary Douglas, whose work on pollution remains extremely influential, pollution refers to matter out of place.[28] In this view, dirt as such does not exist. When we speak of dirt, we are referring to an object removed from its accustomed location, such as mud when it appears on a dining room table. Only by knowing a given culture's pattern of meanings can we know what substances or conditions are considered polluting. The relevance of this view to women in general is not hard to see; qualities associated with women are always out of place in a male-centered system of meanings; hence, they are "polluting." In a female-centered system, by contrast, birth-related substances would not only not be polluting but their absence could also conceivably be construed as a "lack," the way "lack" of a penis is construed in our androcentric culture.

In Westernized cultures that no longer overtly practice rituals designed to control childbirth "pollution," many women absorb only fragments of ancient ideas now divorced from their original, larger contexts. Nonetheless, even this fragmentary exposure to ideas connecting childbirth and pollution suffices to accentuate generalized beliefs that childbearing is a dirty, defiling process. Consider, for instance, the following well-known words from Leviticus 12:1–5, which, taken out of context as they frequently are, appear to single out women, although, in fact, Leviticus as a whole covers a wide range of "defilements":

> The Lord said to Moses, "Say to the people of Israel, If a woman conceives, and bears a male child, then she shall be unclean seven days; as at the time of her menstruation, she shall be unclean. And on the eighth day the flesh of his foreskin shall be circumcised. Then she shall continue for thirty-three days in the blood of her purifying; she shall not touch any hallowed thing, nor come into the sanctuary, until the days of her purifying are completed. But if she bears a female child, then she shall continue in the blood of her purifying for sixty-six days.

Unfortunately, these familiar words still strongly influence Western attitudes toward childbearing women. The language, even in translation, is explicit. The postpartum woman is "unclean" and in need of "purifying." Furthermore, she may not touch "any hallowed thing nor come into the sanctuary." To be told that one is so impure that she cannot touch any hallowed thing is to be totally castigated. How can a woman treated this way possibly feel positive about herself?

And how can she take pleasure in the process of childbearing, which led her to this state? Unless she relishes the role of scapegoat, to be declared impure by her community is extraordinarily painful. Comparisons with all sorts of odious disease states readily come to mind: leprosy, polio, tuberculosis, cancer, and now, of course, AIDS. Granted, the parturient woman, by contrast, is fortunate. She will be allowed to reenter her community. Nonetheless, to be even temporarily excommunicated because one is "impure," particularly at an otherwise joyful time, is to be placed in an extremely ambiguous position.

Women's "polluting" power often extends beyond childbearing in writings of the Early Church Fathers, as this representative misogynistic passage from St. John Chrysostom indicates:

> The whole of her bodily beauty is nothing less than phlegm, blood, bile, rheum, and the fluid of digested food. . . . If you consider what is stored up behind those lovely eyes, the angle of the nose, the mouth and cheeks you will agree that the well-proportioned body is merely a whitened sepulchre.[29]

Such negative imagery raises important questions: Given the traditional low status of women, how does further lowering it by associating us with dirt affect a woman's attitude toward the children she bears through her "disgusting" body? Viewed negatively, through patriarchal eyes, pollution alters childbirth's positive meaning as an act of creation, changing it into an act of elimination as it focuses on bodily fluids as slimy, smelly, unpleasant substances. Rather than being the stuff of life, blood and amniotic fluid disgust and repel. The fetus itself, in this negative view, does not primarily connote new life; instead, like the mother who has just borne it, it exudes filth. Both mother and child exist outside the norms of society. Furthermore, these associations, which define an infant as well as a mother as polluted, are by no means limited to biblically influenced cultures:

> The Hottentots considered mother and child unclean till they had been washed and smeared. . . . Lustrations with water were usual in West Africa. Tatar tribes in Mongolia used bathing, while in Siberia the custom of leaping over a fire answered the purpose of purification. The Mantras of the Malay Peninsula have made the bathing of the mother after childbirth into a ceremonial ordinance.[30]

Similarly, according to a Chinese informant, "The dirt from birth—menstrual fluids—is the dirtiest of all."[31]

Even more unfortunate, such imagery of childbirth as pollution does not simply "contaminate" the process in the eyes of men. Women, whether we give birth or choose not to, are likewise often "infected" by the association, as the following passage shows:

> When my sister was pregnant, she really did disgust me. She kept insisting on showing me how much bigger she had gotten, as if it were an important thing. The experience of pregnancy revolts me. In fact, the whole birth process is undignified. If I had to be pregnant, if for instance Ron wanted a baby, I

would go away by myself to have it; I could not bear to have him see me like that.[32]

A further ramification of such disgust at the "pollution" of childbirth is its propensity to "contaminate" not only a woman's children but her own mother as well: "Everything about her mother filled her with disgust, except the mother's hair. The thought of touching the part from which she came forth at birth was unbearable and nauseated her instantaneously."[33]

Such underlying beliefs that childbirth pollutes are well reinforced by twentieth-century American preoccupations, some would say obsessions, with cleanliness. The sheer messiness of childbirth can seem polluting. A woman whose bag of waters breaks prior to onset of labor may react with horror: "Did I wet the bed?" "Have I wet my pants?" So stigmatized is loss of bladder control that she may be disconcerted, making embarrassment over bodily functions, rather than excitement, a primary focus during labor.

Even a woman spared early seepage of amniotic fluid lacks control during labor. Well prepared or not, she may not anticipate losing control of her bodily fluids. To dribble, spurt, or seep fluids in public epitomizes humiliation in most cultures. Certainly in our own, it is totally unacceptable. Yet here she is, unable to stop her inner fluids from escaping. The words that come to mind accentuate the shameful, "polluting" connotations attached to this condition.

Added to the emotional anguish such culturally induced associations occasion is the physical discomfort of wetness. Any woman whose bag of waters has spontaneously broken or who recalls the artificial breaking of her bag by her attending physician knows that half a pint to two pints is no small amount. Such explosive breaking makes a woman feel as if her insides were flooding out in an unceasing torrential rush. Given the symbols of our patriarchal culture, this feels *wrong*. Such intensity and duration exceed any ordinary release of urine, regardless how long it has been held. A woman may feel that her body is not working correctly, that she is somehow freakish. She may then call what has happened to her "pollution," having no other framework in which to place it.

Even if a woman avoids this discomforting premature rupture of her bag of waters, she may have a "bloody show," as the pregnancy manuals put it. This, the telltale mark of blood on our clothing, is perhaps an even more fearsome labor-connected horror. While this fear ordinarily relates to menstrual blood, it is so deeply rooted that even as highly charged a time as onset of labor cannot automatically counter its humiliating effect. The image of blood "staining," a word commonly applied to sin, does not help.

Some women escape both these signs of beginning labor. For them, loss of body fluids occurs only during active labor, so they circumvent the stigma of being seen by unanticipated observers. Yet, even on a delivery table, a woman patriarchally influenced to abhor her body's "dirt" may still feel contaminated by her fluids. Worse, when she sees her baby all covered with casein, the cheesy coating on newborns, she may view her child as one more slimy exudate, a reaction scarcely calculated to bond her quickly and positively to her infant.

Even if she does not see her child in this negative way, if her own self-image on this major occasion in her life is negatively influenced, a positive response to her baby can be difficult. Squeamishness about her own bodily fluids is unlikely to be mitigated by seeing and touching her equally messy child. On the other hand, if she can reverse the image of childbirth as pollution construed negatively and see it positively, her experience can alter significantly. Now her gushings of wetness, her bloody show, rather than embarrassing her can cause pride. Many feminists, including Mary Daly, Adrienne Rich, Judy Grahn, and Monique Wittig, have called for just such changes. Grahn, for example, says, "Human power was worth-shipped for its origins, the physical stuff of its existence. Menstrual blood, the yoni, the uterus, milk, the placenta, and umbilical cord were all treasured and gave us the concepts of sacredness, worth-ship, and the analogies by which words are attached to ideas and imparted to people as language and wisdom."[34]

Reconstructing negative childbearing images such as those connoting dirt and pollution does not absolutely necessitate creating new words, although some feminists, particularly Daly, do just that. What is desperately needed, however, is a new frame of reference. Toward this end, any woman who does feel opposing pulls of pride in what she is doing—and a great many women do feel pride in pregnancy, labor, and delivery—can consciously focus on her satisfaction. And if she considers the physiological process of childbearing worthy of pride, she can take the next logical step, emphasizing to herself that *all* aspects of childbearing, including those we have been acculturated to believe are "dirty," are equally worthy. That means, for example, that the fluids connected with childbearing, rather than being viewed and experienced as shameful, are really cause for self-affirmation. After all, it is not just the fluids in and of themselves that are viewed negatively, but the particular context in which they arise. Body fluids such as the blood and tears of saints, for example, are believed so powerful that many Roman Catholics venerate them. With any object or concept, *context* determines meaning. Consequently, any woman who seeks to reinterpret childbirth, making it a positive, sacred image, possesses a powerful means for doing so.

If a woman can reach beneath patriarchal encrustations to the underlying power of childbearing and create alternative constructions based on her felt experiences, then she can connect with power rightfully her own. In so doing, she has choices. She can seize the power with accompanying feelings of hostility toward men, hostility which she will then almost inevitably pass on to her children, thus perpetuating the antipathy of the sexes toward each other. Or she can seize the power, recognizing her feelings of hostility but then going one step further to recognize that the layers of patriarchal "meaning" reflect the fierce potency that childbirth has always held for men. In such recognition, she can then work to transform her anger, seeking consciously to break the hurtful chain of negative interaction.

This means that instead of reacting with despair to images that connect childbearing with dirt and pollution, it is just as possible, and far more fruitful, for women to dig beneath the negative exteriors to reveal a positive alternative. For women who make this move, the physiological aspects of pregnancy, labor, and delivery, so troubling to many, acquire a positive dimension. That this is not easy, particularly for women who lack support from understanding partners or other family members, goes without saying. But it is only by such reconstruction that we can make the positive, potentially sacred meanings of childbirth prevail over their negative inversions.

EROTIC DIMENSIONS

A key for further expanding the gynecocentric potential of androcentrically biased images of labor is eroticism. While we take for granted the erotic nature of women's power in general—as the stuff of advertisements, films, and stories never lets us forget—eroticism remains curiously isolated from childbearing. This unnatural separation is vividly embodied in the familiar virgin/whore split, which the 1991 brouhaha over *Vanity Fair*'s cover photo of actress Demi Moore tellingly illustrates. In that controversial photo, the very pregnant actress is shown nude, with a strategically placed hand covering her bare breast. Despite the beauty of the photo, reactions, not surprisingly, were strongly mixed. Of the many commentaries on the subject, perhaps none so incisively captures the issue as Jimmy Breslin's July 25, 1991, column. After briefly summarizing the Demi Moore story, Breslin juxtaposes the following:

> On the other side of the world, the charred body of a woman almost at the end of her ninth month of pregnancy was found in an empty lot . . . in Brooklyn early in the morning of Saturday, July 13. The woman was an Hispanic in her late 20's, and she had been set afire while on her back and with her arms outstretched. The fire had burned much of the skin off her stomach, and the baby she had been carrying could be seen inside.[35]

In the netherworld from which this gruesome portrait comes, pregnant prostitutes are fair game, not just for sex but for brutalization and murder. As Breslin suggests, our culturally shared, collective ambivalence toward eroticism, pregnancy, childbearing, and motherhood leads some individuals to act out their murderous rage over women's procreative power.

So strongly does Western culture try to separate eroticism and motherhood that few of us consider pregnancy and childbirth erotic at all. Even Freud, usually so quick to see Eros everywhere, disconnected the two:

> One would certainly think that there could be no doubt about what is to be understood by the term "sexual." First and foremost, of course, it means the "improper," that which must not be mentioned. I have been told a story about some pupils of a famous psychiatrist, who once endeavoured to convince their master that the symptoms of an hysteric are frequently representations of sexual things. With this object, they took him to the bedside of an hysterical woman whose attacks were unmistakable imitations of childbirth. He objected, however, "Well, there is nothing sexual about childbirth." To be sure, childbirth is not necessarily always improper.[36]

In the last two decades of the twentieth century, ubiquitous emphases on fitness and slenderness heighten the nonerotic image of pregnancy. Although pregnancy is not obesity, the jutting belly is easily confused with it. Furthermore, many pregnant women do gain large amounts of weight, and some grow physically unfit. Women whose mates equate feminine sexual appeal with slenderness may therefore find pregnancy demoralizing, rather than erotic, especially if their men look or wander elsewhere at this time. For any number of reasons, pregnancy strikes many other people as nonerotic as well: individuals of either sex threatened by pregnancy, pregnant women who dislike their bodies, and nonpregnant women whose self-image hinges on slenderness. But for many people, pregnancy is indeed erotic, part of the great lovemaking cycle that precipitated the condition in the first place.

Obviously, no single definition of eroticism is possible. In the largest sense, probably anything—objects, people, situations, ideas, places—can be erotic for someone. But that does not illuminate the concept. One useful way to understand eroticism is to consider the ancient goddesses or gods associated with the erotic, particularly Eros.

Eros comes rather late to Greek thought. He is largely literary rather than popularly rooted. Prior to the classical period no cultic evidence exists for him. Portrayed either as a beautiful youth or young boy, he equally represents homosexual and heterosexual love. Hesiod (c. 739–700 B.C.E.) calls him one of the first gods who, as god of sexual desire, enables the subsequent sexual reproduction of the other deities. That means he must be present from the start, a circumstance borne out in a later cosmogony supposedly by "Orpheus" (c. 500 B.C.E.), which names him Protogonous, Firstborn.

But there is something peculiar about the history of Eros. He is detached from Aphrodite, elsewhere considered to be his mother. This detachment not only makes Eros into a quasiabstraction, surely an oddity for the deity meant to represent sexual love, but also divorces him from women. The appropriateness of this god to fulfill the very role his name implies is therefore somewhat suspect.

But Eros is not the only deity to appear in erotic situations; we must include Aphrodite as well. Originally not Greek, Aphrodite, like the Babylonian Ishtar whom she strongly resembles, was an Asian Queen of Heaven, a creator goddess connected with fertility and war. As with Eros, everyone she visited succumbed to intense sexual longing. Some late myths of literary rather than cultic origin make Eros one of Aphrodite's many children by the war god Ares, with whom she is frequently paired. When Eros becomes her son-lover, the pattern clearly matches the common Asian configuration of mother-goddess and son-consort acting out an endlessly tragic pattern of love, death, and rebirth. The illustrative cases of Ishtar and Tammuz, Cybele and Attis, and Venus and Adonis readily come to mind.

Whether visited by Eros or Aphrodite, for love-struck victims, the world appears altered. Replacing the flatness of ordinary experience is a fullness, physically signaled by engorged body tissue. Eros, the golden boy-god, and Aphrodite, his voluptuous mother, suffuse everything within reach with their warm, pulsating glow. They are the deities who make bodies long to merge. How then can pregnancy be construed as erotic?

As psychological images, both Aphrodite and Eros function somewhat differently in pregnancy from the way they do in lovemaking. Ordinarily either deity can be considered the substance, quality, or spirit that unites two separate individuals. But for fetus and mother, unity exists from the start. Consequently, Aphrodite and Eros are both built into the relationship. In a sense, this situation is too obvious for comment, yet this original erotic unity is too often ignored.

The most common version of this erotic side of pregnancy filters it through male experience. When Norman O. Brown says, 'Coitus successfully performed is incest, a return to the maternal womb,'' [37] his statement is fine for men. But it leaves unanswered the question, What is coitus for a woman? Further, and more to the point in this context, why do so few thinkers turn it around? Sandor Ferenczi in *Thalassa* is a notable exception, and even he, through a complicated sleight-of-hand, turns it into a kind of secondary "compensation" for not being able to "return" to the womb via a penis.[38] Why not say that pregnancy and expulsion of the child from the uterus set the pattern for sexual intercourse? The eroticism of the original experience is what the adult male seeks when he is erotically drawn to a woman. But is the eroticism of a woman's prenatal and natal attachment to her child likewise recapitulated for her in coitus? Or, conversely, does coitus foreshadow the subsequent eroticism of pregnancy and childbirth?

If being in the womb and returning to it are both erotic, what is the situation for the mother whose womb is variously being inhabited or penetrated? In what sense, if at all, are Eros and Aphrodite present for her, both when the baby is within her womb and subsequently when she is expelling it? The pattern of the mother-son dyad, Aphrodite and Eros, or any of their many mythical counterparts shows how childbirth can be erotic for a woman. What then is the relationship between these two cosmic players? Two factors make it difficult at first to see the mother-child relationship in its erotic manifestation. First, we are not accustomed to thinking of the relationship between mother and growing fetus as anything but a biological process of growth. It is very difficult therefore to switch conceptual frameworks and see it as also being highly erotic. Second, the notion that any and all body parts hold erotic potential opposes the puritanical streak in American culture. Although most people now fully realize that mouth, penis, vagina, and breast are not the only erogenous zones, relatively few consider all bodily interiors equally capable of erotic potential.

In pregnancy, this erotic potential may actually be heightened, although until a woman's baby quickens, she will feel nothing from the baby itself. However, if hers is a sensuous nature, the gradual alteration of her body may feel erotic, particularly during the first trimester when her breasts enlarge, sometimes as much as a full size, and her belly remains flat. At this stage, depending on her prepregnant size and shape, she may feel and be more sexually desirable than ever. If *looking* appealing strongly affects her attitude toward her own eroticism, then she may find early pregnancy highly erotic. She may delight in her new contours as she stares at her burgeoning figure, bringing both touch and gaze into play.

A woman may also find pregnancy as such constantly arousing. Phyllis Chesler, addressing her unborn child, tells of just such arousal:

I want to have orgasms without foreplay three or four times every day. I look at your father slyly, passively. I insist he come back to bed, ''now.'' If we're outside, I suggest we borrow a friend's bedroom, or sneak into a hotel restroom, ''for just a minute.''

I am without shame. Never have I been in such sexual heat. Is this natural in pregnancy? Or am I enjoying my lust because I think it unnatural, taboo? What exactly is so arousing, so pleasurably ''lewd'' to me about a woman with a round, fat belly initiating orgasms in Mediterranean heat? Is my body remembering something? Can bodies do this? . . . During and after love-making I watch my stomach, I watch you, like a voyeur, as if I'm not present. There's a direct line from my *consciousness* of your existence to my clitoris. Watching my belly, having my belly seen by another, seems to throb this mysterious line awake.

My serpent rises lazily, a full four feet, then coils back into its clitoral hood. My tiger is gone, my tiger returns, restless, ready to prowl again.[39]

But as Judith Goldsmith points out in her book *Childbirth Wisdom,* engaging in sexual activity during pregnancy troubles many couples. Goldsmith says, ''Most medical authorities are still of the opinion that sex should be avoided for health reasons, especially in the later months, but some are now asking whether this stand is based on strong evidence or just strongly held beliefs!''[40] She also points out that premodern peoples responded to this issue variously, indicating that our own culture's tendency to separate sex and pregnancy is not unique. Nor is it solely a reflection of post-Enlightenment tendencies to endlessly separate in as many spheres as possible.

A woman may also find that quickening opens up a whole new dimension of sexual experience. Here is another human actually inside herself—not just symbolically, as in coitus, but inside her completely. This is the total union of mysticism. What closer bond is there? Mother and fetus are as truly one as it is possible to be, yet the fetus is also a separate human on the way to becoming an individual in its own right. During this time—the four or five months following quickening—the two relate as romance promises all lovers do. This is the bliss every lover craves. Obstetrician Frederick Leboyer describes the relationship like this:

> It was an infinitely sensual, amorous relationship that existed between the child and its mother. . . .
>
> To make love is to return to paradise, it is to plunge again into the world before birth, before the great separation. It is to find again the primordial slowness, the blind and all-powerful rhythm of the internal world, of the great ocean. Making love is the great regression.[41]

This description recalls mystical unions with deity from many religious traditions. Visual evidence indicates that gestation is erotic for some fetuses as well, as several physicians in New London, Connecticut, examining a sonogram of a male fetus were startled to discover when they saw an erection. Since then, these same physicians have documented six more cases.[42]

In Western patriarchal cultures, this particular form of erotic bliss has always been heavily proscribed. We all grow up learning to call it by an ugly name—incest. We also learn that incest is the ultimate taboo, so ultimate, in fact, that until recently if scholars examined it, they typically focused on some primitive tribe, a convenient "Other," whose distance, geographic and cultural, neutralized the topic.

But the erotic dimension of pregnancy does not stop with quickening. Some women find labor equally arousing. In the representative words of a homebirther named Cora, "I began having beautiful, rushing contractions that started low, built up to a peak, and then left me floating. . . . As the contractions got stronger it felt like I was making love to the rushes and I could wiggle my body and push into them and it was really fine." [43] These words, which highlight women's capacity for erotic arousal without need of a partner, combined with a potentially erotic maternal-fetal interrelationship, show why men might indeed feel uneasy. No wonder those who accept Freud's dictum that babies substitute for the penises women supposedly so envy might prefer to gloss over pregnancy's erotic dimension. Pregnancy is simply too overwhelming! It leaves little space, either metaphorically or physically, for the adult male lover. By adding to women's already potent power of incarnation the ability to please themselves sexually, pregnancy can severely threaten masculinity. Such almost unbearable power inevitably provokes sanctions. In a world accustomed to sacrality, these sanctions are taboos; in one predominantly secularized, they degenerate into chauvinistic attitudes.

Once revealed, how can this great power be reconstructed to narrow the gap between women and men rather than increase it? A particularly good model is at hand. A few women have discovered that this "secret" erotic power does not just increase during pregnancy but extends to labor and delivery as well. Furthermore, it can include mates. This extended eroticism, which promises significant hope for reconstructing the erotic dimension of childbirth, appears in numerous examples collected by Marilyn Moran, a leading exponent of the highly controversial unattended homebirthing movement.[44] Moran's two self-published books, *Birth and the Dialogue of Love* and *Happy Birth Days*, and her newsletter, *The New Nativity*, now *A Quarterly Newsletter*, are replete with examples of erotic play during labor. An account written by a homebirther named Georgia Tapp captures the flavor of Moran's findings and her own childbirthing philosophy:

> Hugging and kissing helped so much! If I hadn't read about that, I never would've had such a neat experience. . . . I particularly would daydream of giving birth at dusk. . . . I dreamt of John holding me tenderly during labor and after the baby was born—like RIGHT after. Naturally this happened! It was a natural response to the love and the sexual aspect of birth.[45]

Donn Reed, husband of another homebirther, told Moran: "The birth was not only painless, but very pleasurable. We had never read about this aspect, and it took us both by surprise. As the baby crowned, I knew from Jean's look and sounds that she was having an explosive orgasm, which rolled on and on. What a long way from the pain and agony of conventional myth!"[46]

It is not just Moran who, in collecting hundreds of such accounts, recognizes the erotic potential of childbearing. Another illustrative instance is found in Ina May Gaskin's *Spiritual Midwifery*. These words come from a homebirther named Karen:

> My rushes [contractions] hardly felt heavy at all, but I knew they must be because I was opening up. [My husband and I] just kept making out and rubbing each other. We got to places that we had forgotten we could get to. Since that day we have been remembering. . . . It was like getting married all over again.[47]

Anyone who finds these accounts difficult to believe need only listen to the sounds of the opening section of Frederick Leboyer's video *Birth without Violence*. Without having been told in advance, most people would assume the woman's sounds were orgasmically induced, not the result of labor.

But what about the majority of couples who do not discover Moran's work or stumble upon this ''secret'' on their own? Fortunately, some prenatal classes offer such information. The work of childbirth educator Gayle Peterson is particularly illuminating. In early classes Peterson teaches women to come to terms with their bodies to counter acculturation to mind/body separation. As part of her instruction, she teaches perineal massage. This is done partly to stretch the perineum, but, as Peterson says, ''More importantly, the perineal massage serves to acquaint . . . women with their genitals . . . and to experience awareness of these parts of the body in pregnancy and birth. Perineal massage can be done by the father-to-be as well, [and] . . . gives permission for sexual exploration to be a part of pregnancy.''[48]

Besides a growing body of erotic childbearing accounts, there is testimony of a far different sort. Its unlikely source is romance novels! An article on the front page of the April 12, 1991, *St. Louis Dispatch* entitled ''Mr. Right Is Now Mr. Mom in Romance Novels'' deals with this 1990s development. The article quotes Karin Stoecker, an editorial manager at Harlequin Books, as saying, ''Lately, authors have begun exploring . . . birth . . . as a tender, romantic, and to an extent, sensual event.''[49]

Some readers may consider Harlequin Romances an odd venue for attesting to the erotic nature of childbearing. But one need only recall Ezra Pound's declaration that ''poets are the antennae of the human race'' (using ''poet'' loosely) to realize that this account illustrates the slow cultural penetration of the idea that eroticism is integral to childbirth. The following words, from yet another child-birthing account, reveal how important incorporating Eros into childbearing can be for all concerned: ''We continued to love each other a lot and I felt we were helping the baby to be born into an atmosphere of love.''[50] Reframing childbirth to emphasize its potential eroticism will surely be welcomed by most couples.

8 "Delivery": A Time of Potential Revelation

Second stage labor, which climaxes with the birth of the baby, is commonly known as delivery because in an androcentric model of childbearing the laboring woman is "delivered" *from* her pain, *of* her child, *by* her physician. But "delivery" is a skewed construction, emphasizing the "savior" physician's prowess and deemphasizing what happens for the woman at this important time. Now is when her baby descends through her pelvic bones, down her birth canal, and finally emerges. A far more appropriate way to capture this experience from a gynecocentric perspective is reflected in these words from midwife Ina May Gaskin's moving book, *Spiritual Midwifery:*

> It is possible to reach, in meditation, a level of consciousness which gives deep insight into oneself. Impulses and motivations that may not ordinarily be apparent may become crystal clear. In an even deeper level of meditation, it is possible to reach a level of insight that goes beyond the inner personal wellsprings of thought, words, and behavior into a consciousness of what is universal in humanity. Such insight and power is available to birthing women under the right circumstances. . . . [The] complex of values that attends each birth is so profound and universal that I use the term "spiritual."[1]

Many believe that this time of potential spiritual revelation for the birthing mother is inevitably traumatic for the baby being born. This idea, which underlies many theories of birth, is pernicious in its implicit faulting of women because our bodies permit such "trauma" to occur. Carried to an extreme, this presumed birth trauma becomes death, a condition that potentially confronts both major participants throughout labor and delivery. This is a particularly frightening image for women and thus one especially difficult to retrieve or reconstruct. A common, seemingly far more promising image of childbirth is rebirth. Yet, as patriarchally conceived, rebirth imagery also distorts childbirth, ignoring its feminine source. Thus, retrieval and reconstruction of this significant image demand especially careful attention. Building on ideas of rebirth is a popular New Age technique known as rebirthing. As with many birth-connected images and practices, this one, too, holds ambivalent promise for reconstructing childbirth.

A somewhat less ambiguous image derives from a crucial procedure that takes place very shortly after the emergence of the child—cord cutting. This cutting, by which the child becomes physically separate, has long symbolized major life transitions. Because of its psychological importance, rituals often accompany both cord cutting and the closely related expulsion of the placenta. Such rituals, as significant enactments of the underlying sacrality of childbearing, sometimes must be revisioned to include women rather than centering so exclusively on the child.

"BIRTH TRAUMA"

A particularly controversial conception of delivery asserts that it automatically traumatizes babies. Theories about "birth trauma" are androcentrically conceived counterparts for the child of the presumed pain and suffering of the mother. Yet contemporary findings indicate that birth is not automatically traumatic. For this reason alone, the idea needs close questioning. It should also be questioned because its unconsidered acceptance seriously compromises women. To the extent that women are identified with childbearing, we are also blamed for the trauma that birth supposedly creates. Furthermore, if birth trauma is automatically assumed to be unavoidable, then steps aren't likely to be taken to avert it. In that case, not only will many births inevitably continue to be traumatic but the dangerous imagery associated with that "inevitability" will continue wreaking its havoc on women.

Inevitable birth trauma is the message many myths convey by repeatedly pitting maternal "monsters" against worthy "heroes," as in such birth trauma tales as that of Jonah and the whale or the primeval Mesopotamian dragon mother Tiamat battling her son Marduk.

Freud is generally credited with formally developing the birth trauma theory. In his twenty-fifth lecture in *A General Introduction to Psychoanalysis,* he says,

> We think [a repetition in the anxiety affect] is the experience of *birth*—an experience which involves . . . a concatenation of painful feelings, of discharges of excitation, and of bodily sensations . . . to have become a prototype for all occasions on which life is endangered, ever after to be reproduced again in us as the "dread" or "anxiety" condition. The enormous increase in stimulation effected by the interruption of the renewal of blood (the internal respiration) was the cause of the anxiety experience at birth—the first anxiety was therefore toxically induced. The name *Angst* (anxiety)—*angustice, Erge,* a narrow place, a strait—accentuates the characteristic tightening in the breathing which was then the consequence of a real situation and is subsequently repeated almost invariably with an affect. It is very suggestive too that the first anxiety state arose on the occasion of the separation from the mother.[2]

Freud is, however, careful to say, "Do not imagine that what I am telling you now about affects is the common property of normal psychology."[3]

Freud's one-time pupil Otto Rank, however, is not so careful. He magnifies the birth trauma beyond Freud's Oedipal complex, making it into the ultimate principle of psychology:

> We are led to recognize in the birth trauma the ultimate biological basis of the psychical. . . . The whole psychical development of man [is] shown from the analytically recognized importance of the birth trauma and in the continually recurring attempts to overcome it.[4]

To this day, Rank's claim not only influences psychology but also contributes to a large body of negative views on childbirth and childbearing women. Rank's claim particularly harms women by demonizing our bodies: "There is then . . . only one fixation place, namely, the maternal body, and all symptoms ultimately relate to this primal fixation, which is given to us in the psychobiological fact of our Unconscious."[5] Consequently, although Rank does not precisely say it is "women's fault" that humans suffer psychological symptoms, he strongly implies that because women's bodies give birth, and birth causes psychological problems, women are to blame.

The long tradition in which such antiwoman thinking is embedded is made evident by Rank, for in supporting his theory he extracts much "evidence" from the art and myths of the ancient Egyptians and Greeks. Thus, for example, following a well-established line of androcentric thought, Rank interprets the myth of Theseus, successfully threading the labyrinth as "representing the birth of the Greek ideal human being, the hero, and his detachment from the ancient primal mother,"[6] an emphasis notably different from the gynecocentric interpretation of the labyrinth discussed in the Introduction of this book.[7]

Rank further emphasizes the embeddedness of the birth trauma in the Western misogynistic tradition, whereby childbearing woman is effaced and denigrated, when he discusses the culture hero Prometheus as prototype of the artist:

> [T]he artist . . . like Prometheus, creates human beings after his own image, that is, he brings forth himself amid the maternal pains of creation. So the renowned artistic Greek, who understands woman only as an organ of childbearing, and who pays homage to the love of boys, has raised himself in identification with the mother to creator of men, in that way attempts in his works of art to detach himself gradually and under great resistance, from the mother as all the sphinxlike fabulous beings so convincingly prove. From this "moment" of simultaneously longed-for and yet not wished-for, freeing from the bestial womb, from this eternal sticking fast in birth, which the neurotic constantly experiences afresh, as anxiety of the primal situation, the Greek artist and with him the entire race found the way to idealization by preserving in solid stone this stormy moment, which the Medusa head has kept in all its terrifying significance.[8]

Most relevant to the birth trauma of the misogynist themes presented here is the idea that the womb is "bestial," a theme also prominent in the highly influential, but controversial, work of psychologist Stanislav Grof. Over the past twenty years, Grof has collected data from more than four thousand psychic sessions conducted on a wide range of people—from volunteers to terminal cancer patients. His method is to regress them back to the womb, originally with LSD, more recently by holotropic therapy, a combination of controlled breathing, music, and focused body work. Based on his findings, Grof has named the preborn's experience of the womb during the mother's pregnancy the first perinatal stage. This is the time of "the primal union with mother . . . the original state of intrauterine existence during which the child and mother form a symbiotic unity . . . [characterized by] feelings of sacredness, transcendence of time and space, ineffability, and richness of insights of cosmic relevance."[9] So far so good—in this stage Grof describes the womb positively. In stark contrast, however, is stage two. Here is where the idea of the birth trauma implicitly enters in. Grof's influence is such that the following description appears in an article by scientist Carl Sagan. Now,

> the uterine contractions begin. The walls to which the amniotic sac is anchored, the foundation of the stable intrauterine environment, become traitorous. The fetus is dreadfully compressed. The universe seems to pulsate, a benign world suddenly converted into a cosmic torture chamber. . . . No hope of surcease is offered. The fetus has done nothing to deserve such a fate, an innocent whose cosmos has turned upon it, administering seemingly endless agony.[10]

Note the antiwoman language: "traitorous," "cosmic torture chamber," "such a fate," "cosmos has turned against it," "seemingly endless agony." These are not even vaguely neutral terms. Each strongly suggests a kind of cosmic plot against newborns enacted in the womb of women.

What are we to make of these words? If they do reflect consistent findings, how can the reader fault them, regardless of how distasteful their antiwoman bias? But Grof's "findings" illustrate the slipperiness of scientific objectivity. Many childbirth advocates take issue with Grof because of his methodology. His original work, conducted by administering LSD to his subjects, produced violent imagery. When Grof switched to hypnosis and breath work, he accompanied sessions with martial music, a choice some critics consider to be suspiciously slanted toward reproducing the same kinds of violent images induced by LSD.[11] On the other side, however, Sagan asserts that "oxytocin [a hormone naturally present in laboring women that stimulates delivery] turns out to be an ergot derivative that is chemically related to psychedelics such as LSD."[12] Thus, Grof's original use of LSD is not unreasonable.

If Grof's were the only experiments in birth regression, his "findings," despite his obvious violent imagery of women's bodies, might be less assailable. But this is not the case. Midwives' observations and the regression work of psychologist David Chamberlain both refute assumptions that birth trauma characterizes birth in general. Increasing numbers of fully conscious women and coaching fathers also attest to nontraumatic birthings. In strongly marked contrast to what Grof, following in the tradition of Freud and Rank, repeatedly "finds," these sources often discover quite the reverse: infants who make the transition from maternal uterus to external world with no discernible signs of trauma. An example is Chamberlain's story of Marianne, who recalls birth as feeling "like a tidal wave. . . . I can see that I'm attached to the tidal wave. . . . They are holding my head, but gently; they were gentle. And next thing I know, they're saying, "You just lie right here," and they wrap me up in something."[13] This is decidedly not the cosmic battle Grof describes over and over. When Chamberlain does find trauma, it appears to be specific to a particular family situation, not universal, as when he details the birth account of a child named David, who recalls, "It's very quiet. There's no joy in this room. I feel like nobody's happy to see me."[14] This is not to say that the birth itself is never traumatic, but often when it is, the doctor's intervention, not the mother's body, creates the trauma. A good example is found in an account by Linda, who says the doctor "didn't feel very gentle. He was just trying to get it over with. Then he pulled! It hurt my neck!"[15]

Part of what characterizes the presumed birth trauma Grof refers to is "a sense of total annihilation on all imaginable levels—physical destruction, emotional disaster, intellectual and philosophical defeat."[16] Grof calls this "ego death." Findings by Chamberlain and observations by midwives, birthing women, and coaching fathers categorically refute this notion, too: Preborns do not automatically suffer these psychologically devastating conditions. Quite the contrary, as illustrated by this account from a homebirthing mother: "Aaron Matthew arrived 3:38 P.M., January 24, 1983, and weighed 9 lbs, 11 oz. He was so cool, calm, and collected. Aaron didn't cry or fuss. He just rested beside me growing pinker and pinker. His eyes were wide open, looking about as if wondering why all the commotion."[17] A homebirthing father describes his child's similarly nontraumatic arrival in these words: "After four hours of labor, Lilana finally slid out to my waiting hands. She was delivered to her waist, and as she paused, she wrapped her little hand around one of my fingers and held on tight, forming at that moment a bond of mutual admiration and love that will endure 'til I die."[18] These representative stories counter widely held assumptions that birth automatically traumatizes, thus challenging the implicit misogyny of those who demonize women's bodies as the "monstrous" cause of their children's psychic pain.

A curious twist on arguments that birth traumatizes comes from English professor Alvin H. Lawson, who theorizes that UFO abduction is a fantasized sequence of images and events based on unconscious perinatal memories.[19] Such a theory may sound preposterous, but the alternative is even more so. Consider the fact that in May 1992, the Roper Organization mailed out to U.S. psychiatrists free copies of a booklet entitled *Unusual Personal Experiences* about the UFO Syndrome[20] in connection with a May 1992 TV miniseries on the subject. That report states that two percent of all Americans claim abduction experiences! Believing that so many Americans have been abducted by aliens strains credulity far more than Lawson's intriguing thesis does.

Lawson argues that human fetuses—possibly as early as the embryo stage-possess consciousness sufficient for uterine memories to surface in some children and adults. He bases his theory on a study in which nonabducted individuals ignorant of UFOs were hypnotized and asked to imagine being abducted. Their imagery and descriptions are virtually indistinguishable from those presented by "real" abductees. Both groups typically report sudden loss of control; seeing a bright light; paralysis; being struck by a beam of light; being levitated through a lighted tunnel into a vast, dome-shaped room; and hearing a humming sound.[21] Lawson persuasively juxtaposes perinatal stages, birth memories, abduction stories, and similar imagery from myths, folklore, and fairy tales to make his case. All his arguments, including excellent drawings of fetal-like "alien" abductors, are highly convincing. To take just a few points, he says in discussing tunnel imagery that "of eight cesarean subjects, seven used no tunnel imagery in describing how they boarded or left the UFO," as opposed to frequent descriptions of tunneling up into the UFO by vaginally delivered subjects. Then he connects the ubiquitous imagery of bubbledome headgear to the amniotic sac and claims that reported probings and injections, often felt in the umbilical area by "abductees," recapitulate cord clamping.[22]

Comparisons unequivocally show how strikingly "abductions" resemble what newborns experience. Consider, for example, the following account from one of Chamberlain's regressed subjects, a woman named Marcie:

> I feel I'm being pulled out, head first, gasping for air. Somebody is cutting the cord. It's a strange feeling to be out in the air where all of a sudden I'm kicking and moving my arms. It's like being in a big open space; it's frightening.
>
> I don't like the looks of the people with masks covering their faces. I keep staring at their masks. My mom is the only normal looking one in the room!
>
> Everything is foreign. I feel out of place, like I don't know what to do. Space is overwhelming![23]

While Lawson's UFO reframing of the birth trauma is unlikely to deflect blame from women, it provides an excellent example of the way myth continues, in contemporary dress, to demonize women, turning us yet again into "monsters." A potentially more positive reframing comes from psychohistorian Lloyd De-Mause who, in an interesting variation of the birth trauma, theorizes about what he calls "the fetal drama,"

> which is remembered and elaborated upon by later childhood events. . . . [It] is the basis for the history and culture of each age . . . [and being] traumatic . . . must endlessly be repeated in cycles of dying and rebirth as expressed in group-fantasies which even today continue to determine much of our national political life.[24]

Admittedly, by attempting to give a single, systematic source and explanation for all history, DeMause risks reductionism. But his ideas nonetheless compel consideration for reinterpreting childbearing. DeMause pushes Freudian thought further back, altering the familiar mythic motif of the hero battling the monster into the "suffering fetus" versus the "placental monster." DeMause stresses that our feelings of awe and terror tell us when we are in the presence of the sacred— something "wholly other," as religionist Rudolph Otto puts it—yet also intimately connected to ourselves. This combination, DeMause asserts, is "a perfect description of the placenta."[25] This startling thought forms the centerpiece of his theory, which connects the feelings the fetus once felt in relation to its life-supporting, potentially life-denying placenta to images of deity and kingship. Attempts to "recapture the aura of the placental prototype" lead to worship of a god "from whom all blessing flow" and a leader "from whom all power flows." Furthermore,

> divinity carries far more placental than parental qualities: self-sufficient, arbitrary, hidden, mysterious, omnipotent, unapproachable, unknowable, asexual—all these are not qualities of any living parent but rather of a living, all-powerful "thing" on which one wholly depends but whose arbitrary actions one cannot affect and with which one has constant silent exchanges.[26]

If DeMause is correct in his theorizing, then logically it is not *women* but placentas that function as ultimate images of monstrosity. Whether this shift matters is problematic, given the propensity of androcentric thought, as already described, to transfer negative imagery from body parts to "woman." Nonetheless, the placental theory is extremely interesting to contemplate as a possibility for reinterpreting the idea of birth trauma. Another promising extrapolation from DeMause's ideas is the possibility that if enough babies are eventually born nontraumatically by various contemporary "gentle births," then perhaps some of humanity's seemingly inescapable, repeatedly enacted negative patterns of destructive behavior might be modified.

Even if change on such a dramatic scale does not necessarily follow, DeMause's theory that bloodthirsty rituals of all sorts—scapegoatings, bloody flag wavings, out and out wars—enact the "fetal drama" strongly underscores the need to alter the presumed inevitability of the birth trauma. Such alteration would automatically facilitate some major rethinking of childbirth.

DEATH

Carried to an extreme, the presumed trauma of birth is death. The common association of death with birth is of ancient origin. Putatively, one of the earliest material examples is a terra cotta figure of the goddess Cybele, from approximately 6000 B.C.E., discovered by James Mellaart at Çatal Hüyük in Anatolia. This figurine, which shows the goddess enthroned with a head between her legs, has evoked widely divergent interpretations.[27] Mellaart claims it reveals Cybele giving birth to her divine son, but scholars Wolfgang Hekek and Jurgen Thime see it as the head of a young man killed after intercourse with her. Instead of childbirth, they claim that what the figure depicts is a *Rückgeburt,* an inverted birth, in which the goddess is receiving the dead figure back into her womb. Regardless of the meaning of this particular figure, the idea of *Rückgeburt,* in which a Great Goddess figure not only gives birth but takes back her offspring when it dies, continues on into patriarchal history.

Yet patriarchal thought has distorted this ancient interchangeability of childbirth and death, exaggerating its negative side at the expense of its natural, cyclical quality. In the process, patriarchal thought also revises the natural pattern in such a way that either women or children or both become death's victims.

Of course, not all images of death usurping birth necessarily reflect patriarchal distortion. The death of a mother was once an all-too-common threat to women's lives. A well-known literary example from *Oliver Twist* represents just such an instance:

> The patient shook her head, and stretched out her hand towards the child.
> The surgeon deposited it in her arms. She imprinted her cold white lips passionately on its forehead; passed her hands over her face; gazed wildly round; shuddered; fell back—and died.[28]

This excerpt, like its many nineteenth-century counterparts, appears "merely" mimetic. Yet so many fictional images, from myths and fairy tales through contemporary stories, project this theme that the question nags: Why do so many writers, especially males, kill off their female characters in childbirth?

The suspicion that repeated images of childbirth as death reflect more than factual representation is heightened by examples such as the bizarre twist in Hemingway's short story "Indian Camp." This story details young Nick Adams's introduction to childbirth as death when his physician-father delivers an Indian woman following two days of nonproductive labor. Among many misogynist motifs, Hemingway features the woman's screams, her lack of anaesthesia, and the physician's lack of concern for both:

> "Oh, Daddy, can't you give her something to make her stop screaming?" asked Nick.
> "No, I haven't any anaesthetic," his father said. "But her screams are not important. I don't hear them because they are not important."[29]

Besides highlighting the doctor's professed indifference to his patient's pain, the story emphasizes the physician's skills, not the woman's experience:

> "That's one for the medical journal. . . ." he said. "Doing a Caesarean with a jack-knife and sewing it up with nine-foot, tapered gut leaders."[30]

These stereotypical macho qualities combined with sadistic attitudes and implicit anti-Indian bias create an atmosphere congruent with the real story—the death of a man—for unexpectedly, it is not the laboring woman who dies, but her husband. After bragging about his medical prowess, Nick's father says, "Ought to have a look at the proud father. They're usually the worst sufferers in these little affairs. . . . I must say he took it all pretty quietly." But when the doctor pulls back the blanket covering the Indian's head he receives a shock:

> His hand came away wet. He mounted on the edge of the lower bunk with the lamp in one hand and looked in. The Indian lay with his face toward the wall. His throat had been cut from ear to ear. The blood had flowed down into a pool where his body sagged the bunk. His head rested on his left arm. The open razor lay, edge up, in the blankets.[31]

How oddly this twist strikes a woman reader. Bad enough that death substitutes for childbearing. Still worse are suspicions that male writers have sometimes used this substitution as revenge against laboring women. But here, in a macabre turn, Hemingway imposes yet a different pattern. Reducing the importance of the laboring mother to almost nothing, he focuses on the wordless "fight" for male competence between "superior" and "inferior" male, savior physician versus helpless husband. The Indian, unable to alleviate his wife's agony, must sit by while two white men and a boy take over. He thereby loses so much face as a male that he takes his own life. Implicit in this suicide, however, is the idea that the Indian, having thereby honorably sacrificed himself, has "won." Few stories better illustrate the familiar patriarchal distortion and displacement of a woman's childbearing story, as it is made incidental to the "real" one of male prowess and bloody self-sacrifice.

The negative patriarchal view of the connection between childbirth and death raises the horrifying spectre that in patriarchies death dealing functions for men as childbearing does for women. Certainly, as the next section indicates, the common phenomenon of all-male warbands and the nearly universal, patriarchally idolized "Holy Warrior" who fights for the greater glory of his god suggest that, historically, death dealing has served men as a "heroic" counterpart or substitute for childbearing. Islam makes this connection explicit in its teaching that only men who die in holy war and women who die in childbirth will go directly to Paradise. Such a transformation of the primary image of feminine sacrality into its opposite represents patriarchal distortion of childbirth in its most extreme, most dangerous form. No other alteration separates childbirthing imagery so thoroughly from its original meaning.

Yet even this destructive distortion can be reconstructed by understanding that the birth-death connection far exceeds the limitations of inherited patriarchal imagery. Some women giving birth recall experiencing this larger interchangeability for themselves. Stanislav Grof, for example, describes such a recollection from one of his subjects:

> Susanne started feeling nauseous . . . she clearly associated it with pregnancy; she experienced herself as the pregnant mother, but simultaneously identified with the baby in the womb. She was hypersalivating and experiencing the water in her mouth as amniotic fluid. . . . . She started experiencing sequences of dying and being born in many variations, a strange mixture of the agony of dying and the ecstasy of birth.[32]

As her experience progresses, this woman identifies with all children and all child-birthing mothers, thereby achieving an extraordinary communion with human life as a whole. In her experience, the associated imagery of birth and death reaches such intensity that she lives out the sacred meaning of childbirth. Instead of death being sharply severed from such presumed opposites as life and birth, it is understood as an integral part of both. Integrated this way, death functions not as a terrifying ending to be avoided, but as a natural part of an ongoing cycle that connects us all. This is the cycle underlying all religious images of life after death.

While this understanding of the life-death cycle in no way promises *individual* rebirth, it places every individual in a context that promises continued birth of life in general, a promise that gives each individual a role in a continuing drama larger than any single consciousness. Women lucky enough to experience giving birth at this level of intensity gain entry into a sacred realm through the process of child-bearing itself. For them, no artificially created rituals are needed. They themselves experience firsthand what most humans feel only at a remove. At this level, a woman is truly one with the most elemental of all powers, the powers of death and creation.

REBIRTH

Just as birth and death are often mythically interconnected, the two are also frequently associated with rebirth. Common to many cultures, the intricate pattern that turns the death-birth childbirth complex into rebirth would appear to celebrate birth and counteract negative patriarchal connotations. Unfortunately, this is not entirely the case. Historically, rebirth is almost invariably envisioned as coming through a man; thus, it often minimizes or even altogether eliminates women's role.

Many traditional cultures consider rebirth necessary for individuals to become fully "human," usually meaning fully male. Young men in premodern cultures typically endure ordeals culminating in ritual rebirth from their male elders, as in the Hindu rite of *Upanayama:* "When the teacher receives the [Brahmanical disciple] . . . he places him as a foetus inside (of his body). He carries him for three nights in his belly: when he is born the gods gather about to see him."[33]

Yet, even as the Brahmanical concern for rebirth overtly negates the original model of birth from a woman, it nonetheless covertly reinforces maternal child-bearing through appropriation. This circumstance is also apparent in the well-documented case of male "birthing," dramatized in the mystery cult that celebrates the mythic rebirth of Dionysus from the thigh of his father, Zeus. According to classicist Jane Harrison, followers of Dionysus, in their rituals, chant this birth from a male mother: "Come, O Dithyrambos, enter this my male womb." She adds, "The child [Dionysus] is to be born anew, not of his mother Semele, but of his father Zeus."[34]

Some of the specifics of the Dionysiac mysteries further illustrate their capacity to appropriate and alter women's childbearing. The Dionysiac, or Bacchic, mysteries of the Roman age featured an oblong winnowing basket, commonly used as a baby cradle, filled with fruit surrounding a cloth-covered, erect phallus. In this dramatic initiatory image the phallus usurps the baby's place as the male birth giver appropriates the mother's. Of the various elements associated with Dionysiac festivals, two are particularly significant: blood and enactment of a *hieros gamos*. Blood not only symbolizes the dismemberment of Dionysus and the red wine associated with him, it also connotes the menstrual and birth-giving blood of women's mysteries. And the sacred marriage of the festival queen, given as wife to Dionysus, ritualizes the generation of new life.

The male appropriation merely implicit in Dionysiac rebirth imagery even more prominently characterizes initiations into *Männerbünde*, secret male warbands common to such geographically distant Indo-European cultures (c. 3500–700 B.C.E.) as India, with its Ksatriya, and Germany, with its beserkers. *Männerbünde* reveal some peculiarly distorted connections between childbirth and the common initiatory practice of ritualized homosexual intercourse. Such ritualized homosexuality, also found among Australian and Native American tribes and in various Pacific, African, and Asian cultures, turns the fertility marriage into a very different ritual with absolutely no room for women or childbearing.

Of various institutionalized types of homosexuality—age-structured, gender-reversed, and role-specialized—only the age-structured form applies to *Männerbünde*. Best known to contemporary readers from the ancient Greeks, age-structured homosexuality formed part of Dorian (ca. 800 B.C.E.) initiatory practices. At the start of the ceremony, a Dorian boy would be ritually captured for a member who would then become his older lover, replicating the mythic incidents of the capture of the beautiful youths Ganymede and Khrysippos, respectively, by Zeus and Laios, the father of Oedipus in Euripides' tragedy *Khrysippos* (411–409 B.C.E).[35]

Instead of recognizing woman's life-giving power, as when Zeus gave birth to Dionysus, in this homosexual ritual the androcentric power *aretē* predominates. *Aretē* denotes a warrior-athlete's skill, strength, and heroic valor, qualities for which the warrior willingly sacrifices his life.[36] Through the love relationship of man and boy, the *aretē* of the older passes on to the younger, much as nourishment passes by means of the placenta from mother to fetus.

An exception to the common patriarchal pattern in which male rebirth supersedes female childbirth occurs in Judaism, where childbirth is considered very important. Yet, while women are expected and encouraged to have children, only men are specifically enjoined to do so. More precisely, they are commanded to have at least two. According to the school of Shammai, these two were to be males; according to the school of Hillel, whose decision held sway, they were to be a male and a female, with the couple thus reproducing themselves. Especially relevant to the translation of childbirth into rebirth is the ceremony of *brit milah*, ritual circumcision, from which women are excluded. One can argue that in some way this ceremony, by creating a bond between father and son, between all Jewish men and God, "takes" boys from their mothers, thereby superseding the significance of the mother-son bond created through pregnancy and childbirth in much the same way that initiation rites of rebirth do.[37]

The search for a better way of existing in the world by means of initiatory rebirth is universal. Mircea Eliade and other comparative religionists have pointed out that an outstanding feature of mythical premodern thought is the belief that what happened at the beginning of time is sacred. Divine forces created everything from the earth to the plants, animals, and humans that inhabit it to the processes of human life itself. Because it is human, what happens ever after is a necessarily flawed recapitulation of those original events. As Eliade says, "This 'sacred history'—mythology—is exemplary, paradigmatic: not only does it relate how things came to be, it also lays the foundations for all human behavior and all social and cultural institutions.''[38] Given this logic, whereby the original event is forever exemplary, a crucial question in attempting to retrieve childbirth has to be, Why, then, if this is so, is childbirth in *its* original form—that is, from a woman's body—not more venerated?

The accepted answer, repeated throughout the history of patriarchy, is apparent in this excerpt from Eliade's words:

> through initiation the candidate passes *beyond the natural mode* [emphasis added]— the mode of the child—and gains access to the cultural mode; that is, he is introduced to spiritual values. . . . It could almost be said that, for the primitive world, it is through initiation that men attain the status of human beings; before initiation, they do not yet fully share in the human condition precisely because they do not yet have access to the religious life.[39]

But these words make sense only in an androcentric mode of thinking. From a gynecocentric perspective, the words are *secondary* to a "truth" from which they originally derive. Childbirth is a biological function that provides women with a natural means of experiencing sacrality. Through all its associated conditions—conception, pregnancy, and giving birth—a woman functions in a curiously twofold way. This makes her experience simultaneously representational and symbolic. It is both the actual occurrence itself and a replaying of a highly significant event enacted millions of times before.

What is so surprising, to a gynecocentric way of thinking, is that androcentric thought readily seizes upon childbirth as a metaphor, but then immediately distorts it for its own purposes. Although the desire for appropriation points to the great importance of the image, the *way* childbirth is reinterpreted undercuts the positive impulse. Thus, in countless myths and rituals of initiation, it is birth from the male that counts, not birth from the female. In fact, the latter is typically construed as inferior, if not outright "bad."

Underlying these rituals is a pattern of beliefs centering around the idea that this world, the world of nature into which we are all born, is somehow lacking. Biblically, this theme appears in the Genesis story of the Fall. But because of the disobedience of the first humans, the original paradise, where everything created was "very good," was forever lost to us in our earthly, mortal form. Humanity is left, as we respectively give birth in pain or toil all our days, with only the memory of that original, far better place.

This image of some other place, not here and now, but then and there, totally distinct from the world of nature, occurs in the stories of almost every culture. By recognizing a hope for something better, these stories all implicitly denigrate this material world and, by contrast, elevate an "other," purely imagined world, typically either created or personified by a remote father god such as the Judeo-Christian Yahweh or the Greek god Kronos. Rarely does a female deity occupy this position, for female deities are almost always so closely associated with the earth itself as to make identification with some "other" world virtually impossible. Ordinarily, the separation of this sinful, fallen, imperfect world from that other, perfect one forms part of a larger pattern, in which a similar dualism separates humanity by sex: Women are connected with this fallen material world, men with that elevated spiritual one. In this dualistic way of thinking, it is scarcely surprising, then, that men should wish to be reborn. They want to sever all connections with this contaminated world.

Such dreams of self- and world improvement can be looked at in two ways. Surely everyone wants to improve in some way—spiritually, educationally, socially, economically. Furthermore, socially conscious individuals often want to improve living conditions for others as well. Few would denigrate either idea. What is not acceptable, however, from a gynecocentric perspective, is the simultaneous devaluation of what already exists.

Gynecocentrically speaking, it makes no sense for *this* world that we physically inhabit, the world almost universally connected in myths and philosophical systems to "woman," nature, and physical birth, to be consistently denigrated throughout much of patriarchal history while some *other* world, of which no one has actual, verifiable experience—dreams and visions excepted—is touted as better. Of course, that imagined other world is a wish fulfillment. And males, biologically excluded from the childbearing so intimately connected with the material world, have historically been most prone to theorize about that better world. More readily accessible to males, that other world typically excludes females, whether in Roman Catholic banishment of women from the secrets of the priesthood or in archaic male initiation mysteries such as those of the Australian Kurnai, which must never be revealed to women: "You must never tell this. You must not tell your mother, nor your sister." [40] From an androcentric perspective, of course, such emphasis makes perfect sense, for in *that* world it is men who most often become gods. The Satapatha Brahmana (3.1.1.8), for instance, clearly states, "He who is initiated approaches the gods and becomes one of them." [41]

But not all rebirth focuses so exclusively on a theoretical other world. A contemporary variant, currently popular with New Age adherents is "rebirthing." Rebirthing is a human growth movement which, according to its leading U.S. proponents, Leonard Orr and Sondra Ray, grew out of a retreat Orr conducted in 1974, although he did not actually invent this practice. [42] Being rebirthed may or may not involve immersion in water, "dry births" being common now that Orr and other rebirthers have decided that "conscious breathing," not water, effectively counteracts the "birth trauma" occasioned mainly by suddenly breathing air instead of amniotic fluid. [43] The purpose of rebirthing is "to remember and reexperience one's birth; to relive physiologically, psychologically, and spiritually the moment of one's first breath and thereby release the trauma it caused." [44]

Personal accounts from people who have been rebirthed illustrate the experience and subjectively show how the practice continues implicitly to blame women for an originally imperfect birth. Here is an excerpt from a long rebirthing story told by a man named Garry:

> Back on the waves and troughs I have the sudden realization that I am no longer in control. I look around. It's true. No oars, no paddles, no outboard. I'm breathing in a rich deep rhythmic racehorse pant and I'm totally out of control. I couldn't stop this if I wanted to. A moment of panic flashes by. . . . I'm approaching

the rapids. I'm nearing the falls and there isn't any goddamned thing I can do. Suddenly I know I'm going to die and I'm mighty pissed about it all. My breathing has reached high gear. My back arches up in a paroxysm of pain and anger. My throat clamps down and instinctively I gape, my mouth wide open. . . . I'm dying. . . . Confusion, bewilderment. Followed by oblivion. I arch up in one final glorious spasm. No pictures. No emotions. No thoughts. My last conscious memory is the dying climactic strains of Wagner's Love-Death theme from *Tristan und Isolde*. Then it's over.[45]

Despite the representative negativity toward childbearing women latent in Garry's account, some women are nonetheless using rebirthing to create their own twist on the procedure. They do so by being rebirthed during pregnancy or labor, or both, ideally in tandem with their mates. The practice is becoming more common as New Age beliefs filter into the culture at large. Quite apart from the assumed gains to both mother and father, the preborn is thought to benefit as well. One of the interesting twists here is that infant benefit is postulated on the grounds that the birth trauma results as much from psychic contamination from the parents' collective birth traumas—greater emphasis, however, still being placed on that of the birthing mother—as from the preborn's own experience. Consequently, the infant's birth trauma does not result solely from its own mother's body. It also comes about partly because one or both parents retain unresolved images from their births. More important, rebirthing will supposedly stop the endless chain of traumatic births.

In a still more promising variation for recreating childbirth, rebirthing is also being used to expunge mothers' negative associations from earlier childbearing experiences. Rebirthing is being transformed into a vehicle for positive woman-centered change. This altered usage of rebirthing means that a mother need no longer be a passive victim of androcentric animus. Instead, she can discard her own negative birth-related experiences and move on.

What follows is an example of a rebirthing ritual as it is used in labor. In this instance, the ritual was designed to allay the fears of a second-time mother whose first birthing experience resulted in a cesarean delivery after more than 29 hours:

Rima [the rebirther] put a tall candle on the floor, and we all made a circle around it, and, at Rima's direction, we started stating our fears, one by one, and then throwing them into the fire to symbolically release them. Everyone present participated, and the fact that Rima, Steve, and Zak [both also rebirthers] were so unselfconscious and natural about the whole thing made it easier for me not to feel silly about throwing things I couldn't see into a tiny flame.

The ritual was very cathartic, especially for me, because one of the fears I had was that I couldn't communicate with Robert [her husband], that he would think I was being ridiculous during labor and wouldn't support me.

But when he started doing the ritual like everyone else, and stating his own fears, I felt a sudden rush of openness between us. After the ritual was over, I went to him crying, and he really opened up to me and held me for a long time, just standing there in the living room in our magic circle.[46]

This account vividly contrasts with the previous story of Garry and the more traditional images of rebirth common to myth and religion. Traditional images, typical of patriarchal cultures as a whole, do not focus on *women's* power. Furthermore, they emphasize birth altered to become *male* birthing. In this woman's account, the only alteration involves cleansing past birth-related fears and negative associations. This changes both the emphasis and the purpose. Furthermore, unlike many patriarchally influenced rebirths, this one, like those of the New Age rebirthing movement in general, is not geared towards some other world. Instead, it is intended to make life in this world better. For women able to overlook the extreme fervor, terminology, and beliefs of rebirthing advocates, rebirthing techniques may help to ritually reconstruct childbirth.

SEPARATION: CUTTING THE CORD AND EXPELLING THE PLACENTA

Shortly after every child is born, two very important procedures must be performed: the umbilical cord must be severed and the placenta must be safely expelled or removed. These are essentially two parts of the same process whereby baby and mother are physically separated. Of the two, severing the umbilical cord has generally assumed greater symbolic import in Western cultures. The process is, after all, the one that visibly and irrevocably changes the infant into a physically separate individual no longer attached to its own private life support system. As with most childbirth-related images, however, these two interrelated separation processes are not unambiguous. Being physiologically necessary but psychologically painful, cord cutting comes metaphorically to signal both achievement and loss. The loss involved often reflects negatively on the mother, who is stereotypically castigated for "not letting go." Furthermore, cord cutting is one of the common metaphors of childbirth which, like the death-rebirth motif, so continuously repeats itself in the lives of both mother and child that it cannot be ignored or avoided. This image therefore plays a crucial role in reinterpreting childbirth. Some women describe their grief at the cord cutting, which foreshadows countless future separations, as an "empty womb feeling." As Simone de Beauvoir says, "The newly empty and now flabby belly symbolizes the now 'lost,' separate baby: Some women suffer from the emptiness they now feel in their bodies: it seems to them that their treasure has been stolen. . . . There is an astonished melancholy in seeing him outside, cut off from her. And almost always disappointment."[47]

A woman who reacts this way may also subsequently mourn each developmental stage starting with her child's first word, on to its first day of school, and through the many steps leading to permanent departure from home. Some maternal sadness at these repeated cuttings is inevitable. But how a woman handles them matters enormously, for her response affects the developing selfhood of her child. In each cutting, the child is fighting for its separate existence while the mother, if she opposes it, is fighting for the close, symbiotic quality of their previous relationship. Feminist theorist Carol Gilligan's work suggests why mothers often fail, from a patriarchal perspective, with these necessary cord cuttings.

Gilligan asserts that whereas male-biased developmental theories value separate selfhood, a relational model of selfhood accords more with women's experience.[48] As with other aspects of childbearing, a mother's struggle to separate from her child partly involves the mother's being ignored. Although the cord connects *two* people, its religio-cultural significance often features only the baby.

Such ritual focus on the infant is readily apparent in most premodern cultures' disposal of cord and placenta, either of which can house the child's separable soul. What happens to cord or placenta therefore affects the child's whole life. Consequently, proper disposal is critical. In this regard, both "connect" exclusively to the child. How both might also affect the mother's life is typically overlooked. For example, when a high-status New Zealand Maori baby arrives, an attendant first severs its umbilicus with a sharp stone of flint or obsidian typically handed down in the family for just this purpose. Then she ties it off, smears it with oil, and applies a bandage of special bark from the hohi tree before placing it over the umbilicus and covering both with a large beltlike bandage.[49] The next step entails a special rite in which the severed umbilicus is baptized. Then it is either buried, placed in a rock or tree cleft, inserted into a post, or pushed into a pod and floated on water with an accompanying spoken charm. Some upper-class families even inherit a special plot where all family umbilical cords and placentae are buried in a place sufficiently removed from common activities that no one is likely to walk over them.

Whereas in ritual the cord symbolizes only the child, somewhat paradoxically, in myth, it does not. In myth, the image of the umbilicus, and by analogy the placenta, figures in most cultures as the world navel.[50] Also sometimes depicted as a world tree, this unmovable spot represents an imagined opening between this world we inhabit and the "other" one, presumed home of deity. (For those who have never closely looked at a placenta, it may come as a shock to note that it does indeed closely resemble a branching tree when viewed from the fetal side.) Through this world navel flows the life substance, variously imaged as food, energy, or grace, an obvious metaphoric adaptation of its maternal origin. But instead of providing a needed image of the mother's experienced loss, this imagery instead does something different: It "steals" both placenta and cord from parturient women and turns them into patriarchal symbols connected to a far-off, better world typically ruled by a god or gods, not a goddess or goddesses. Furthermore, when the world navel becomes blocked, stuck, or tangled—all variants of a common patriarchal mythic motif—it is not a mother or midwife who frees it. It is a male hero, perhaps an Oedipus or a Fisher King. In so doing, he invariably saves a people devastated by this blockage wasting their land.

This particular image of childbearing therefore contains a double threat for women. In ritual, the image functions exclusively to represent the life and selfhood of the infant, totally ignoring the interrelationship of the mother with her child. The act of cutting simply excises her from the relationship. At the same time, in myth, where this connective capacity and the maternal side of the equation both remain evident, the image is predictably seized and altered for patriarchal ends. Reframing and reconstructing cord cutting therefore demands concerted effort.

One of the most dramatic ways cord cutting can be reconstructed is through nontraumatic cutting. This is a central tenet of gentle birthing, so central in fact that almost every account of home birthing, whether attended by midwives or husband alone, emphasizes it. Consider, for example, these words of a father who caught his baby in an unassisted home birth: "After waiting a little time for the blood to empty from the cord, I tied and cut it." [51] And a mother, describing her unassisted birth, says: "After a while we checked the cord and saw that it was white and not pulsating. We tied it off and cut it about two inches from the navel." [52] What these representative examples reflect is contemporary understanding derived from Leboyer's insistence that all aspects of childbirthing must be "gentle," that cord cutting is potentially traumatic. Therefore, it must not be rushed.

Concern for appropriate "delivery" of the afterbirth is slightly different. Here it is not the baby but the mother who stands to suffer if the procedure is not well handled. She may bleed to death if the placenta does not come out intact. In her directions to midwives, Ina May Gaskin says: "The thing to remember about delivery of the placenta is not to get impatient or uptight about it because that kind of vibration directly inhibits rushes. The midwives on The Farm have a saying, 'The placenta always comes out.' " [53] These words show Gaskin applying "gentle" rather than interventionist techniques to the mother, not just to the baby as Leboyer does.

Besides "gentle" delivery of the placenta, reframing part of childbirth can occur in a dramatically different way. Some women who give birth at home choose to ritualize disposal of the afterbirth. Like women in many premodern cultures, they cook and eat it. While this practice is unlikely to attract many contemporary women, there are physiological reasons for consuming the placenta. It is full of nutrients and thought to counter postpartum hemorrhaging. [54] Symbolically, such a ritual can become part of any woman's thinking. It represents not just acceptance but also positive celebration of this tangible sign of women's connection to our infants and, more generally, to the life-force. By eating the placenta, or more likely, by eating a specially prepared cake, as some women do, a woman engages in a holy communion that symbolically reconnects her to her now physically separate infant. She thereby highlights the relational aspect of what is otherwise a separation. And for once her celebration ties her to a female image of ultimacy, allowing her to enact a genuinely maternal response to the otherwise painful process of separation.

Reframing the often linked separations of cord and placenta can involve both "gentle" birthing techniques and, in many cases, ritual enactments. But possibly even more significant, at least in the case of the umbilicus, is a highly suggestive theoretical potential. Consider, for instance, the contemporary feminist stress on "difference," which in a feminist context refers primarily to sexual characteristics differentiating female from male and secondarily to a host of other differences— racial, economic, social, and linguistic—beyond the scope of this book. The idea, developed theoretically, is drawn from two distinct sources, the French linguist Ferdinand de Saussure and the Freudian revisionist psychoanalyst Jacques Lacan. Lacan contends that "patriarchal order is represented by the phallus and language is *phallocentric* or structured around the controlling centre of the symbolic phallus. . . . Male identity is constructed in positive terms as the norm, female identity in negative ways as the 'other,' as lacking a phallus and thus negatively differentiated."[55] But it may be that thinking about difference based on presence or absence of a penis, the physical source of the symbolic phallus, is not primary. Recent writing by the German physician Hans Rausch, in pre- and perinatal psychology, suggests a different source. Rausch argues that "the castration complex defined by Freud as Oedipal is not the primary origin of the fear of losing the phallic sex organ . . . but is . . . the consequence of the too early loss of the umbilical cord.[56] Like others such as Grof, Verny, and Chamberlain, working in pre- and perinatal psychology, Rausch believes preborns possess feelings, body ego, consciousness, and sensory organs. He therefore reasons that it is not fear of losing the *penis* that constitutes the primal human body loss fear—a theory always problematic for women anyway—but rather the traumatic loss of the umbilicus! The idea is extremely compelling, although Rausch does not pull his material together in a fully systematic way. Following the direction he suggests, however, the male emphasis on the penis then would not be primary at all but derivative. The primary "signifier" would then be the universal one of the umbilicus! Instead of being based on distinctions between male and female, the issue becomes the difference between self and mother, an area many thinkers, feminist and otherwise, have explored but not, to my knowledge, with specific reference to the symbolic importance of the umbilicus.

Reframing cord cutting and, to a more limited extent, removal of the placenta, along the lines suggested here, holds great promise for also reframing a major psychological theory of child development. This could be a significant shift in moving from phallocentric to gynecocentric theorizing.

9 The Postpartum Period

In the weeks and months immediately following childbirth—called the postpartum period or the fourth trimester—a woman typically experiences intense mood swings. These result from a combination of hormonal changes, confusion (particularly after a first baby), exhaustion, and isolation from adults and accustomed professional responsibilities. Mild "blues" afflict most women; extreme emotional disturbance does not. A seldom acknowledged contributing factor to the severe depression that devastates some women is displacement from our own birth-giving experience. Being cast out of the picture is enormously harmful, not only for a mother but for her child and, ultimately, for society as a whole. Devaluing a role most cultures outwardly profess to admire only heightens the covert antichild sentiments in our complex society.

By contrast, lactation and bonding, two other major features of the postpartum period, are positive experiences that often allow women to connect with the sacred nature of the childbearing experience. The importance of these two tightly interlinked images for reframing childbirth cannot be emphasized enough. Not just for women but also for men and children, these images possess great potential.

DISPLACEMENT

The sadness a woman may feel at the cutting of her baby's cord often intensifies between the second and fourth days after delivery, when she typically experiences a mild to severe depression:

> Immediately after the birth of my first baby I felt high and exhilarated. But that night I got sad. I cried all night long. During the next few days I lay on my bed thinking of how I would kill myself. . . . I felt like I'd never feel anything again but this incredible despair, that it would never end. . . . I don't know why I had these dreams and impulses. I have a happy marriage and it was a wanted pregnancy.[1]

Many factors contribute to this condition: the transformational crisis occasioned by pregnancy, labor, and delivery; constant fatigue; difficulty in coping with a child; changes in life style; social pressures; and hormonal changes. These factors, separately or combined, can create havoc with a postpartum woman's psyche. But these tensions are usually released fairly quickly during the so-called normal post-partum blues, which last only a few days. There may be, however, indifferent or negative family and social responses to a new mother's status and her central role in childbearing. Instead of focusing on her and the stages of labor and delivery, which demand so much of her, attention may immediately center on her child. Such a shift harms both mother and child by setting a lifelong pattern in which the mother is essentially effaced, her child perhaps spoiled as the object of undue attention.

The most familiar of all such woman-effacing births in Western culture must be that of Jesus. Despite the elaborate myth surrounding it—the shepherds, the stable, the wise men, the animals, the star in the East—Mary's part is ignored, although popular tradition proffers its own nonphysical counterpart in stories of her immaculate conception and perpetual virginity. Luke 2:1–7, for example, the only Gospel to give even a tiny bit of the birth story, passes over Mary's child-bearing like this:

> In those days a decree went out from Caesar Augustus that all the world should be enrolled. This was the first enrollment, when Quirinius was governor of Syria. And all went to be enrolled, each to his own city. And Joseph also went up from Galilee, from the city of Nazareth, to Judea, to the city of David, which is called Bethlehem, because he was of the house and lineage of David, to be enrolled with Mary, his betrothed, who was with child. And while they were there, the time came for her to be delivered. And she gave birth to her firstborn son and wrapped him in swaddling cloths, and laid him in a manger, because there was no place for them in the inn.

What matters in this account is not the perinatal experiences of Mary but only their outcome—her child. In a certain sense, of course, it is always the child who matters in childbirth, but here, from a gynecocentric point of view, the emphasis is clearly skewed. Whereas in pre-Christian stories portraying the births of Divine Children, the mother, as a great goddess figure, receives equal or even greater prominence, in the canonical Christian birth story she is almost totally ignored, her status reduced to that of receptacle for the divine impregnation. Totally gone is any recognition of the mother's once-dominant goddess role. Even stories built around the prominent Old Testament theme of babies born to seemingly barren women such as Rebekah, the wife of Isaac, always center on the child, despite the miraculous nature of birth in such a circumstance. Instead, both the mother and her experience essentially vanish, resulting in the nearly universal motif of the miraculous birth of a Divine Child. Popular emphasis on Mary's special status as the one woman able to give birth without sacrificing her virginity could be interpreted as restoring the mother to her rightful prominence.[2] But Mary's per-petual virginity scarcely does justice to the physical process of childbearing. Thus, the applicability of Mary's popular elevation is difficult to connect to real wom-en's experiences.

A currently popular, similar diminishment of women's role occurs in the New Age idea that "Divine Children" or "Great Ones," as they are often called, choose to come to earth from time to time when they feel their presence is needed to help bring about a "New Age": "A whole new order of beings is incarnating on Earth. . . . They are coming into the human forms of our children, our infants, our unborns, our fetuses, our yet-to-be borns. They are coming to speed up the process of planetary evolution."[3] As with the Christian story of the Divine Child, Jesus, New Age manifestations deemphasize the mother and focus almost exclusively on the child.

Quite apart from mythical and New Age emphases on the Divine Child archetype, an ordinary, nonmythicized woman may find her childbearing experience displaced in other ways. Her mate, family, birth attendants, or even contemporary cultural predilections for professional activities all may threaten her childbearing role. If she is so displaced, her labor seems to net her little. She is ignored, while her infant is separated from her and idolized. The depression caused by such displacement may be exacerbated by jealousy. Maternal jealousy is not that unusual. Psychiatrists underscore the difficulties either parent may experience with infants because of unresolved childhood feelings. For a woman who received little attention during childhood, indifference to her own crucial maternal role may precipitate resentment at the care lavished on her baby. If she felt slighted in favor of her siblings, she may now react ambivalently. On the one hand, here is a child on whom she can exact vengeance; on the other, here is an infant of her own flesh and blood through whom she can vicariously experience the attention she never received. In fact, even a woman not deprived in childhood may resent being eclipsed by her own newborn. And such resentment can further fuel postpartum depression.

Such depression- and resentment-inducing childbirth places women in a terrible double bind. Traditional cultures teach us from infancy that, like it or not, our destiny is motherhood. And yet when we fulfill that destiny, scant notice rewards us. Only when we fail, either by refusal or disability, to achieve motherhood are we noteworthy, and then we are "abnormal." Yet the norm of motherhood makes us anomalous when our birth giving is ignored. What should be a kind of miracle is reduced to a routine, demanded by culture and husband alike.

Theoretically, few contemporary Western women should be affected by this minimalization of childbearing. But this is not so. It may even be women ourselves who most deeply assimilate this denigrating view. The sharp dichotomy between "significant" professional activities and "insignificant" childbearing automatically made by many women reflects the influence and espousal of a demeaning patriarchal view of childbearing. This does not mean that all women should be mothers any more than it means that all women should be professionals: It means *both* choices should be freely recognized for their differing kinds of meaning.

Detrimental beliefs that labor and delivery signify little in and of themselves reinforce two very different gender-based value systems. In the historical separation of women's work from men's, women's is trivialized and men's valued. The worth given to work in our culture reflects the status of whichever sex typically performs it. And as this entire book seeks to point out, the history of women's reproductive labor is rife with examples of *male* preeminence, even in this sphere where the work can only be performed by women.

To automatically accord less importance to whatever a woman does is both insulting and suspect. How better to denigrate women's childbearing work than to ignore it? If men do not acknowledge women's role, concentrating instead on *male impregnation* and *its* eventual outcome—babies—then they can ignore their own comparative lack of intimate involvement, for who wants to perform something so little valued (i.e., the labor of childbirth) that it scarcely receives mention? Sadly, some women respond in the same way to the labor of childbearing: "No, I *could* do it all right, but who would *want* to? It's like—it's like having a tooth out or something. You can do it and it's not going to kill you, but why would you want to if you didn't have to?"[4] Some women who choose childlessness associate motherhood with incompetence.[5] To whatever extent even women who do give birth share this attitude, they are bound to feel some threat to their self-esteem, making postpartum depression likely.

The idea, espoused by some feminists, that childbirth is insignificant actually reflects the familiar patriarchal devaluation of women's role in childbearing. Some feminist theorists have even seen women's bodies as tyrannous, an opinion long promulgated by patriarchal thought.[6] Instead of accepting patriarchal norms, which selectively value the labor of *pro*duction while disvaluing that of *re*production, we can distinguish them nonhierarchically. Why must one kind of labor supersede another? Why should the virtues of work be touted, the labor of childbearing belittled? As long as the two are construed this way, women struggling with the issue of work versus family are consigned to feelings of displacement and depression.

Such questions point to a second issue created by the common view that childbearing is insignificant. Much productive labor is valued because it requires individual talent; not everyone can teach topology or cook pasta with pancetta and peas. Such tasks gratify the ego, allowing the performer to proudly say, "*I* did it." By contrast, how many people connect talent to pregnancy and childbirth (although infertile women may well believe some missing "talent" is involved). Fortunately, some people, such as obstetrician Paul Grover, are rethinking this issue: "When that baby looks at his mother and father and appears to perceive them intelligently, their immediate, instinctual response is to tell themselves: 'We've done well.' "[7] As these words suggest, the hard, creative work of pregnancy, labor, and delivery should not be ignored. Thinking otherwise denies the importance of the very secret of life. Ironically, the many voices in our culture that cover up an antiwoman stance by claiming to be "pro-family" merely reverse a *truly* pro-life stance. As long as "pro-family" inverts its supposed meaning by trying to keep women in "their place," our culture will continue to displace childbearing women, putting them in a double bind from which prolonged postpartum depression appears to represent almost the only escape. In that condition, the sacred potential of childbearing appears remote indeed.

How, then, can this still common tendency to eclipse women even in our supposed sphere be countered or reframed? One of the best answers, fortunately, forms a natural part of most childbearing situations. The very same hormones that are partially responsible for postpartum depression also help trigger the mechanism whereby the breasts fill with milk. As the next section shows, two often closely connected aspects of the fourth trimester—lactation and bonding—oppose the displacement some women experience during their own childbearing. As with so many negative images and behaviors long associated with childbearing, displacement involves yet another form of separation and isolation. In fact, one way of construing it is as a separation of mother and child so complete that the mother is virtually removed from the picture. By contrast, bonding and lactation both represent reconnection. As we will see, they epitomize a powerful means for countering the depression-inducing condition whereby some women are essentially excluded from their own childbearing experience.

LACTATION AND BONDING

A sharp contrast to the extreme separation experienced by a mother displaced in childbirth is provided by imagery including *both* mother and child. A mother is often depicted holding or suckling her infant; often their eyes are locked in mutual admiration. Such imagery, recognizably religious when it shows Mary and Jesus, also appears in many a family photo. Whether the context is sacred or secular, mother and child together touch a deep chord in most of us. Perhaps the combined image triggers buried recollections of our own infant bonding.

Bonding is the term generally used to describe the all-important mother-child attachment. (The whole idea of bonding has been challenged by a 1993 study by Diane Eyer.)[8] It starts immediately after birth, although some researchers now place it even earlier, in the uterine stage. Bonding is much like imprinting, a phenomenon first identified by ethnobiologist Konrad Lorenz with ducks and geese in the 1930s, by which newborn animals form an irreversible attachment to the first moving thing they see after birth. Like imprinting, bonding appears to be partly instinctual. Knowledge about it comes largely from experiments by Marshall H. Klaus and John H. Kennell conducted on hundreds of newborns and their parents, which demonstrated that hormones released in the last stages of labor heighten a mother's awareness and thus make her particularly receptive to her baby while it is being born.

During a child's early years, bonding continues as a form of communication between mother and child: "What we see in the evolution of the human bond is a language between partners . . . in which messages from the infant are interpreted by his mother and messages from the mother are taken as signals by the baby. This early dialogue of 'need' and 'an answer to need' becomes a highly differentiated signal system in the early months of life; it is, properly speaking, the matrix of human language and of the human bond itself."[9]

Yet like so much else related to childbearing, even bonding has not always been readily accessible to women. Standard Westernized hospital practices up through the 1970s often worked against it, despite the persuasive findings of scientists such as Swedish researcher Peter Umea, who suggests that the longer a mother is kept from her child after its birth, the more difficult it is for her and her infant to bond. In light of these findings, most medical personnel now admit the need for private time for the mother (and the father) to be alone with the baby very soon after its birth. To assume that, because her infant has been inside her womb, a mother fully knows her child, and vice versa, is not entirely warranted. Time is required for each to grow comfortable with the other in their newly separate states. After all, despite the physical closeness of their relationship during the previous nine months, they remain in some ways strangers. Just exactly "who" the other is continues to be partly a mystery.

The extremely deep, partially unconscious nature of this essential bonding process is apparent in the following account:

> I heard the nursery door open and a crying baby being brought out to the mother. My uterus clamped down as it had when I heard my newborn's first cry. My breasts tingled and there was a definite gush of blood from my uterus which came from the contraction caused by the sound of the crying baby. When I realized that this was the first baby being brought out I thought it must be a baby belonging to someone else and would be going down to the other end of the ward, but with another sound of that cry my uterus again clamped down and I felt complete bewilderment and a sense of demand for my baby. Within an instant he was being brought in to me by a different nurse. My body had known this child to be mine. . . .
>
> I feel that when a woman first sees and hears her child at the moment of birth—which is another kind of consciousness—that she is bound to her baby already in a capacity beyond what I think we are willing to admit. I feel this is part of our survival.[10]

The closeness of the bonding connection described here is accentuated for women who choose to breast-feed. In this case, too, patriarchal attitudes frequently intervene negatively, causing women to stop nursing or to feel guilty if they continue. An early 1990s case in point is the fate of the unpopular "Today Show" host, Deborah Norville, whose "fateful decision to breast-feed her newborn son in front of a *People* magazine photographer was the last straw. You'd have thought the woman had just posed for *Hustler,* so outraged was the network's reaction."[11] While lack of immediate postpartum bonding time is not ideal, it does not ordinarily set an irreversible lifelong pattern. By contrast, when women are discouraged from breast-feeding, that decision cannot be reversed. Once a woman's milk has dried up, it does not normally come back, leaving her no option but to bottle-feed. Nowadays, negative attitudes toward nursing are not as explicit as they were in midcentury, but even a woman who is not told by family, friends, or medical personnel that nursing is inappropriate and who is fully determined to breast-feed still requires overt encouragement. Nursing, though natural, is not easy. Until a mother's milk flow is well established, her baby may be constantly hungry, and in hospital settings that limit feeding times to set hours—typically every four if that practice is followed—most infants require supplementary feedings. But once a pattern of supplements is started, a mother's task becomes that much harder. Because milk flows faster from a bottle, most babies find it harder, by contrast, to suck at the breast. Consequently, a baby may not try hard enough, thus decreasing its mother's milk supply. In turn, chances of breast-feeding failure are intensified. Not only is the frustrated breast-feeder denied yet another component of her own childbearing experience, she feels inadequate as well. Here is something she "should" be able to do without effort, yet she cannot do it. By extension, she may feel, "I cannot even learn to nurse; how can I possibly learn to mother appropriately?"

Frequently antinursing biases reflect "the deep disgust many members of our contemporary society feel toward all body secretions. . . . There remains a deep unshaken emotion that a nipple, with its profusion of secretions, must be soaped or otherwise tampered with. Several other lactation rituals are similarly harmful to milk secretion—and similarly, in spite of objective evidence to the contrary, they continue to be practiced.[12] Instead of being viewed as a miraculous substance, breast milk is often categorized as "dirty" along with sweat and excrement. A tragic twist on this theme emerged a few months before the 1992 furor over the danger to women of breast implants. In a June 2, 1991, article, the *New York Times* reported that a cancer-causing chemical had been discovered in the milk of a nursing mother who had breast implants covered with polyurethane foam.[13] When news of this sort breaks, a nursing mother is not seen as participating in a communion through which she bestows her life-giving substance on her child. Instead, she appears to be harming her child, sometimes even performing a "dirty," shameful act:

> Viva, a closet nurser, was confronted by a friend who was "horrified to find Emma (Viva's daughter) still sucking tit at fifteen and a half months." Persuaded to wean the baby immediately, Viva sought medical help. . . . Appalled by the "obscene" spectacle of a sixteen-month-old fondling her mother's nipples right in front of him, [the pediatrician] prescribed a breast pump. Viva described the aftermath: "The next day was again sheer hell. . . . Big drops of milk were seeping out and soaking my T-shirt. . . . Emma looked longingly at the breast nearest her head and burst into tears. There seemed to be no reason at all to wean her. . . . What if I never had another child and would never again experience a baby sucking milk at my breast? . . . Knowing . . . that I was more concerned about the experience ending for me than for the baby, I felt guilty and selfish on top of everything else."[14]

A potentially beautiful experience has been transformed into something ugly and obscene. Obviously what one person, in this case the pediatrician, considers offensive, another, the nursing mother, does not. Such relativity partially reflects individual opinion. But it is also likely that *ugly* and *obscene* are words applied patriarchally to many experiences that women, allowed to live out our own experiences without patriarchal mediation, might consider beautiful. The discrepancy may have devastating effects on both mother and child.

Occasionally patriarchal hostility against women's capacity to nurse enlarges to become punishment, a reaction, as noted earlier, similar to that aroused in some men by the ability of women to give birth:

I actually had an American doctor come into my room and, when he found me nursing, said: "You know, Mrs. Rose, there's evidence in test animals that breast-feeding causes cancer in the infant." So I looked at him and said: I had a boy! And he said that makes no difference. Can you imagine 24 hours after giving birth having that kind of exchange with someone![15]

All traces of sacredness have been squeezed out of this woman's experience and replaced by guilt.

An especially devastating variation on this theme that nursing is ugly or obscene sometimes even hinders the bonding experience for women who don't nurse. When this happens, what is defined as "obscene" or "aberrant" is not breast milk but the child itself. Any mother who perceives her baby as somehow aberrant or monstrous, even if this "monstrosity" is only in her own mind, may have such difficulty bonding that she rejects her child. This circumstance is mythicized in the figure of the Greek goddess Hera relative to her son Hephaestus. So ugly and puny did Hephaestus appear to Hera that she flung him from Olympus, making him lame. Thus was added a second "monstrosity" to heighten the condition that led his mother to reject him in the first place.

Obviously, such rejection in our contemporary world is by no means always patriarchally induced nor even done deliberately. But given the delicate nature of the entire bonding process, all efforts to encourage bonding need cultural fostering. At the very least, birth attendants should actively support rather than undermine bonding by encouraging new mothers to hold, touch, nurse (if they desire), and cherish their newborns. The words of a mother, given no warning that she has borne a child with a harelip and cleft palate, indicate just how important the medical attendants' attitude is: "It was a terrible shock to see such a baby; he was like something out of a horror film."[16] How easily this woman's shock could have been lessened with a few judiciously chosen words. Research indicates that parents who are adequately prepared for a disabled child commonly find the actual baby far less terrifying than the fears they have conjured up in their minds. Consequently, their relief that the anomaly is not any worse than it is usually enhances bonding rather than provoking the intense aversion revealed above.[17] This is not to blame others for absence of bonding but to stress how much the surrounding cultural context (in this case strongly represented by the birth attendants) contributes to the process.

Without bonding, the necessary "glue" to attach one generation to the next vanishes, and with it, the ability of the young to develop their full human potential. Furthermore, in its absence, a woman's capacity to mother, hence to enter into a meaningful relationship with her child, is impaired. To reconstruct the powerful image of mother bonded with child is crucial. In this age in which women have increasingly learned how to function in a male-dominated world, but comparatively few men have chosen to learn the complementary pattern, the sacred aspects of our reproductive experience could become extinct.

Far from imprisoning women in a now-obsolescent confinement to hearth and home, the image of mother and child can actually strengthen us. In it, we have a model of relationship at its fundamental level. What seems to be repeatedly ignored is the potentially positive experience for a woman when bonding works. It is not, after all, only the child who benefits, the mother who is "enslaved," as some antinatalist thinking suggests. Quite the contrary, if a mother and child bond positively, this relationship will probably be the closest one she ever experiences or, if her relationship to her own mother was close, a recapitulation of that. Even closeness with her mate may be less intense than this bond. Indeed, bonding, which exemplifies the erotic side of childbearing, is one of the most positive of all life-affirming symbols. In the words of one mother:

> On the third morning I was sitting in bed, nursing Rufus, and looking down at his beautiful face. His eyes, nose and mouth were perfectly shaped and seemed to be set so very perfectly into his smooth face that I could barely comprehend such great beauty. It seemed an ideal, an archetype of beauty. This image of his face burned itself into my brain. Then suddenly I felt as though I had stepped off a roller coaster and landed, smack, on solid ground again. The labor and birth, the next two days, had been tumultuous. Birth doesn't end when the baby comes out. . . . I realized—Hey, I did it! I wanted to have the baby at home and I read the books to figure out how and then I really did it! It worked! I didn't have to go to the hospital at all; the doctors didn't touch me! Then I realized that if I could do that great thing, perhaps I could do other things as well.[18]

What can possibly be more empowering to a woman than this?

Conclusion

"I felt God creating life through me and I felt that I was God."[1] These words, spoken by one woman to describe her childbearing experience, like other women's reactions we have considered in this book, vividly depict the spiritual nature of childbearing. As such, they epitomize the book as a whole. But some readers may think, This is all well and good, but of what practical value, ultimately, is childbirth viewed as a sacred event? And how do woman-centered reinterpretations benefit society? Furthermore, are ritual reconstructions of childbirth merely late twentieth-century manifestations of inward-looking, individually salvationist religious consciousness? I would answer all these questions with a loud no. Reinterpreting and reritualizing childbirth not only restore to women our natural and deeply spiritual birthright but they also demonstrate possibilities for responding to one of society's most pressing contemporary problems: the plight of our children.

The poverty, broken homes, educational deprivation, low self-esteem, addictions, physical and emotional abuse, and even incest that so many children endure have many causes. But surely one is our culture's implicit devaluation of mothers and children. Despite rhetoric to the contrary, lack of social support services for working mothers and young children reveals where our culture's real priorities still lie, in the "real" world of business and professionalism. Yet if childbirth is truly understood as a sacred experience, then social application can logically follow.

One practical social application of sacred childbearing to the plight of our children is called "visionary obstetrics." The idea comes from pre- and perinatal psychologist David Chamberlain, who suggests a future "where doctors actually receive feedback from babies and the two collaborate in meeting emergencies at birth."[2] Chamberlain bases his prognosis on a thirteen-year study of birth memories, which grew out of unanticipated findings in his practice of hypnosis on clients with various problems.[3]

One of the most striking consistencies of Chamberlain's findings is the way his subjects repeatedly indicate that it is the baby who is in charge of birth. For instance, in his book *Babies Remember Birth,* a subject named Deborah says, "The doctor has black hair and a white coat and he's looking at a tray of instruments. He's turned away from me. I don't think he knows I'm coming out. Somebody better tell him I'm going to come out! I think I'm just going to do it by myself" (p. 152). Nor is it only regressed adult subjects who make such statements. Some of Chamberlain's evidence comes from recollections spontaneously generated by small children, such as a memory revealed by a boy named Jason, who "told his mother that he heard her crying and was doing everything he could to get out" (p. 103). A similar incident is reported from a totally different source, anthropologist Robbie Davis-Floyd, who told me that a two-year-old she knows told his mother, "When I got born, I pushed with my hands and kicked with my feet and I did it, I got out."

A cogent example of what Chamberlain has in mind when he speaks of applying birth memories to a visionary obstetrics comes from Kit, who was 37 at the time Chamberlain hypnotized her. Kit initially consulted Chamberlain for "a mysterious breathing problem involving a heavy feeling in her chest and the inability to get enough oxygen into her system." Under hypnosis, Kit recalls nearly suffocating at birth. Not only does she claim to be aware of what was happening at the time, she recalls trying to communicate with the attending physician. She remembers knowing that her mother was hemorrhaging long before the doctor did. Trying to block the flow of blood with her own body, Kit feared that if she turned herself the way she must to be born, her mother would die. She says:

> There's too much blood all over. Nobody knows it yet. [My mother] is completely filled with it and I'm the only one keeping it from coming out! (sobs)
>
> Ohhh. . . . If I come out and she dies, she'll never know how much I love her! I want to know her. She talked to me a lot before I was born but nobody else knew because they'd think she was silly. . . .
>
> I felt like I was going to drown, and I knew I wasn't supposed to. (sobs) I don't know what I should do. (p. 160)

After she was born, Kit recalls, her mother was transfused. At the time, Kit recalls wishing "they'd hurry up! I'm stiff as a board." When the doctor pushed a breathing tube too far down her throat, Kit "knew" the procedure was wrong and that she was powerless to help him. As she reexperiences the physician's second attempt with a larger tube, she says, "I'm getting a little bit, but it still isn't enough. (Repeated gasps) If he could only get it down a little bit deeper!" At one point—whether in or out of hypnosis Chamberlain does not make clear— Kit remarks that "babies can *communicate* and they don't need words to do this" (pp. 159–61). It is on the basis of repeatedly unearthing such birth memories, combined with testing fetuses for their reactions, that Chamberlain suggests the possibility for a visionary obstetrics. Whether drawn from hypnotized adults or generated spontaneously by preschoolers, such memories, if accurate, go far beyond anything promoted by mainstream science.

If findings such as Chamberlain's do truly reflect preborn capabilities, it would mean that contemporary understandings of childbirth are even more at odds with the sacred potentialities of childbirth—for both mother and child—than has hitherto been suspected. While research of this sort is on the edge of credibility for many people, it nonetheless suggests a powerful practical application for sacred childbirth, based on the intrauterine connection of mother and child. Even for readers who find the idea of such "memories" problematic, just the possibility that preborns may be more capable of responding to their surroundings than is usually assumed holds enormous promise. What a vital new image this is for expanding ideas of childbirth beyond their accustomed boundaries.

Yet some readers may see a problem with the idea upon which visionary obstetrics is based. Examined superficially, birth "memories" in the aggregate suggest a familiar baby-centered interpretation of birth. Yet it is important to reflect that, as with many of the models of childbearing we have discussed, this is only a partial view. The focus can easily be shifted from the baby alone to the combined birth experiences of mother and child. When that happens, a much larger perspective emerges that is critical when applying reinterpreted childbirth to society as a whole. If we think again of the pervasive mind/body split in our culture, it is not hard to see that a variation of this same split typically separates first mother and fetus, then mother and child. What we usually see as separate, however, can just as easily be reconceptualized as a unit. Seen that way, the mother's subjective feeling that *she* is doing all the work of birthing, and the baby's recollected subjective feeling that *s/he* is doing it, need not be opposed. Instead of each memory being analyzed separately and then being set up in a mutually exclusive dualistic pattern, the two can be seen as complementary. The separate memories of each then become two "parts" of a larger whole.

Seeing these birth memories as mutually supportive and interactive counters the kinds of antagonisms that have repeatedly separated mother and child in myth and history right on into the present. Those antagonisms can be re-visioned by turning the two major childbirth players into co-protagonists, rather than antagonists, in this initial drama. Starting off with a nonantagonistic mother-child relationship would certainly obviate feminist criticisms of current relationships, such as Dorothy Dinnerstein's in *The Mermaid and the Minotaur*.[4] And establishing a nonantagonistic mother-child relationship before birth might help prevent some of the terrible psychological problems that trouble our country's children. In turn, if those problems could be prevented, perhaps funding now used to relieve them could be used to prevent some of the devastating social problems that trouble so many of our children after birth—lack of opportunity, lack of education, exposure to drugs, and so on. And if we can also begin applying some of the sacred potential of childbearing through techniques such as visionary obstetrics, then the words with which this Conclusion opened might one day be applicable to all childbearers, whether they are biological or metaphoric: "I felt God creating life through me and I felt that I was God."

NOTES

INTRODUCTION

1. Rebecca Rowe Parfitt, *The Birth Primer: A Source Book of Traditional and Alternative Methods in Labor and Delivery* (Philadelphia, Pa.: Running Press, 1977), p. 8.

2. Andre Droogers, *The Dangerous Journey: Symbolic Aspects of Boys' Initiation among the Wagenia of Kisangani, Zaire* (The Hague and New York: Mouton, 1980), p. 46.

3. Gerda Lerner, *The Creation of Patriarchy* (New York and Oxford: Oxford University Press, 1986), pp. 238–39.

4. The essays in Alice Jardine and Paul Smith, eds., *Men in Feminism* (New York and London: Methuen, 1987), provide a helpful discussion of poststructuralism and feminist theory relevant to this issue.

5. Ann Cornelison, *Women of the Shadows* (New York: Vintage Books/Random House, 1977), p. 132.

6. For further discussion of Stanislav Grof's work and some of the reactions to it, see "Birth Trauma" in chapter 8.

7. David Chamberlain, *Babies Remember Birth: And Other Extraordinary Scientific Discoveries about the Mind and the Personality of Your Newborn* (New York: Ballantine Books, 1988), p. 176.

8. Kenneth Ring, "Near-Death Studies: An Overview," in *The Near-Death Experience: Problems, Prospects, Perspectives,* ed. Bruce Greyson and Charles P. Flynn (Springfield, Ill.: Charles Thomas, 1984), p. 5.

9. Margot Edwards and Mary Waldorf, *Reclaiming Birth; History and Heroines of American Childbirth Reform* (Trumansburg, N.Y.: Crossing Press, 1984), p. 187.

10. Dorothy Dinnerstein, *The Mermaid and the Minotaur: Sexual Arrangements and Human Malaise* (New York: Harper & Row, 1976), p. 28.

11. Dinnerstein, p. 34.

12. Dinnerstein, p. 25.

13. Mary O'Brien, *The Politics of Reproduction,* (Boston: Routledge & Kegan Paul, 1981), p. 8.

14. O'Brien, p. 105. The original is from Hegel, "On Love," in his *Early Theological Writings.*

15. Emily Martin, *The Woman in the Body: A Cultural Analysis of Reproduction* (Boston: Beacon Press, 1987).

16. Sarah Ruddick, *Maternal Thinking: Toward a Politics of Peace* (Boston: Beacon Press, 1989), p. 48.

17. Ruddick, p. 48.

18. See especially Chamberlain on this point.

19. Penelope Washbourne, *Becoming Woman: The Quest for Wholeness in Female Experience* (New York: Harper & Row, 1977), p. 90.

20. Julia Kristeva, "Stabat Mater," in *The Kristeva Reader,* ed. Toril Moi (New York: Columbia University Press, 1986), p. 179.

21. Sylvia Brinton Perera, "The Descent of Inanna: Myth and Therapy," in *Feminist Archetypal Theory: Interdisciplinary Re-Visions of Jungian Thought,* ed. Estella Lauter and Carol Schreier Rupprecht (Knoxville: University of Tennessee Press, 1985).

22. Patricia Reis, *Through the Goddess: A Woman's Way of Healing* (New York: Continuum, 1991), p. 181.

23. Kathryn Allen Rabuzzi, *Motherself: A Mythic Analysis of Motherhood* (Bloomington: Indiana University Press, 1988), pp. 205–6.

24. Marta Weigle, *Creation and Procreation: Feminist Reflections on Mythologies of Cosmogony and Parturition* (Philadelphia: University of Pennsylvania Press, 1989), p. xi.

I. PRECONCEPTION(S)

1. Suzanne Arms, *Immaculate Deception; A New Look at Women and Childbirth in America* (Boston: San Francisco Book/Houghton Mifflin, 1975), p. 144.

2. Frederick Leboyer, *Birth without Violence* (New York: Alfred A. Knopf, 1975), pp. 30–31.

3. See, for example, Emily Martin, *The Woman in the Body: A Cultural Analysis of Reproduction* (Boston: Beacon Press, 1987), and Robbie E. Davis-Floyd, "Birth as an American Rite of Passage," in *Childbirth in America: Anthropological Perspectives,* ed. Karen L. Michaelson (South Hadley, Mass.: Bergin & Garvey, 1988).

4. *Encyclopaedia Britannica,* under "Childbirth," 1961 ed.

5. See, for example, Dawson Church, *Communing with the Spirit of Your Unborn Child* (San Leandro, Calif.: Aslan, 1988).

6. Robbie E. Davis-Floyd, prepublication copy of "The Technocratic Body and the Organic Body: Cultural Models for Women's Birth Choices," in *The Anthropology of Science and Technology,* a special issue of *Knowledge and Society,* vol. 9, ed. David J. Hess and Linda L. Layne (Hartford, Conn.: JAI Press, in press), 21.

7. Davis-Floyd, p. 21.

8. Gena Corea, *The Mother Machine: Reproductive Technologies from Artificial Insemination to Artificial Wombs* (New York: Harper & Row, 1985), p. 170.

9. Corea, p. 39.

10. Quoted in Corea, p. 47.

11. Shulamith Firestone, *The Dialectic of Sex: The Case for Feminist Revolution* (New York: Bantam Books, 1970), p. 238.

12. Deborah Lipp, "Mothering after Incest," in *Mothering* 363 (Spring 1992), p. 119.

I I. CONCEPTION

1. Hesiod, *Theogony,* trans. Norman O. Brown (Indianapolis: Library of Liberal Arts/ Bobbs-Merrill, 1953), p. 56.

2. Karl J. Narr, "Paleolithic Religion," trans. Matthew J. O'Connell, in *The Encyclopedia of Religion,* 1987.

3. For a full discussion of this hypothesis, see Richard E. Leakey and Roger Lewin, *People of the Lake: Mankind and Its Beginnings* (Garden City, N.Y.: Anchor Press/Doubleday, 1978).

4. Plato, *The Symposium,* in *Dialogues of Plato,* trans. Benjamin Jowett (London: Sphere, 1970), 189e–191e.

5. Charles Long, "Cosmogony," in *The Encyclopedia of Religion.*

6. Euripides, *Melanippe the Wise* [Nauck, frag. 484, trans. Gilbert Murray], quoted in Jane Harrison, "Themis," in *Epilegomena to the Study of Greek Religion and Themis: A Study of the Social Origins of Greek Religion* (New Hyde Park, N.Y.: University Books, 1962), p. 463.

7. *Hymns of the Rgveda,* trans. Ralph T. H. Griffith (New Delhi: Munshiram Manoharlal, 1987), Hymn 121.

8. Paul Radin, *The Trickster: A Study in American Indian Mythology* (New York: Schocken Books, 1976), pp. 22–23.

9. Of all subsistence strategies—hunting-gathering, horticulture, agriculture, pastoralism, industrialization, technocracy—pastoralism is the most intensely patriarchal. Men owned

the herd animals, and women symbolically became equated with those animals. As chattels, women also belonged to the men. Because so many of our inherited origin myths come from the Hebrews, our culture could hardly escape those patriarchal influences.

10. Aristotle, *De Mundo,* in *The Basic Works of Aristotle,* ed. Richard McKeon (New York: Random House, 1941), chap. 5, 396b7, refers to this Heraclitean insight by saying:

> Perhaps Nature has a liking for opposites and produces concord out of them and not out of similars, just as for instance she brings male together with female and not with members of the same sex. . . . It was this same thing which was said in Heraclitus the Obscure.

11. Aristotle, *Metaphysics,* in *The Basic Works,* 986a22–25.

12. Aristotle, *Generation of Animals,* trans. A. L. Peck (Cambridge: Harvard University Press; London: Heinemann, 1943), 737a28.

13. For more information on this topic, see Narr.

14. For a helpful overview of Neolithic religion, see Dragoslav Srejovic's entry in *The Encyclopedia of Religion.*

15. Bruce Lincoln, *Emerging from the Chrysalis: Studies in Rituals; Women's Initiation* (Cambridge: Harvard University Press, 1981), p. 80.

16. Sigmund Freud, *The Standard Edition of the Complete Psychological Works of Sigmund Freud,* trans. and ed. James Strachey (London: Hogarth Press, 1953–1974), pp. 29–30.

17. From a Pyramid text, quoted in David Maclagan, *Creation Myths: Man's Introduction to the World* (London: Thames & Hudson, 1977), p. 15.

18. Samuel Taylor Coleridge, *Biographia Literaria; or, Biographical Sketches of My Literary Life and Opinions,* ed. George Watson (London: Dent; New York: Dalton/Everyman's Library, 1971), p. 167.

19. Dawson Church, *Communing with the Spirit of Your Unborn Child* (San Leandro, Calif.: Aslan, 1988), p. 12.

20. June G. Goodfield, *Playing God: Genetic Engineering and the Manipulation of Life* (New York: Random House, 1977), p. 57.

21. David White, "Indian Alchemy," in *The Encyclopedia of Religion.*

22. This material is from Joseph Fletcher, *Morals and Medicine: The Moral Problems of the Patient's Right to Know the Truth; Contraception, Artificial Insemination, Sterilization, Euthanasia* (Boston: Beacon Press, 1954), pp. 104–105.

23. Amy Zuckerman Overvold, *Surrogate Parenting* (New York: Pharos Books, 1988), pp. 59–60.

24. Ellen Lewin, "By Design: Reproductive Strategies and the Meaning of Motherhood," in *The Sexual Politics of Reproduction,* ed. Hilary Homans (Aldershot, England: Gower, 1985), p. 134.

25. George J. Annas, "Baby M: Babies (and Justice) for Sale," *Hastings Center Report* (June 1987): 14.

26. Material on the myth of Balarama is from the *Encyclopedia of Religion.* The connection with the surrogate womb is entirely my own.

27. Andrea Dworkin, *Right-Wing Women* (New York: Perigee Books, 1983), pp. 181–82.

28. Information on the frozen storage of embryos is from the *Wall Street Journal,* 26 September 1989, editorial page, and from E. Peter Volpe, *Test-Tube Conception: A Blend of Love and Science* (Macon, Ga.: Mercer University Press, 1987), pp. 57–62.

29. Volpe, p. 86.

30. Volpe, p. 91.

31. Volpe, p. 95.

32. Aldous Huxley, *Brave New World* (New York: Bantam Books, 1932), p. 3.

33. Volpe, p. 97.

34. *Syracuse Post-Standard,* 9 May 1986, p. 2.

35. Joseph E. Sokoloski and Don P. Wolf, "Laboratory Details in an *in Vitro* Fertiliz-

ation and Embryo Transfer Program," in *Human in Vitro Fertilization and Embryo Transfer*, ed. Don Wolf and James Quigley (New York: Plenum Press, 1984), p. 281.

36. Gwen Davis, "The Private Pain of Infertility," *New York Times Magazine*, December 1987, pp. 106–21.

37. Bobbie Ann Mason, *In Country* (New York: Harper & Row, 1985), pp. 191–92.

III. MIRACULOUS CONCEPTIONS

1. Edward Albee, *Who's Afraid of Virginia Woolf?* (New York: Pocket Books, 1969).

2. G. G. Margolin, *Pathophysiological Processes in Psychosomatic Concepts in Psychoanalysis* (New York: International University Press, 1953, quoted in *Modern Perspectives in Psycho-Obstetrics*, ed. John G. Howells (New York: Brunner/Mazel, 1972), p. 55.

3. Margolin in Howells, p. 60.

4. Peter Barglow and Edward Brown, "Pseudocyesis: To Be and Not to Be Pregnant, a Psychosomatic Question," in Howells, p. 60.

5. Barglow and Brown in Howells, p. 59.

6. Joyce Maynard, "Domestic Affairs," *Syracuse Post-Standard*, 3 December 1985, D-1.

7. S. L. Wykes, "Animal Instincts; Koko Says It's Time for Responsibilities of Motherhood," *Syracuse Post-Standard*, 7 April 1988, D-1.

8. For an interesting and comprehensive discussion of couvade, see Alan Dundes, "Couvade in Genesis," in *Parsing through Customs: Essays by a Freudian Folklorist* (Madison: University of Wisconsin Press, 1987), and the chapter on "Couvade and Parturition" in Marta Weigle, *Creation and Procreation: Feminist Reflections on Mythologies of Cosmogony and Parturition* (Philadelphia: University of Pennsylvania Press, 1989).

9. Sigmund Freud, "Analysis of a Phobia in a Five-Year-Old Boy (1909)," *The Standard Edition of the Complete Psychological Works of Sigmund Freud*, vol. 10 (London: Hogarth Press, 1953–1974), pp. 86–87.

10. Freud, "On the Sexual Theories of Children (1908)," *Standard Edition*, vol. 9, pp. 2–23.

11. Diodorus Siculus, Bibliotheca Historica, 1.80, quoted in Theodore Reik, "Couvade and the Psychogenesis of the Fear of Retaliation," in *Ritual: Psycho-Analytic Studies*, trans. from the 2d German edition by Douglas Bryan; *The Psychological Problems of Religion*, vol. 1 (Westport, Conn.: Greenwood Press, 1946), p. 28.

12. Sir Edward Burnett Tylor, *Researches into the Early History of Mankind and the Development of Civilization* (London: J. Murray, 1870), p. 302.

13. Col. Henry Yule, *The Book of Ser Marco Polo* (London: J. Murray, 1871), Vol. 2, p. 52, quoted in Reik, p. 28.

14. *Aucassin and Nicolete,* trans. Andrew Lang (New York: Holiday House, 1936), p. 89.

15. John Desmond Gimlette and H. W. Thomson, *A Dictionary of Malayan Medicine* (London: Oxford University Press, 1939).

16. W. H. Trethowan, "The Couvade Syndrome," in Howells, p. 73.

17. Otto Rank, *The Myth of the Birth of the Hero, and Other Writings,* ed. Philip Freund (New York: Vintage Books/Random House, 1959).

18. Alan Howard et al., "Traditional and Modern Adoption Patterns in Hawaii," in *Adoption in Eastern Oceania*, Monograph No. 1, ed. Vern Carroll (Honolulu: University of Hawaii Press, 1970), p. 1.

19. Ward H. Goodenough, "Epilogue: Transactions in Parenthood," in Carroll, p. 394.

20. Howard et al., in Carroll, p. 22.

21. William and Joanna Woolfolk, *The Great American Birth Rite* (New York: Dial Press, 1975), p. 197.

22. Woolfolk, p. 197.

23. Wayland D. Hand, *Magical Medicine: The Folkloric Component of Medicine in the*

Folk Belief, Custom and Ritual of the Peoples of Europe and America (Berkeley, Los Angeles, and London: University of California Press, 1980), p. 165.

IV. MISCONCEPTIONS

1. Suzanne Arms, *Immaculate Deception; A New Look at Women and Childbirth in America* (Boston: San Francisco Book/Houghton Mifflin, 1975), pp. 107–108.

2. *New York Times*, 17 May 1992, A-22.

3. Sherry Lynn Mims Jiminez, *The Other Side of Pregnancy: Coping with Miscarriage and Stillbirth* (Englewood Cliffs, N.J.: Prentice-Hall, 1982), pp. 28–29.

4. Jonathan B. Imber, *Abortion and the Private Practice of Medicine* (New Haven and London: Yale University Press, 1986), p. 105.

5. Ina May Gaskin, *Spiritual Midwifery*, 3d ed. (Summertown, Tenn.: Book Publishing, 1990), p. 58.

6. Gaskin, p. 58.

7. Claudia Panuthos, *Transformation through Birth: A Woman's Guide* (South Hadley, Mass.: Bergin & Garvey, 1984), p. 161.

8. *Wall Street Journal*, 29 November 1989, A-1.

9. Margaret Atwood, *Surfacing* (New York: Fawcett/Crest, 1972), pp. 168–69.

10. Magda Denes, *In Necessity and Sorrow: Life and Death in an Abortion Hospital* (New York: Basic Books, 1976), pp. 102–103.

V. PREGNANCY: A NATURAL INITIATION PROCESS

1. Mircea Eliade, *Rites and Symbols of Initiation: The Mysteries of Birth and Rebirth* (New York: Harper & Row, 1958), p. x.

2. Reva Rubin, *Maternal Identity and the Maternal Experience* (New York: Springer, 1984), p. 74.

3. Rubin, p. 75.

4. Bruce Lincoln, *Emerging from the Chrysalis: Studies in Rituals; Women's Initiation* (Cambridge: Harvard University Press, 1981), p. 94.

5. Lincoln, p. 95.

6. A woman from the Onondaga tribe informed me that she comes from a matriarchal culture.

7. Lincoln, p. 95.

8. John G. Howells, "Childbirth Is a Family Experience," in *Modern Perspectives in Psycho-Obstetrics*, ed. John G. Howells (New York: Brunner/Mazel, 1972), pp. 141–42.

9. R. Kumar, "Neurotic Disorders," in *Motherhood and Mental Illness* ed. I. F. Brockington and R. Kumar (London: Academic Press; New York: Grune & Stratton, 1982), pp. 81–82.

10. Grantly Dick-Read, *Childbirth without Fear: The Original Approach to Natural Childbirth* (New York: Harper & Row, 1944), p. 41.

11. Rubin, pp. 48–49.

12. Martin Buber, *I and Thou*, 2d ed., trans. Ronald Gregor Smith (New York: Scribner's, 1958), p. 7.

13. The term *bind-in* is used by Rubin in *Maternal Identity*.

14. Rubin, p. 9.

15. Nancy Friday, *My Mother/My Self: A Daughter's Search for Identity* (New York: Dell, 1977), pp. 270–71.

16. Many childbirth educators stand out. Among the most influential are renowned English anthropologist, reformer, and lecturer Sheila Kitzinger; holistic psychotherapist Gayle Peterson, and Claudia Panuthos, founder and director of OFFSPRING, a comprehensive childbirth counseling center.

17. See Carl Simonton and Stephanie Simonton, *Getting Well Again* (Los Angeles: Tarcher, 1978).

18. Claudia Panuthos, *Transformation through Birth: A Woman's Guide* (South Hadley, Mass.: Bergin & Garvey, 1984), p. 108.

19. Gayle Peterson, *Birthing Normally: A Personal Growth Approach to Childbirth,* 2d ed. (Berkeley, Calif.: Shadow & Light, 1984), p. 28.

20. Patricia Reis, *Through the Goddess: A Woman's Way of Healing* (New York: Continuum, 1991), p. 183.

21. Anne Roiphe, *Torch Song* (New York: Farrar, Straus & Giroux, 1977), p. 205.

22. Michael Czaja, *Gods of Myth and Stone: Phallicism in Japanese Folk Religion* (New York: Weatherhill, 1974), p. 207.

23. Leslie Fiedler, *Freaks: Myths and Images of the Secret Self* (New York: Simon & Schuster, 1978), p. 230.

24. Lincoln, p. 26.

25. Phyllis Chesler, *With Child: A Diary of Motherhood* (New York: Thomas Crowell, 1979), pp. 38–39.

26. *New Yorker,* 11 August 1980, pp. 21–22.

27. Ann Oakley, *The Captured Womb: A History of the Medical Care of Pregnant Women* (Oxford, England: Basil Blackwell, 1984), p. 85.

28. Marshall H. Klaus and John H. Kennell, *Parent-Infant Bonding,* 2d ed. (St. Louis: C. V. Mosby, 1982), p. 67.

29. Roiphe, p. 205.

30. Robbie E. Davis-Floyd, prepublication copy of "The Technocratic Body and the Organic Body: Cultural Models for Women's Birth Choices," in *The Anthropology of Science and Technology,* a special issue of *Knowledge and Society,* vol. 9, ed. David J. Hess and Linda L. Layne (Hartford, Conn.: JAI Press, in press).

31. Freud, *The Standard Edition of the Complete Psychological Works of Sigmund Freud,* vol. 9, trans. and ed. James Strachey (London: Hogarth Press, 1953–1974), p. 114. See also Freud's essay "The Acquisition and Control of Fire," in *Standard Edition,* vol. 22.

32. *Syracuse Post-Standard,* 18 June 1992, A-4.

33. See Davis-Floyd, "Technocratic Body," for a helpful discussion of "having" versus "being" a body.

34. Tamar Lewin, "Pregnant Women Increasingly Fearful of VDT's," *New York Times,* 10 July 1988, p. 19.

35. Thomas R. Verny with John Kelly, *The Secret Life of the Unborn Child* (New York: Simon & Schuster/Summit, 1981), p. 39.

36. Verny, p. 31.

37. Verny, p. 30.

38. Verny, p. 30.

VI. MODELS OF LABOR AND DELIVERY

1. Barbara Katz Rothman, *In Labor: Women and Power in the Birthplace* (New York and London: W. W. Norton, 1982), p. 33.

2. Dr. Pierre Vellay, *Childbirth without Pain,* trans. Denise Lloyd (New York: E. P. Dutton, 1960), p. 170.

3. Sheila Kitzinger, *The New Good Birth Guide* (Harmondsworth, Middlesex, England: Penguin, 1983), p. 95.

4. Dyanne D. Affonso, *Impact of Cesarean Childbirth* (Philadelphia: F. A. Davis, 1981), p. 44.

5. Irwin Chabon, *Awake and Aware: Participating in Childbirth through Psychoprophylaxis* (New York: Delacorte Press, 1966), pp. 157–58.

6. Quoted in Valmai Howe Elkins, *The Rights of the Pregnant Parent* (New York: Schocken Books, 1985), p. 353.

7. Elkins, p. vii.

8. Rayna Rapp, "The Power of Positive Diagnosis: Medical and Maternal Discourses

on Amniocentesis,'' in *Childbirth in America: Anthropological Perspectives,* ed. Karen L. Michaelson (South Hadley, Mass.: Bergin & Garvey, 1988), p. 110.

9. Susan Borg and Judith Lasker, *When Pregnancy Fails: Families Coping with Miscarriage, Stillbirth, and Infant Death* (Boston: Beacon Press, 1981), p. 150.

10. Jackie Pringle, ''Hittite Birth Rituals,'' in *Images of Women in Antiquity,* ed. Averil Cameron and Amelie Kuhrt (Beckenham, Kent: Croom Helm, 1983), p. 133.

11. Pringle, p. 135.

12. Barbara Ehrenreich and Deirdre English, *Witches, Midwives, and Nurses: A History of Women Healers* (SUNY at Old Westbury, N.Y.: Feminist Press, 1973), pp. 12–13.

13. Marta Weigle, *Spiders and Spinsters: Women and Mythology* (Albuquerque: University of New Mexico Press, 1982), p. 127.

14. Ina May Gaskin, *Spiritual Midwifery,* 3d ed. (Summertown, Tenn.: Book Publishing, 1990).

15. Elizabeth Davis, *Heart and Hands: A Midwife's Guide to Pregnancy and Birth,* 2d ed. (Berkeley, Calif.: Celestial Arts, 1987), p. 37.

16. Rahima Baldwin, *Special Delivery: The Choices Are Yours* (Berkeley, Calif.: Celestial Arts, 1979).

17. Michel Odent, *Birth Reborn* (New York: Pantheon Books/Random House, 1984), p. 53

18. Marilyn French, *The Women's Room* (New York: Harcourt Brace Jovanovich, 1978), p. 71.

19. Words of David Kliot, M.D., quoted in Nancy Berezin, *The Gentle Birth Book: A Practical Guide to Leboyer Family-centered Delivery* (New York: Simon & Schuster, 1980), p. 43.

20. See E. Sidenbladh, *Water Babies* (New York: St. Martin's Press, 1982), for a detailed account of Charkovsky's work.

21. Binnie A. Dansby, ''Underwater Birth: The Ultimate Alternative,'' in Thomas R. Verny, ed., *Pre- and Perinatal Psychology: An Introduction* (New York: Human Sciences Press, 1987), pp. 160, 164.

22. Nelle Morton, ''The Dilemma of Celebration,'' in *Womanspirit Rising: A Feminist Reader in Religion,* ed. Carol P. Christ and Judith Plaskow (San Francisco: Harper & Row, 1979), p. 163.

23. Marilyn A. Moran, *Birth and the Dialogue of Love* (Leawood, Kans.: New Nativity Press, 1981), pp. 31, 42.

24. Dorothy Dinnerstein, *The Mermaid and the Minotaur: Sexual Arrangements and Human Malaise* (New York: Harper & Row, 1976), p. 28.

25. Moran, pp. 73–74.

26. Berezin, pp. 53–54.

27. Grantly Dick-Read, *Childbirth without Fear: The Original Approach to Natural Childbirth* (New York: Harper & Row, 1944), p. 272.

28. Robert Bradley, *Husband-coached Childbirth,* 3d ed. (San Francisco: Harper & Row, 1981), quoted in *The Whole Birth Catalog: A Sourcebook for Choices in Childbirth,* ed. Janet Isaacs Ashford (Trumansburg, N.Y.: Crossing Press, 1983), p. 40.

29. Bradley in Isaacs, p. 40.

30. Nathan Cabot Hale, *Birth of a Family: The New Role of the Father in Childbirth* (Garden City, N.Y.: Anchor Press/Doubleday, 1979), pp. 21, 15.

31. Sheila Kitzinger, *Education and Counseling for Childbirth* (New York: Schocken Books, 1979), p. 11.

32. Kitzinger, *Education,* p. 4.

33. Frederick Leboyer, *Birth without Violence* (New York: Alfred A. Knopf, 1975), pp. 24–26.

34. Marjorie Karmel, *Thank You, Dr. Lamaze* (New York: Harper & Row, 1959), pp. 85–86.

35. Odent no longer operates his clinic in Pithiviers; he now attends homebirths in London.

36. Odent, p. 43.

37. Odent, p. 58.
38. Karmel, pp. 43–44.
39. Karmel, pp. 43–44.
40. Sheila Kitzinger, *The Experience of Childbirth,* 4th ed. (Harmondsworth, Middlesex, England: Penguin Books, 1978), p. 143.
41. Karmel, p. 49.
42. Leboyer, pp. 76–77.
43. Odent, pp. 27–28.

VII. PHASES OF LABOR

1. Barbara Katz Rothman, *In Labor: Women and Power in the Birthplace* (New York and London: W. W. Norton, 1982), pp. 259, 260, and 262.
2. See Rothman, pp. 160, 168, and 251–52, for an interesting discussion of this topic.
3. Simone de Beauvoir, *The Second Sex,* trans. and ed. H. M. Parshley (New York: Bantam Books, 1961), pp. 26–27.
4. Margaret Mead, *Blackberry Winter: My Earlier Years* (New York: William Morrow, 1972), quoted in Rebecca Rowe Parfitt, *The Birth Primer: A Source Book of Traditional and Alternative Methods in Labor and Delivery* (Philadelphia: Running Press, 1977), p. 39.
5. Dr. Pierre Vellay, *Childbirth without Pain,* trans. Denise Lloyd (New York: E. P. Dutton, 1960), p. 134.
6. Marshall H. Klaus and John H. Kennell, *Maternal-Infant Bonding* (St. Louis: C. V. Mosby, 1976), p. 48.
7. Isidore Bonstein, *Psychoprophylactic Preparation for Painless Childbirth* (New York: Grune & Stratton, 1958), p. 17.
8. Sheila Kitzinger, *The Experience of Childbirth,* 4th ed. (Harmondsworth, Middlesex, England: Penguin Books, 1978), p. 231.
9. Sheila Kitzinger and John A. Davis, eds., *The Place of Birth: A Study of the Environment in Which Birth Takes Place with Special Reference to Home Confinements* (Oxford, New York, and Toronto: Oxford University Press, 1978), p. 208.
10. Suzanne Arms, *Immaculate Deception: A New Look at Women and Childbirth in America* (Boston: Houghton Mifflin, 1975), p. 115.
11. Carolyn Fishel Sargent, *Maternity, Medicine, and Power: Reproductive Decisions in Urban Benin* (Berkeley: University of California Press, 1989), p. 169.
12. Sargent, p. 7.
13. Judith Goldsmith, *Childbirth Wisdom from the World's Oldest Societies* (Brookline, Mass.: East West Health Books, 1990), pp. 86–87.
14. Arms, p. 118.
15. Vellay, p. 120.
16. Louise Henking Wejksnora, "Unexpected Forceps," in *Birth Stories: The Experience Remembered,* ed. Janet Isaacs Ashford (Trumansburg, N.Y.: Crossing Press, 1984), p. 98.
17. Vellay, pp. 134–35.
18. Robbie E. Davis-Floyd, prepublication copy of "The Technocratic Body and the Organic Body: Cultural Models for Women's Birth Choices," in *The Anthropology of Science and Technology,* a special issue of *Knowledge and Society,* vol. 9, ed. David J. Hess and Linda L. Layne (Hartford, Conn.: JAI Press, in press), p. 24.
19. Davis-Floyd, p. 28.
20. Davis-Floyd, p. 45.
21. Davis-Floyd, p. 25.
22. Stanislav Grof, *The Adventure of Self-Discovery* (Albany: State University of New York Press, 1988), p. 26.
23. *The Hymns of the Rgveda,* trans. Ralph T. H. Griffith (Benares: E. T. Lazarus, 1896), Book X, Hymn 90, verses 10–13, quoted in David S. Noss and John B. Noss, *Man's Religions,* 7th ed. (New York: Macmillan, 1984), p. 76.

24. Quoted in Mircea Eliade, *From Primitives to Zen: A Thematic Sourcebook of the History of Religions* (San Francisco: Harper & Row, 1967), pp. 106–7.

25. Grof, p. 29.

26. Lloyd DeMause, "The Fetal Origins of History," in *Pre- and Perinatal Psychology: An Introduction,* ed. Thomas R. Verny (New York: Human Sciences Press, 1987), p. 247.

27. DeMause, p. 255.

28. See Mary Douglas, *Purity and Danger: An Analysis of Concepts of Pollution and Taboo* (Harmondsworth, Middlesex, England: Penguin Books, 1966), for a comprehensive discussion of pollution.

29. Quoted in Marina Warner, *Alone of All Her Sex: The Myth and the Cult of the Virgin Mary* (New York: Pocket Books, 1976), p. 58.

30. Sir Edward Burnett Tylor, *Religion in Primitive Culture* (New York: Harper & Row, 1958), p. 518.

31. Margery Wolf and Roxane Wike, eds., *Women in Chinese Society* (Stanford, CA: Stanford University Press, 1975), p. 195.

32. J. E. Veevers, *Childless by Choice* (Toronto: Butterworths, 1980), p. 44.

33. Wilhelm Stekel, *Disorders of the Instincts and the Emotions: The Parapathic Disorders; Frigidity in Woman in Relation to Her Love Life* (1926; New York: Liveright, 1943), p. 211.

34. Judy Grahn, "From Sacred Blood to the Curse and Beyond," in *The Politics of Women's Spirituality: Essays on the Rise of Spiritual Power within the Feminist Movement,* ed. Charlene Spretnak (Garden City, N.Y.: Anchor Books/Doubleday, 1982), p. 266.

35. Jimmy Breslin, *Syracuse Post-Standard,* 20 July 1991, editorial page.

36. Sigmund Freud, *A General Introduction to Psychoanalysis,* trans. Joan Riviere (New York: Washington Square Press, 1960), p. 312.

37. Norman O. Brown, *Love's Body* (New York: Vintage Books/Random House, 1966), p. 133.

38. See Sandor Ferenczi, *Thalassa: A Theory of Genitality,* trans. Henry Alden Bunker (New York: W. W. Norton, 1968).

39. Phyllis Chesler, *With Child: A Diary of Motherhood* (New York: Thomas Crowell, 1979), p. 50.

40. Goldsmith, p. 142.

41. Frederick Leboyer, *Birth without Violence* (New York: Alfred A. Knopf, 1975), p. 62.

42. David Chamberlain, *Babies Remember Birth: And Other Extraordinary Scientific Discoveries about the Mind and the Personality of Your Newborn* (New York: Ballantine Books, 1988), p. 56.

43. Ina May Gaskin, *Spiritual Midwifery,* 3d ed., (Summerton, Tenn.: Book Publishing, 1990), p. 63.

44. See "Place-centered Models" in Chapter 6.

45. Marilyn Moran, *Happy Birth Days: Personal Accounts of Birth at Home* (Leawood, Kans.: New Nativity Press, 1986), p. 45.

46. Moran, p. 34.

47. Gaskin, p. 53.

48. Gayle Peterson, *Birthing Normally: A Personal Growth Approach to Childbirth,* 2d ed. (Berkeley, Calif.: Shadow & Light, 1984), p. 48.

49. I am grateful to Marilyn Moran for giving me this newspaper account.

50. Rahima Baldwin, *Special Delivery: The Choices Are Yours* (Berkeley, Calif.: Celestial Arts, 1979), p. 141.

VIII. "DELIVERY": A TIME OF POTENTIAL REVELATION

1. Ina May Gaskin, *Spiritual Midwifery,* 3d ed. (Summertown, Tenn.: Book Publishing, 1990), p. 9.

2. Sigmund Freud, *A General Introduction to Psychoanalysis,* trans. Joan Riviere (New York: Washington Square Press, 1960), p. 404.

3. Freud, p. 403.

4. Otto Rank, *The Trauma of Birth* (New York: Harcourt, Brace, 1929), pp. xiii–xiv.

5. Rank, p. 211.

6. Rank, p. 155.

7. For more on this topic, see Patricia Reis, *Through the Goddess: A Woman's Way of Healing* (New York: Continuum, 1991), chap. 6.

8. Rank, pp. 156–57.

9. Stanislav Grof and Joan Halifax, *The Human Encounter with Death* (New York: E. P. Dutton, 1977), p. 48.

10. Carl Sagan, "The Amniotic Universe," in *The Near-Death Experience: Problems, Prospects, Perspectives,* ed. Bruce Greyson and Charles P. Flynn (Springfield, Ill.: Charles Thomas, 1984), p. 148.

11. This information was provided to me by anthropologist Robbie E. Davis-Floyd.

12. Sagan, p. 145.

13. David Chamberlain, *Babies Remember Birth: And Other Extraordinary Scientific Discoveries about the Mind and the Personality of Your Newborn* (New York: Ballantine Books, 1988), p. 123.

14. Chamberlain, p. 137.

15. Chamberlain, p. 112.

16. Stanislav Grof, *The Adventure of Self-Discovery* (Albany: State University of New York Press, 1988), p. 30.

17. Marilyn A. Moran, ed., *Happy Birth Days* (Leawood, Kans.: New Nativity Press, 1986), p. 43.

18. Moran, p. 49.

19. Alvin H. Lawson, "Perinatal Imagery in UFO Abduction Reports," in *Pre- and Perinatal Psychology: An Introduction,* ed. Thomas R. Verny (New York: Human Sciences Press, 1987), p. 261.

20. Roper Organization, *Unusual Personal Experiences* (Las Vegas: Bigelow, 1992).

21. Lawson, p. 262.

22. Lawson, p. 267.

23. Chamberlain, pp. 124–25.

24. Lloyd DeMause, "The Fetal Origins of History," in *Pre- and Perinatal Psychology,* ed. Thomas R. Verny (New York: Human Sciences Press, 1987), pp. 243–44.

25. DeMause, p. 218.

26. DeMause, p. 248.

27. Maarten J. Vermaseren, *Cybele and Attis: The Myth and the Cult* (London: Thames & Hudson, 1977), p. 16.

28. Charles Dickens, *Oliver Twist* (Philadelphia: John Wanamaker, n.d.), p. 3.

29. Ernest Hemingway, "Indian Camp," in *The Nick Adams Stories* (New York: Bantam, 1973), p. 17.

30. Hemingway, p. 19.

31. Hemingway, p. 20.

32. Grof and Halifax, p. 86.

33. *Hymns of the Atharva-Veda with Extracts from the Ritual Books and the Commentaries,* trans. Maurice Bloomfield (New York: Greenwood Press, 1969), quoted in Mircea Eliade, *A History of Religious Ideas: From the Stone Age to the Eleusinian Mysteries,* vol. 1 (Chicago: University of Chicago Press, 1978), p. 215.

34. Jane Harrison, "Themis," in *Epilegomena to the Study of Greek Religion and Themis: A Study of the Social Origins of Greek Religion* (New Hyde Park, N.Y.: University Books, 1962), pp. 34–35.

35. Information on both incidents occurs in K. J. Dover, *Greek Homosexuality* (Cambridge: Harvard University Press, 1978).

36. Werner Jaeger, *Paideia: The Ideals of Greek Culture,* trans. from the 2d German edition by Gilbert Highet (New York: Oxford University Press, 1939), p. 4.

37. This information was given to me by Ellen Umansky, associate professor of religious studies, Emory University.

38. Mircea Eliade, *Rites and Symbols of Initiation: The Mysteries of Birth and Rebirth,* trans. Willard R. Trask (New York: Harper Torchbooks, 1958), p. xi.

39. Eliade, *Rites,* p. 3.

40. Eliade, *Rites,* p. 10.

41. Quoted in Eliade, *History,* p. 221.

42. The history of rebirthing can be traced to hypnosis experiments in the nineteenth century, which occasionally produced presumed regressions to birth. Freud also touches on rebirth with his speculations that traumatic birth might effect traumas later in life, a theme taken up more fully by Otto Rank in the 1920s (see "Birth Trauma" in Chapter 8 for more details on that subject). In the 1950s, the American analyst Nandor Fodor repeatedly found birth-related materials in the memories of his adult patients, and in the 1970s, psychologist Arthur Janov strongly emphasized birth pain as one of the primal hurts common to emotional problems. Some of the other leaders in this field from the 1970s on are obstetrician David Cheek, psychologist Leslie leCron, Stanislav Grof, and psychologist David Chamberlain.

43. Leonard Orr and Sondra Ray, *Rebirthing in the New Age* (Berkeley, Calif.: Celestial Arts, 1983), p. xvii.

44. Orr and Ray, p. 71.

45. Orr and Ray, pp. 125–26.

46. This material is from an unpublished childbirthing account called "Knowing: A Story of Two Births," by anthropologist Robbie E. Davis-Floyd, p. 89.

47. Simone de Beauvoir, *The Second Sex,* trans. and ed. H. M. Parshley (New York: Bantam Books, 1961), p. 476.

48. See Carol Gilligan, *In a Different Voice: Psychological Theory and Women's Development* (Cambridge and London: Harvard University Press, 1982).

49. Elston Best, *The Whare Kohanga (The "Nest House") and Its Lore: Comprising Data Pertaining to Procreation, Baptism, and Infant Betrothal, &c. Contributed by Members of the Ngatai-Kahungenu Tribe of the North Island of New Zealand* (Wellington, New Zealand: A. R. Shearer, 1975).

50. For more information on the concept of the world navel, see Joseph Campbell, *The Hero with a Thousand Faces* (Cleveland and New York: World, 1949), pp. 32, 40–46.

51. Moran, p. 49.

52. Moran, p. 39.

53. Gaskin, p. 363.

54. I am grateful to Robbie E. Davis-Floyd for this information.

55. For further discussion of this difficult material, see Roger Webster, *Studying Literary Theory: An Introduction* (London: Edward Arnold, 1990).

56. Hans Rausch, "The Castration Complex and the Trauma of Birth," in *Pre- and Perinatal Psychology: An Introduction* (New York: Human Sciences Press, 1987), pp. 234–35.

IX. THE POSTPARTUM PERIOD

1. The Boston Women's Health Book Collective, *Our Bodies, Ourselves: A Book for and by Women* (New York: Simon & Schuster, 1971), p. 208.

2. For a provocative discussion that emphasizes the psychological rather than the physical aspects of this issue, see Julia Kristeva, "Stabat Mater," in *The Kristeva Reader,* ed. Toril Moi (New York: Columbia University Press, 1986).

3. Dawson Church, *Communing with the Spirit of Your Unborn Child: A Practical Guide to Intimate Communication with Your Unborn or Infant* (San Leandro, Calif.: Aslan, 1988), pp. 6–7.

4. J. E. Veevers, *Childless by Choice* (Toronto: Butterworth, 1980), p. 46.

5. Veevers, p. 50.

6. See, for example, Shulamith Firestone, *The Dialectic of Sex: The Case for Feminist Revolution* (New York: William Morrow, 1970).

7. Quoted in Nancy Berezin, *The Gentle Birth Book: A Practical Guide to Leboyer Family-centered Delivery* (New York: Simon & Schuster, 1980), p. 55.

8. Diane Eyer's book *Mother-Infant Bonding: A Scientific Fiction* (New Haven: Yale University Press, 1993) came out after this book went to press. In it, Eyer disputes the notion that bonding exists, seeing it partly as a patriarchal threat to women who wish to work outside the home. The idea that mothers and their children ideally form a close attachment nonetheless remains valid no matter what it is called or exactly when or how it is formed.

9. Selma Fraiberg, *Every Child's Birthright: In Defense of Mothering* (New York: Basic Books, 1977), p. 57.

10. Suzanne Arms, *Immaculate Deception: A New Look at Women and Childbirth in America* (Boston: San Francisco Book/Houghton Mifflin, 1975), p. 108.

11. Syracuse *Post-Standard*, 17 April 1991, C-2.

12. Niles Newton, *Maternal Emotions* (New York: Paul Hoeber, 1955), p. 45.

13. *New York Times*, national edition, 2 June 1991, p. 26.

14. Quoted in Margot Edwards and Mary Waldorf, *Reclaiming Birth: History and Heroines of American Childbirth Reform* (Trumansburg, N.Y.: Crossing Press, 1984), p. 93; original in Viva, "Hooked on Weaning," excerpt from "The Baby," *Ms.*, April 1975, pp. 51–54. For a more recent case, see the letter in *Mothering*, Spring 1992, pp. 8–9, from Denise Perrigo of La Fayette, N.Y. Perrigo's two-year-old daughter was taken from her by the Department of Social Services in 1991 and placed in foster care for 359 days after Perrigo, who was nursing the child, telephoned La Leche League to ask if it is normal to feel sexually aroused while nursing.

15. Eunice Mitchell, quoted in Arms, p. 18.

16. Sheila Kitzinger and John A. Davis, eds., *The Place of Birth: A Study of the Environment in Which Birth Takes Place with Special Reference to Home Confinements* (Oxford, New York, and Toronto: Oxford University Press, 1978), p. 209.

17. Marshall H. Klaus and John H. Kennell, *Parent-Infant Bonding*, 2d ed. (St. Louis: C. V. Mosby, 1982), p. 230.

18. Janet Isaacs Ashford, "Doing It Myself," in *Birth Stories: The Experience Remembered* (Trumansburg, N.Y.: Crossing Press, 1984), p. 80.

CONCLUSION

1. Ina May Gaskin, *Spiritual Midwifery*, 3d ed. (Summertown, Tenn.: Book Publishing, 1990, p. 45.

2. David Chamberlain, *Babies Remember Birth: And Other Extraordinary Scientific Discoveries about the Mind and the Personality of Your Newborn* (New York: Ballantine Books, 1988), p. 159.

3. Chamberlain, pp. 105–11. To minimize the likelihood that such memories were merely fantasies, Chamberlain paired mothers with their grown children, using only those capable of hyperamnesia, the ability to remember completely with strong images. Children, who necessarily had to be verbal, ranged from ages nine to twenty-three, mothers from thirty-two to forty-six. To qualify, mothers had to establish that they had never discussed birth details with their children. Sessions held separately for each mother and child usually lasted one to four hours, with Chamberlain trying to avoid leading questions. In ten pairings, the degree of correlation between mothers' and children's memories was startling.

4. Dorothy Dinnerstein's entire book, *The Mermaid and the Minotaur: Sexual Arrangements and Human Malaise* (New York: Harper & Row, 1976), is devoted to critiquing exclusively maternal childrearing practices.

INDEX

KATHRYN ALLEN RABUZZI is author of *Motherself: A Mythic Analysis of Motherhood* and *The Sacred and the Feminine: Towards a Theology of Housework*. She was one of the founding editors of *Literature and Medicine*.